"If you're burnt out on hustle culture and tired of second-guessing your intuition, *How Are You, Really?* is a must-read. Jenna Kutcher will help you redefine success and reshape your life, on your terms."

—MARIE FORLEO, #1 *NEW YORK TIMES* BESTSELLING
AUTHOR OF *EVERYTHING IS FIGUREOUTABLE*

*"How Are You, Really?* is the perfect read for every person who has ever felt stuck between where she is and where she wants to be. In short? Everyone I know."

—MARIA MENOUNOS, *NEW YORK TIMES* BESTSELLING AUTHOR
AND HOST OF PODCAST AND DIGITAL SERIES *BETTER
TOGETHER WITH MARIA MENOUNOS*

"In *How Are You, Really?* Jenna Kutcher walks us through what it means to live a life that doesn't just look good but feels good too. This book is an absolute gift, one that is profoundly necessary in our world right now."

—TIFFANY ALICHE, *NEW YORK TIMES* BESTSELLING
AUTHOR OF *GET GOOD WITH MONEY*

"This book is a version of Jenna you can hold in your hands: frank, kind, funny, and inspiring, full of personal stories and hard-earned wisdom. *How Are You, Really?* is an energizing read for anyone trying to make their dreams come true."

—MARTHA BECK, PHD, *NEW YORK TIMES*
BESTSELLING AUTHOR AND LIFE COACH

*"How Are You, Really?* is your personal guide to cut straight through the noise, distraction, and busyness around you, and start living your life with intention, courage, and purpose!"

—JAMIE KERN LIMA, *NEW YORK TIMES* BESTSELLING
AUTHOR OF *BELIEVE IT* AND FOUNDER OF IT COSMETICS

*"How Are You, Really?* guides us to ask the hard questions like, 'What do I want?' and 'How can I enjoy this more?' With every page, Jenna Kutcher leads you to your own answer as you unlock the keys to a good life. One that you'll love, you'll trust, and you'll want to share."

—ARLAN HAMILTON, FOUNDER AND
MANAGING PARTNER OF BACKSTAGE CAPITAL

"Empowering, insightful, thought-provoking! *How Are You, Really?* is a beautiful balance of stories, guidance, and grounding that gives you the courage to pave your own way, define your own success, and wake up to the life you were meant to live."

—AMY PORTERFIELD, HOST OF TOP-RATED
PODCAST *ONLINE MARKETING MADE EASY*

"Jenna Kutcher captures your heart and mind through her own personal experiences and resilience. Allow Jenna to show you her relatable approach to helping all women succeed."

—CANDICE KUMAI, JOURNALIST, WRITER, BESTSELLING AUTHOR OF *KINTSUGI WELLNESS*, AND HOST OF THE *WABI SABI* PODCAST

"*How Are You, Really?* is a soulful, charming guide to crafting a life based on the true, unique beauty of who you are. Between these pages you'll find questions you never thought to ask yourself, so you get the answers your soul has been craving."

—KATE NORTHRUP, BESTSELLING AUTHOR OF *DO LESS*

"*How Are You, Really?* is a road map for choosing a path on your own terms. Jenna Kutcher teaches us to turn to our intuition and answer the questions that matter most: our own."

—BARBARA CORCORAN, FOUNDER OF THE CORCORAN GROUP AND SHARK ON ABC'S *SHARK TANK*

"*How Are You, Really?* is one of those books that you find yourself saying, 'Nah that's not me,' but then you can't stop reading because it is so uncomfortably you to a tee. Jenna tells it like it is and cuts to the chase all while inspiring that fire inside each of us. I immediately wanted to go reinvent myself and do a life inventory after reading this *gem*."

—ALLI WEBB, FOUNDER OF DRYBAR AND *NEW YORK TIMES* BESTSELLING AUTHOR

"A transformational page-turner. If you're looking to create the perfect life recipe that feels right, Jenna has done it. This book is smart, relatable, and will tell you exactly HOW to create a life you love."

—MEL ROBBINS, LEADING MOTIVATIONAL SPEAKER AND *NEW YORK TIMES* BESTSELLING AUTHOR OF *THE HIGH 5 HABIT*

"When it comes to combining work with woo, Jenna Kutcher gets it. *How Are You, Really?* is a brilliant disrupter for reimagining what an enriched life can look like—and how to get there."

—REBECCA MINKOFF, DESIGNER AND CO-FOUNDER OF FEMALE FOUNDER COLLECTIVE

"Jenna has a way of writing that brings her into the room next to you, slides up a chair, and chats like the girlfriend you need. *How Are You, Really?* is honest, touching, and guiding in all the right ways."

—ARIELLE ESTORIA, POET, AUTHOR, AND ACTOR

"Jenna Kutcher is a breath of fresh air, reminding us that self-help really does start with self!"

—KAITLYN BRISTOWE, TELEVISION HOST AND ENTREPRENEUR

HOW ARE YOU, REALLY?

**DEY ST.**

*An Imprint of* WILLIAM MORROW

# how are you, Really

## Living Your Truth
## One Answer at a Time

### JENNA KUTCHER

HarperCollins books may be purchased for educational, business, or sales promotional use. For information, please email the Special Markets Department at SPsales@harpercollins.com.

FIRST EDITION

*Designed by Renata De Oliveira*

Library of Congress Cataloging-in-Publication Data has been applied for.

ISBN 978-0-06-322194-9

22 23 24 25 26 LBC 7 6 5 4 3

FOR MY GIRLS:
*May you always be able to ask curiously,*
*answer honestly, and live wholly*

# contents

# introduction

## CAN WE TALK?

Confession: I'm not one for small talk.

(Please, if we ever meet, don't ask me about the weather. *There are apps for that!*) I'd rather talk to you about your impending divorce, the new organizational hack you just learned, that viral TikTok caprese salad, your toddler's tantrum, or the odd shape of that mole under your armpit that you really should get checked. Small talk drains me. It sucks the life out of me. I'm like a scuba diver that wants to venture wayyyy down into the depths, like ear-poppingly deep. Leave that surface stuff to the snorkeler floating at the top with their butt bobbing out of the water, you know?

And yet, these days, small talk feels like it's the norm. Whether it's the cashier at Target, the neighbor in your cul-de-sac, or that friend you haven't had a chance to sit with in over a year, it seems like it's hard to get past the "good" and "busy" responses to the question that most people ask (but don't really have enough time to hear the response): *How are you?* But let's be honest; it's easy to see why many of us don't really know how to answer that question. We're not going to dive straight into the aches and pains of our plantar fasciitis with the barista in the Starbucks window. (With some relationships, you have to snorkel *before* you can deep dive.)

But the rest of them? Those inner-circle relationships with the people who have our back? We must be willing and wanting to explore the depths a little more. Sometimes, our brains simply stay in the habit of trying to connect the dots for the easiest, quickest response to offer. And sometimes we're afraid to burden a close friend with the truth, or are scared to show a different side of us that stays hidden when we talk about the weather or the local football team or that one soup recipe on Pinterest.

We tend to take the most direct route to *Get me out of this conversation before I expose myself,* just like we let Siri reroute us around the rubble of road construction. We avoid the curves, the dips in the road, and the dust of our lives in conversation. We quickly reroute to safe territory or take the quickest exit to keep us safe from answering the bigger question. It's like we want others to pay attention, but not so closely that they ask us about the real stuff, the personal stuff, the *It's a long story, so who would even want to listen to it?* stuff.

Beyond getting really honest about the things that might not be okay, we stifle the things that make us come alive. It's like we all end up chattering about on this banged-up planet carrying these big dreams and audacious goals and boundary-breaking ideas, *and we keep them quiet.* All throughout the week—in the checkout line, on the conference call, around the dinner table—we are walking around with wild parts of ourselves left unspoken.

But have you ever felt the feeling that comes when you cut the fluff, get past the small stuff, and are asked, "How are you, *really?*" Just the addition of that one precious word, that small invitation to cut the crap and stop with the niceties and be real with yourself and whoever is brave enough to ask it? It feels like a gulp of oxygen, like coming to the surface and seeing the light again. *So why don't we do this every moment we can?* What are we running from, drowning out, and keeping under lock and key?

The *answer.*

The truth is, we're scared of what might come out if we pause to pose the question with honesty—not only to the people in our lives, but to ourselves. We're scared of what we'd hear if we got quiet enough to ask ourselves the questions that matter. *Is there more out there? Is this it? Am I actually happy? What now? What's next? What's wrong?*

When these questions come to the surface, most of us shove them back down, grab the smoothie, run out the door, and get on with our day, keeping ourselves busy so we don't actually pause long enough to have to sit with the responses. But the answers to our deep questions somehow find their way into our lives. They return to us in the middle of the night, or when we're driving to that thing we wish we hadn't committed to. They come after the toddler spills the Cheerios on the floor or the teenager rolls her eyes for the seventeenth time that day.

And like we've been conditioned to do, we just keep going, keep pushing, keep smiling, and keep reminding ourselves that we are lucky, we are blessed, and we should be thankful. That same old song with the cheap lyrics. We tell ourselves so many others have it far worse than us. Or it's probably our fault we aren't content or happy, and we should just "choose joy" like the coffee mugs and water bottles say.

Listen: not every feeling is a choice. As if life is simply a menu of delicious options and we just need to choose! As if the world isn't burning and the oceans aren't rising! As if our pain can't exist because others have pain, too. As if accessing more difficult, complex emotions like sadness, discontent, or futility means we're doing this all wrong.

(Hear me loud and clear: it doesn't.) There will be times in our lives where joy is not an emotion we can access in the moment, and in those times, the goal isn't to just *choose* it. The choice we do have is to ask ourselves when we last felt it, and to dig hard for that answer.

But when we shame ourselves for not choosing the convenient response (#*blessed*), or for not displaying what we think is the socially acceptable response to whatever situation we're in, we distract from the real work. We try to outrun the longings, try to forget about our wants, try to silence every deep doubt and deeper dream. Or we reach for whatever might numb the feelings we *can't* silence. Because sometimes seeking out the answers becomes too painful, especially when we think we have to ask them in the shadows where we won't bother anyone. Where no one can hear that we're actually admitting we're not happy or that life hasn't turned out how we thought it would.

How many times have we woken up at 3:00 A.M., mind racing with hundreds of these unacknowledged responses pinging in our brains? It's like that error we get when we send a text and whatever wizard it is that runs the magical cloud these days bounces us right back to earth: "Message failed to send." The times we didn't ask for what we needed. The times when we weren't honest about our boundaries. The times we pretended we weren't in pain. The times we felt shame for still being in pain. The times when we didn't apologize. (The times we did apologize, but for something we didn't *at all* need to.) The times we trivialized our accomplishments. The times we said, "No worries!" when we felt betrayed. The times we said to our doctor, "It's probably nothing, but . . ."

We're overflowing with these unsent messages and these unanswered questions. Our bodies are storing them, our *lives* are storing them, and there's no cellular 5G plan on earth that can handle that sort of backup. We're carrying them around, all day and all night, all of these unfelt feelings and unexpressed words and unexplored dreams.

And we wonder why we wake up so damn tired. Like, the bone-deep kind. The beyond-needing-a-quick-catnap kind. Tired of trying to keep up with expectations. Tired of the relentless games of hustle culture. Tired of hating our bodies while trying to find time to move and nourish them anyway. And if you're anything like me, you're *really* tired of all those dust bunnies your ten-pound dogs leave in every corner of your space.

It's no surprise we're exhausted. Before we're even fully awake, we start scrolling through everyone else's opinions and ideas and solutions—our news feeds, our Facebook page, our Instagram feeds. We crowdsource our life to push us toward something else, to distract us, to lose those 3:00 A.M. thoughts in the comforting chaos of the latest craze. We set goals we think we're supposed to, we buy the bestselling planner, we create the resolutions that sound nice to (and for) everyone else, and we hope for the promise that on Monday it'll all be different.

But most of the time, on Monday, we wake to reality, again—that the five-star magic diet plan didn't work. Those meditations still haven't sunk in. We've been grinding our teeth again. That same stressor keeps getting in the way every single time you attempt to journal, strategize, or manifest your way to happiness.

And we decide that surely the problem is *us*? Surely we're doing something wrong? It always comes back to us and the many ways we assume we're incapable. We wonder, do we just need, like, three more yoga classes to make it click? Do we just need to wake up earlier?

The fill-in-the-blank, $99.99 solution is working for everyone else, isn't it? At least, that's what the ads say. That's what the wellness guru preaches. That's what the book promised.

So *why* isn't it working for me?

Spoiler alert: that thing you're doing isn't working for you because it didn't *come from* you. That "answer"—the diet, the planner, the four-step-manifestation plan—came from something (or someone) *outside of you*. It came from Amazon. It came from an influencer or that wellness guru. It came from your sister or your sister's neighbor or her sister's neighbor's best friend.

We can't always solve our own problems with someone else's solutions. We can't always find our own selves using someone else's directions. And we sure as hell can't always question our lives clearly if we don't close our eyes to the nonstop jazz hands of every other answer parading by.

When we look to the crowd to answer our deepest questions, we move in whatever direction we're carried. We stop looking within, stop checking in, stop carrying our own visions, because what is inside of us perhaps doesn't match the identities our world keeps telling us to clothe ourselves in. Instead, our gaze catches the motions of the crowd and we sync up. We become people who know how to go with the flow more than anything else. And we end up exhausted and bruised, numb to ourselves, lost down a path we don't even remember turning on.

But this time it's going to be different. This time, you're going to hear *your* voice—not your best friend's, not your mother's, and not that one girl's on Instagram. (Yeah, that includes me.)

In this book, I'm going to gently shake your shoulders and remind you to wake up to your life, to start listening to yourself and trusting yourself more. I'm going to tell you to be ready to question what you thought couldn't (or shouldn't) be questioned, and to lean into your curiosities because they're about to get noisy. I'm going to ask you the question that you should be asking yourself, each and every day: *How are you, really?* And I'll help you prepare to dig deep for the answers.

As the world tells us that in order to get what we really want, we need to empower ourselves (a beautiful notion and movement in and of itself, certainly), my question is: *When did we ever allow ourselves to lose the power?*

The power has always been within us. It's always been available to us, deep below the surface. We know our power is there because it whispers to us in the quiet, and it screams at us when we need it to, and it shows up in a million different ways. Goose bumps. Pinpricks. Laughter. Pain, amazement, boredom, restlessness, wide-eyed wonder.

Accessing our power might not begin with marching in the next protest or donating thousands of dollars to a worthy cause, and it might not happen on stages or in front of the masses. Uncovering your own power may begin to take shape in a more discreet, personal way. It might happen behind the doors of your home or in a circle with neighbors. It might happen at a bus stop or in the grocery store or a church basement. It might even happen while you read this book. Maybe years after or in mere minutes.

Whatever power will come forth in these pages, it will be *yours*. It will be full of your own questions and your own answers—a life recipe that is yours and yours only. *One that doesn't just look good but feels good. Feels right.*

A life that refuses to delay joy.

One that redefines success.

One that celebrates wins.

One that admits the hardships.

One that invites rest and time for play.

One that stops hiding, stops shrinking.

One that doesn't numb the pain.

One that gives permission to feel.

One that turns up the volume on intuition.

One that creates space for enjoying the benefits of what your work provides for you.

One that knows how—and *where*—to find exactly what you're looking for.

As you read, don't just listen to me; listen to you. That inner narrative or dialogue (or if you like, a fairy godmother in the form of, say, Dolly Parton sitting on your shoulder) will be a guiding light that can show you where you're at. That's why, in every chapter, you'll find a writing prompt included. Answer those prompts. Journal them on paper, or record a voice memo to yourself. Get quiet. Get specific. Get honest. *And watch what happens next.*

Because your truest answers are already here. They've been in you, all along, ready for an invitation to spill out, to come alive, to bring forth. Ready to be asked.

*How are you, really?*

PART ONE

# who
# you
# are,
## *Really*

## A LETTER FROM JENNA:

life has taught me that there are an infinite number of paths for us to take. Some are well traveled, led by tour guides who know the lay of the land, while others are less clear, traversed alone as we bushwhack our way through.

When we look for answers about our lives and seek truth, we often turn to others, but I hope this section of the book helps you to silence the noise and first look within.

Before we dive into the tactical stuff or my own stories, we have to first take a hard look at the stories you may have been telling yourself when it comes to who you are. I've learned that if we don't first start with knowing ourselves, we will struggle to show up authentically in all aspects of our lives.

We have to learn how to silence our inner playground bully and turn up the volume on our intuition. If you can get quiet enough to let the deepest part of you speak, you might be surprised by what you hear.

Your newfound confidence is about to swallow up your disbelief.

Buckle up!

Jenna

# 1

# the softer question:

## HOW TO FEEL YOUR FEELINGS

**If you do not tell the truth about yourself you cannot tell it about other people.**

**—VIRGINIA WOOLF**

When's the last time you took stock of your life? Like, full-on, full-sweep, forensic accounting–style inventory? A staring-contest-with-the-mirror kind of activity? I'm guessing if I asked you how often you take time out of your day to consider your feelings, your own preferences, your unique needs, and your deepest desires, you'd round way up, wouldn't you? Kind of like I do at the dentist when my hygienist asks me how often I'm flossing. "Every night-ish?" I muffle. (*As if they can't tell.*)

Hear me say this as gently as I possibly can. As of right now, this very moment, we're done fudging the numbers. Today's the day to wake ourselves up to two hard truths: (1) we're def not flossing enough, and (2) we're asleep for too much of our own lives.

As an online educator and advocate for female entrepreneurs, I hear from women all over the world who move through long bouts of the week where everything feels like it's running on autopilot. Surprisingly, we're fine. *Good! Busy!* The sun's shining. The toddler didn't come into our bed last night. The boss loved the pitch. The vacation is booked. The garden is planted. The jeans zip *and* button.

But in moments of quiet, we feel discontent, exhausted, frazzled, or even trapped. Something's missing and we just can't put our finger on it. We don't know what it is. We're equal parts overwhelmed and bored. Ambitious and feeling guilty about it. Overstimulated and lonely. We're exhausted from dragging the mental load of it all to and from the car pool, the grocery store, the office, the gym, and back into bed at night.

We know something's off, but we can't put our finger on it. So we experiment with ways to make life "better." We try morning pages, mushroom tea, and yoga. We join the Y. We buy (mostly) organic. We plan date nights. We quit our job, try a Dry January, sign up for a spin class. We take a parenting course. We hire a house cleaner.

We decide to declutter, minimize, and make do with less. We get a new meal plan and a new finance plan and a new floor plan. We create routines that stack up on top of each other like Jenga blocks, never pausing once to question whether or not we're actually enjoying anything about the days we're living.

Because if we did pause to ask ourselves the question *How are you, really?* we'd know that sometimes the answer would be this: *we are not okay.*

The way we are living is not sustainable for a human soul. Constantly covering up who we are just means we inevitably get buried. We are not okay anymore with just *looking* like we're okay. We're not okay with pretending to feel okay. We are not okay with holding on for one more day like Wilson Phillips told us to. We might not know exactly what to do next, we might not have all the right thoughts to piece together, but we can at least make out the words "not okay."

I remember when I first started hearing that buzz. When I first realized I was not okay, too. I didn't want to hear it, I didn't want to pay attention. But from the very first moments of recognizing my own unsustainable life, I couldn't unhear it.

Long before I launched a chart-topping podcast and carved myself a CEO position educating women around the world on business and marketing strategies, usually from the comfort of my own home, I was a ten-year-old middle child in Minnesota thinking about what most ten-year-old minds were focused on in the late nineties: windbreakers, homework that was actually on paper, and new Rollerblades. I was also a fifth grader with a knack for eavesdropping on late-night family convos. My parents called me "radar ears" for the way I could make out whispers and mumbles from across the room.

The grown-up world fascinated me to no end, and I couldn't help but beg myself to stay awake *just one more minute* as I faux-napped on the family room sofa and tried my darndest to decode adult concepts like 401(k)s and varicose veins. From my perspective then and even now, I notice that most adults tend to speak like kids aren't listening and don't care what's being said. I tend to think that's simply incorrect.

It was one of these overheard "adult" conversations that changed the trajectory of my life—and the life of someone I loved. I tagged along with my mom to visit my cousin Mike, who lived alone as a quadriplegic. His choice to live independently required massive amounts of strength and ingenuity, and we were all in awe of how he was able to creatively adapt to an environment that presented so many challenges. At that visit, I learned that late nights were especially hard for him because if he was thirsty, he had to wait for a drink of water until morning when his aide arrived. After hearing him share that discomfort, I felt a tiny ping. A micro-call to action. A gut feeling.

*That's not okay!* was my first thought.

*Maybe I can help?* was my second.

The very next day, while thinking about Mike, I dreamed up a prototype for what would become my state-of-the-art invention: the Handy Helper Sipper Upper. (Yep, you can 100 percent laugh.) I readjusted the butterfly clips in my hair, scribbled the idea on paper, and got to work. My parents didn't laugh away my idea, and instead they fully supported my desire to help find a solution. My mom helped me find an IV stand, and I created a bladder for drinking water using an IV bag. My dad welded a connection to the stand that could reach a hospital bed. I asked my dental office if they could spare a few of those suction things they use to suck the spit out of your mouth. Within weeks, I rigged it all up and voilà, my cousin now had access to drinking water in the middle of the night.

> ## Want to hear from more goal diggers whose dreams began by responding to a need in their own lives? Check out
>
> WWW.JENNAKUTCHER.COM/MORE

It was my first foray into this notion that making an impact can be as simple as recognizing and responding to an immediate need—yours or someone else's. That a simple idea could potentially change a life (again, yours or someone else's). The truth is the Handy Helper Sipper Upper earned me a showcase spot at Minnesota's statewide Inventors Fair. And it gave my relative a more restful, comfortable night.

But here's what I want you to take from this story: What might have happened if I hadn't listened to that tiny ping in my mind? That quiet hunch? That feeling that pointed to a problem in my own small world—one I became aware of and one I wasn't afraid to try to overcome? What if I'd explained it away, or distracted myself long enough to forget about it, or assumed someone else could solve it? What if I'd ignored it entirely?

It's so easy to do; to talk ourselves out of what we feel, to disqualify ourselves as a part of the solution or to deny the issues that we see. How many times do we move throughout our day and ignore the first inkling of *that's not okay*? How many times do we swallow down that feeling instead of following it up with an idea that could potentially help take the *not okay* and make it *okay*?

This response to talking ourselves out of our feelings is ingrained in most of us, from the very first moment we fall down on the playground and a loving caretaker wipes away our tears and tells us not to cry. While, yes, we can be grateful for every adult who carried us through childhood with what they perceived as good intentions embedded into our brains, we can also question whether or not we want to carry those same intentions with us in our own adulthood. Let's face it. Most of us grew up from that playground and internalized some version of the same beat: *Don't overstep! Don't ruffle feathers! Don't make waves! Don't! Be! Emotional!* So, we swallow the hunch. We ignore our feelings. We put on a happy face. We smile, we nod, we carry on.

Here's a feather worth ruffling: *your perspective*. Your noticings and your questions and your doubts. Your thoughts. Your longings. Your physiological responses to the good, the bad, the amazing, and the absolutely intolerable. Your feelings. And while feelings aren't always facts, they 100 percent matter. They're pulsating through your veins for a reason, and that reason is not just to keep you alive. It's to keep you coming alive—again and again and again.

I'll lean on the succinct words of clinical psychologist Dr. Lara Fielding: "The fact is our emotions serve an essential function in connecting us to what is truly important. Emotions signal a need . . . each one is informing us of what it is we value and hold dear."[1]

And that's precisely why so many of us are walking this planet as strangers to our own selves, not knowing who we are or what to do about it. We've numbed the feelings along the way and stopped asking ourselves the important questions: What do we value? What do we hold dear? What do we absolutely never want to do again? *How are we, really?* Hell, even if we know, we're too busy smiling and nodding at the guy who just stole our damn parking spot.

And sometimes, we move through life not knowing who we are *because we don't even know how we actually feel.* The world slings slogans around telling us how we *should* feel or encouraging us to ignore our feelings, not respect them. *Mind over matter! No pain, no gain! Push it, push it real good!* (Okay, that last one was Salt-N-Pepa, but you get me, right?)

We're told to gloss over the hard parts. To laugh it off, to lighten up. *Smile more!* (Honestly, a marketing slogan that tells me to smile usually makes me want to do the opposite.) And we never pause to question the thing we've been told, like: Why does happiness have to be my default? Why do I have to shut up every emotion that might make others uncomfortable? Why can't I scream from the rooftop: *THAT'S NOT OKAY?!*

Spoiler alert: because then . . . I might have to actually do something about it.

Our acknowledgment that there's a problem opens us up to the fact we might need to step up as part of the fix. We often avoid even pausing to *notice* a problem because we're afraid to sign ourselves up as that person with a solution, even when those solutions could change our own lives. Being part of a solution requires a lot from us—the added pressure and responsibility, the time investment, the risk of how people react. Let's face it; it's a lot easier to come up with the reasons why we can't do something than it is to muster up the time/energy/brain power to try.

Problems and solutions aside, step into your feelings for a quick beat. How are you, *really*? Do you need to cry a big, messy cry? Do it. Do you need to come to terms with the fact that life doesn't feel the way you thought it would? Do it. Do you need to admit that you're not okay? Do it. Just as I encourage my toddler to feel her feelings, get quiet enough with yourself long enough to know whether or not you want to *be quiet* in the first place. Recognize that happiness should not and will not always be your final destination. Each feeling is teaching us something, telling us about who we are *right now*.

We can't move forward if we don't pause long enough to see where we are. We can't process what's hidden from us. We can't learn to cope until we know what we're really coping with.

The truth is, it is time. It's time for us to get really honest with ourselves. It's time for us to change our tune and put on a little Aretha. R-E-S-P-E-C-T those emotions, no matter how small. It's time we pay attention. Notice. Feel the damn feeling. Sit with it. Listen to it. Receive it like a tiny text message, a little ping of info. *Alert! Breaking news! Listen up!* I mean, we all know what happens when we ignore our texts, amen?

When our normal way of living in this world is to abandon how we feel, we have to slowly course correct. We have to unlearn in order to relearn. Paying attention to how you're really feeling isn't an overnight transformation. It's taken me years (and will take many more!) of practice to get honest enough with myself, my body, my limitations, my ambitions, and my human nature to not only feel my feelings, but to hear them. I know that sounds like a trite concept, so let me unpack what I mean.

Emotions are a compass that will point you straight to your path. Starting with that first foray at the Inventors Fair, nearly every venture I've ever attempted, every problem I've tried to solve, and every success I've ever reached has stemmed from this question: *How does this feel?* Read that carefully. The sentence wasn't "How does this *make* me feel?" These questions may sound so similar, but that one small edit can dramatically transform how we answer them. When you take out the "make," you're asking a question with zero blame but full curiosity. It removes the chance for us to blame ourselves for our feelings. It's the stripped-down version.

I haven't always gotten this right. It's our natural human inclination to rush right into the reasons we might be feeling a certain way. We might try to place the blame, slap on a solution, and call it a day. But this is one of those questions that's worth slowing down for. *How does this feel? How does my life feel?* The space to answer those questions feels bigger, doesn't it?

And when you get brave enough to ask yourself, you owe it to yourself to be patient enough to listen. Your first response might be like the first layer of an onion; you'll have to peel away the layers to get to the most raw version of it. But it's worth all the peeling it takes to be as wholehearted and honest as possible when asking this question, because of how truly potent the answer will be. (Yes, potent, like an onion.)

Asking myself *How does this feel?* has been the catalyst for every chance I've taken, every leap I've attempted, and every dream I've chased. *How does this feel* has sparked the beginning (and sometimes, the ending) of every story that has mattered to me, both the ones in my heart and the ones in this book. Moments like buying the $300 camera that pointed me toward the path of becoming a wedding photographer. Or sending me on a journey of launching marketing courses for women entrepreneurs. Or leading a team of ten brilliant women. Or hitting record on the first ever episode of what would become the number-one marketing podcast in the country, *The Goal Digger* podcast (originally produced from my car, no less).

Asking myself this question has gotten me out of bad friendships. It's helped me pivot when the feelings I felt indicated I needed a change and it forced me to set real boundaries in my life. It taught me that I was capable of rest, and it showed me how to redefine success over and over again. This question reminded me that grief is not linear, that seasons change. Most of all, it taught me that my own voice was the only one who needed to answer that question, every time.

When I say *How does this feel?* oftentimes my brain can't always knit words together that feel true, at least not right away. So, I give my brain a break and take a minute to check in with the rest of my body. What sensations are present? Are my shoulders tense? Am I holding my breath? Does my head feel hot, light? Is my gut swirly? Is my vision swimmy? That's what I mean by the stripped-down version of this question. How do I actually, physiologically, *feel?*

Our bodies know. Every single time. So keep asking. And the

kicker is? We often lean on our brain and write off our bodies as a part of the equation of self-awareness. But the truth is, we get to (and sometimes need to) feel the feelings before we can decide what to do with them. We call the shots. We can label our sweaty pits nervousness or excitement. We can categorize those goose bumps as fear or intuition or curiosity. We can feel our toes tingle and call the sensation good or bad or—my personal favorite—both/and/neither. It's our choice, our answer—*as long as we're willing to be brave enough to ask it.*

When was the last time you asked yourself how you truly feel, how you really are, and waited long enough for an honest response? I know it may be uncomfortable. I know we generally want to avoid getting still with ourselves, I know sometimes we're afraid to face the answers, and sometimes we don't even realize we're avoiding this all together. I know it's easier to numb the feelings with another glass of merlot, another scroll through Instagram, another *Ted Lasso* episode. (Okay, that last one might be definitely worth it, though.)

But here's a thought. Maybe the most high-octane parts of our day—the ones we try to shove and swallow and smooth over—aren't just the minor inconveniences, annoyances, or distractions we've been taught to bypass, to shoo away like a fly. That racing heart, the sweaty pits, the fight-or-flight reactions we experience day after day—small and large? They aren't meant to be ignored. Maybe our *THAT'S NOT OKAY!* moments are trying to point us toward something new, something better, something truer, and maybe we are the ones defiantly standing in our own way without even realizing it.

When we go through life numbing our feelings, ignoring our longings, avoiding opportunities, and silencing our inner voice, we're avoiding what it can feel like to truly come alive, to be awake to the entire experience. Just as life is meant to be lived, feelings are meant to be felt.

HOW ARE YOU, REALLY?

When was the last time you felt 1,000 percent
AMAZING? On top of the world? Vibrant, giddy, alive?
Where were you and what were you doing? What
did it feel like in your body? What might it take
to get that feeling back?

It's time for a life inventory. A feelings file. Because I'm certain that at least a dozen or two wise people through the ages have said something along these lines: you can't know where you're going until you know *where you are*. So, what's a good way to establish a true and honest relationship with yourself? Document where you are *today*. Like dropping a pin on your life map and really getting the lay of the land you exist in right now, you're making it easier to see the ways in which you've grown as you've gone from there to here and as you go from here to wherever is next.

If you've ever read a journal entry (or a whole pile of diaries) from a part of your life you're no longer in, you know *exactly* why this process matters. Get out a pen. Your journal. The back of an envelope. Whatever. Start asking and answering.

You don't have to do this all at once. These questions will be here for you, available to you, whenever and wherever you need to check in with yourself. Pick one, a few, or all. There is no pass or fail on this; it's not a midterm, so let any and all of those "classroom anxieties" roll right off you. This part is just for you. Getting to know yourself is a lifelong process. This isn't a Tinder swipe. It's slow. It's meaningful. And it's 100 percent essential.

# life inventory

Answer without apology, without judgment. Your responses and gut reactions aren't things to "keep in check"; we're not worried about coloring in the lines here. Your honesty won't get in the way. Your hunches aren't just random curiosities. What you write down are messages your brain is trying to deliver straight to your heart.

Here's your chance to see yourself. To be yourself. You're not going to get mad at or shame yourself for not knowing how you've been feeling. You're not going to waste more time lingering in the part you cannot change or control.

### WHAT INSPIRES YOU?

### WHAT MAKES YOU RAGE?

### WHAT MAKES YOU SNORT-LAUGH?

### WHAT MAKES YOU CRY WITH JOY?

## WHAT MAKES YOU FEEL EMPOWERED?

## WHAT MAKES YOU NOD IN AGREEMENT?

## WHAT MAKES YOU DANCE WITH GLEE?

## WHAT DO YOU FEAR MOST?

## WHAT DO YOU FIND UNFAIR?

## WHAT PROBLEM DO YOU WISH YOU COULD SOLVE?

## WHAT DO YOU WANT TO CREATE IN THE WORLD?

Need help with this step? Clarify what you can control and equip yourself with a plan at
WWW.JENNAKUTCHER.COM/MORE

The truth is, sometimes we don't listen to how we're feeling because we can't yet "hear" and we haven't yet learned how. Sometimes the noise of the world just drowns out our souls. Sometimes we don't wake up to how we're feeling because we didn't know we could set an alarm. But other times? We don't listen *because we don't want to*. The messages are not easy to hear.

Resentment rising in the back of your throat when you get passed over for a promotion. Invisibility sinking into your gut when your partner stays up late arguing on Twitter instead of coming to bed. Dread when you reach that date on your calendar where you overcommitted yourself. Doubt banging in your head when you finally get the courage to research that new position at work.

Let me ask you this: How long? How long are you willing to ignore the ping? How long can you avoid the hard convo or leap of faith? How long can you convince yourself that you are okay with sleepwalking through life? Is it one week? One year? One life?

There's an old wives' tale that, as we age, our bodies grow heavy from the unacknowledged lives within us. Our skin expands and sags from the weight of ignored emotion. Our joints scream at us to listen.

To *feel*. As the story goes, crow's-feet are just bird tracks from every single time we allowed ourselves to be walked all over.

And while I'd never argue every single feeling is worth acting on, I will always, unabashedly say this: every feeling is worth feeling. Because when we ask *How does this really feel?* and we get quiet enough to listen for the answer, there's something else happening simultaneously. We're telling ourselves the feeling is real. In doing so, we recognize *we* are real. We stop erasing ourselves. We don't run and hide from our questions. We let them command our attention and, thus, we speak.

The more we listen to the feelings when they speak, the clearer they get. Like learning a new language. And while the world at large has its heartbreakingly big needs, ones that require our activism, anger, and attention—those needs are not to be compared to *your story*. You do not diminish in their shadow, no matter how big or small they might feel by comparison. Feelings don't exist to be compared. They exist for *you*. You don't need to write off your own pain because others are experiencing worse. Perhaps most importantly, you don't need to waste your energy convincing yourself that what you've got is fine enough—*unless, of course, it is.*

And if it's not? If everything is *not* okay enough, what you need right now isn't a booming loudspeaker over which to broadcast how you're going to fix yourself. How you're going to make everyone proud. Your ten-step plan to be okay. You don't need to run straight to your reasons, to find the blame, to search for your cloud's silver lining at the hit of the first raindrop. You don't need a big reveal, a perfect plan, a quick answer that everyone can hear and clap for.

You need a softer question. And the space to hear it speak in the quiet. It knows who you are. Listen closely, because you'll soon recognize that the voice is familiar. It's *yours*.

# 2

# golden handcuffs:

## HOW TO DITCH THE *SUPPOSED TOS*

**Success is only meaningful and enjoyable
if it feels like your own.**

**—MICHELLE OBAMA**

"I can't imagine leaving . . . but I also can't fathom staying," my friend said about her career as she grabbed a handful of truffle fries. Around the table, we all nodded in unison. Been there, done that with work, with relationships, with just about everything. We've followed the road we were accustomed to—*the beaten path instead of the best one.*

Sometimes, when we fail to check in with ourselves about what we want, we blindly go down the trail of expectation: get a degree, work a nine-to-five, pay your dues, go camping on the weekends, punch the clock, contribute to your 401(k), and retire with enough time to take an afternoon nap in your La-Z-Boy.

It's a perfectly suitable path, and who the heck would ever complain about a comfy recliner? But in quiet moments of honesty, we know—for some of us—that a safe and comfy leather expectation might instead feel like a bed of nails. Like we're already on the conveyor belt that'll drop us right into our caskets.

At least, that's what the expected path felt like for me. Once upon a time, years ago, I set off on my own path of leathery comfort expectation. I went to college, double majored, graduated, and got a job as I marched along toward what I thought would be fulfilling, meaningful work. I found myself with a retail executive management position, and over the next few years I worked my way up from role to role within the company.

Looking back, I can't tell you precisely how or why I ended up in my own windowless HR office with a red nameplate on the door and a candy bowl on top of my filing cabinet. Actually, strike that, the title on the nameplate feels like a lot of fancy words strung together but I can tell you *exactly* why I ended up with that candy bowl (#priorities).

My life was Post-its, meetings, weekend-interrupting phone calls, perfecting the fast-walk, and getting familiar with orthopedic insoles. The back seat of my Honda was a graveyard of to-go containers, coffee tumblers, and bras—the ones I'd whip off as soon as I plopped into my car after a particularly tough day. Those days when the upper half of me was like, *I need more oxygen and space,* stat.

My hard work and constant grind was paying off. I was on the fast track to promotions and marginal changes in my responsibilities and paychecks. While the thought of pleasing others, "making the company proud," and stacking up new titles gave me a tiny dopamine hit, there always felt like something was missing. If I'm being honest, I had a lot of somethings missing. I wasn't happy. I was not okay.

Looking back, it's no surprise I was depleted. I commuted an hour each way, worked a minimum of ten-hour days, and didn't have the time or energy to enjoy the new city I was living in. I picked one coffee shop, one grocery store, stopped at each when I needed to, and came home only to drive across town to hang out with my fiancé Drew and plan our wedding with the last few drops of gas in my emotions tank reserved for him. My fancy apartment had a pool I never dipped a toe in, included a roommate I never saw, and had a gym I had every intention of using but only visited once or twice. A human can only run on short, bright bursts of adrenaline for so long.

When I got quiet enough to realize things didn't feel like I thought they should, I usually ended up blaming myself. I thought what I needed to do was wrestle with my gratitude. To suck it up, hustle hard, fake it till I made it, and not sweat the small stuff . . . all phrases programmed within my DNA for as long as I could remember. Surely it was me, right? I just needed to "Count my blessings!" like that plaque on many a grandmothers' wall. I thought I should just be grateful for what I had, even if it wasn't what I wanted.

What I now know is this: you can count your blessings, acknowledge the good in your life, recognize the gift of it all, while simultaneously counting on those blessings to drive you just a little bit crazy, especially when they aren't totally aligned with what it is that you *really* want.

The more I questioned the direction of my life, the less cut-and-dried the answers became. Could I be simultaneously grateful yet still want more? Could I push against what I was told to want and instead go after what I really wanted? Could I admit that this was good . . . but not good *enough*?

Here's the thing: we all know that bad days are inevitable, they will come, and we will survive them, like we've survived all the hard days we've already encountered. But I'm not talking about a few bad days here and there; I'm talking about the hard days that turn into hard weeks, months, and even years. When the bad days become the norm, when they outnumber the good ones, and you can't really remember the last time you felt true joy or were excited to get out of bed in the morning, then it might be a sign that you need a change.

The truth was, I worked really hard.

And I could be proud of that.

The truth was, I was miserable.

And I was allowed to change that.

I remember one particular meeting with my boss that still finds its way back to me to teach me something, even now. We were sitting in her office and I glanced at the various bits of document debris and decor commingling on her desk, and I spotted something I hadn't noticed before—a photo of her smiling with two little blond kids in her lap.

I pointed to the photo and asked her about her children. She beamed and shared the normal things proud moms share. Then she told me that if she was lucky, she got to spend an hour with them each night before they went to bed. After her confession, she quickly moved the conversation along, opting out of what I know now in my soul would have been a painful subject to stay in. I pushed my own heartache for her away at that moment, too. Because it felt like the same future I was headed toward if I stayed on the path that was expected of me.

I could see the trajectory of my life in that moment in my boss's office: Late nights catching up with my husband, Drew, on what I'd missed while working the weekend. Searching for the energy to see friends. Sitting frustratedly in traffic as I felt like it was uncorking and draining away what little precious time I had left of the day. I might be sitting at my boss's desk someday, waiting to get off work and scurry home. Wondering why they don't put windows in these offices . . . and then realizing exactly why they don't.

The conversation continued, pulling me from my vision of where I was headed as my boss started to present my next promotion opportunity. The next five to ten years of my life with a stable job plan all mapped out, on paper, ready to be stapled together. Vacations planned. Retirement age set. Yearly salary in stone. Bonuses outlined. The office chair basically already had my butt-print perfectly molded into it.

I was flattered they labeled me with the word "potential," and I promptly thanked her and left her office saying I needed to mull some things over. I sat at my desk surrounded by my own detritus of a job half loved. I looked around at the files, the two archaic overheating computers, fans cranking out hot air. I felt the blisters on the back of my heels from the new leather shoes I bought to feel ready for that promotion. And then I reached over and plucked up the framed photo of Drew, with me staring at him. His warm smile. His glowing brown eyes. His little mole right above his lip.

I wanted adventures with this man. Maybe even a family someday. I wanted to make every moment count. I wanted to take another picture just like this one when we were old and gray, more smile lines, more seasons of life worn onto our faces. I stared at that photo and I saw that magic in our eyes, the kind that says, *You are all I need, and I mean it.*

I knew we were about to start our married life together, I knew life was bound to bring more challenges our way, and I knew we'd pivot through every one of them together. So how could I say yes to a life on autopilot? Weren't we supposed to be the pilots? Weren't we going to choose where we were headed . . . together?

Like a lightning bolt, I felt these words strike my heart: *Jenna, this promotion isn't for you.* If continuing the ladder climb would mean a fancier title and a corner office (still no guaranteed windows) where I would spend my days looking at the things that mattered the most to me in photos but not being able to experience them, I knew I needed to figure out a way to step off.

I was beginning to adopt this belief: I'd rather be on a journey that is the one I am personally called to, not the one defined by someone else. A life where I could call the shots, where I was an active participant, making tough choices about what mattered most to me. This belief is one a lot of us are awakening to. That even if the outcome isn't what you expect, carving out your own prototype is better than caving as a puppet. Even if the 401(k) package looks mighty tempting. Even if the cushy promotions feel promising. Even if that windowless office comes with a big ol' bowl of company-expensed M&M's.

That day I began a war with myself. I felt guilty for questioning the opportunity, for considering saying no, for feeling that way in the first place. Was I really ready to just throw out all my hard work and sacrifices? Was I ready to leave the security of a five-year plan that included all the financial gain and security I was taught to crave? Was I ready to walk away from the glory of becoming a rising star in the corporate setting?

I knew somewhere along the way I had started to journey down the wrong path. I knew I wanted to leave, but the process of walking toward the exit door felt . . . complicated. I worried I would get the timing all wrong. I worried I'd mess it up (whatever "it" was) for the coworkers I really liked. And even though it's a phrase we all hear, I worried about how I would exit "gracefully."

Those tugs, those doubts, and those questions rose deep from within me, making me wonder if somewhere along the way I got (or stayed) on the wrong path. But immediately after that feeling, the guilt would wash over me. An acknowledgment that I should be grateful for the opportunity, for all the blessings, for the consistent paycheck, in the first place.

This inner battle and these feelings aren't unique to me. It's a battle I bet you also know, and it's a battle I recognized in the eyes of my dearest friend as we dined over truffle fries not so long ago. As I dunked a fry into the ranch, I listened to my friend try to defend the company she had pledged her loyalty to, the same one that was robbing her of her life. She had been with the firm for nearly a decade. She poured in her time, sweat, talent, and tears as they stretched her, asked more of her, and demanded she rise to every occasion.

If she dared to grumble, they'd remind her that she had a great benefits package, epic perks, personal days; she even got to fly first-class when she traveled. The company made her feel silly for even pondering the idea of cutting back or, worse, leaving. They gaslit her thoughts before she could even wonder if there was a better job out there for her. They dangled the carrot in front of her and she stayed.

All of this is what *Inc.* magazine calls "the golden handcuffs." The salary is good, the benefits are good, the retirement plan is good, "everything is so good that you're willing to sit in a cubicle hating your life for 8 hours a day simply because, on paper, you're 'living the life.'"[1]

Golden handcuffs. It's not just a career thing, it's an *everything* thing. We chain ourselves to good-on-paper. As thirty-somethings or eighty-somethings, as people called to love others, as women exploring faith and sex and love and life, we never stop to consider: What do we want to leave behind? What never made sense to us, but we did anyway? What felt wrong to us, but we kept doing all the same?

My friend stayed at her job when she had panic attacks, she stayed when the late-night calls made her crack open her laptop when she desperately needed sleep, she stayed when she had to miss day care pickup, she stayed through meetings that should have been emails, she stayed when others left. She simply *stayed.*

From a young age an idea had been ingrained in her: seek security at all costs, keep moving up and up and up, bear the weight of your exhaustion, count your blessings, don't complain, and never be a quitter. But what if when we start to really question whether this is how we want to spend our days, and ultimately our lives, we realize we already have our answer: *no, not me.*

I carefully asked her, "Those perks they keep reminding you of, do you even enjoy them? Are they things that add value to your life? Do you take those vacation days?" Turns out, she didn't. A lot of things the world positions to us as shiny, as desirable, are actually quite dull. They're the things that have been drilled into our heads as things we need, things we should be looking for, paying for, saving for. And once we get them, of course we believe we'd be fools to let them go.

I watched her mentally battle herself, trying to justify why she kept staying, even when it felt uncomfortable. Painful even. She looked over at me and said, "You took the risk, you made the leap when other people would have stayed. . . . How did you do it? How did you trust *yourself*? How did you leave?"

What I told her is this: I knew if I stayed any longer, I'd be living someone else's vision for my life. So I let curiosity lead me to consider a different story playing out, one where I was the leading role, one where I penned the plan. I checked in with myself and questioned whether or not I wanted this path in the first place. And if not this, then what? I had to learn to trust in my own vision, even when it wasn't fully formed. I needed to believe that I would figure *something* out, build in my own perks, give myself a nameplate I'd be proud of, even if it didn't sound fancy. If I stayed, I'd be another butt in a seat, another person wearing a necessary title on their chart, and another person wandering down the path they were paving for me, the one they tried to disguise with important-sounding words, the one that was headed somewhere I didn't want to go.

Have you ever felt that way? It's not our fault this happens to us more times than we can count. It's easy for us to start adopting other people's visions for our lives and tricking ourselves into believing they are our own. This doesn't just happen in an office, either. It can happen everywhere. The picket fence, the 2.5 children, and the minivan—we've mocked those clichés before, but we never got rid of them. It happens with the church choir, the book club, the fundraisers, or the way we talk about what retirement is *supposed to* look like. With cute kids who serve us mud cakes and mums blooming on the front porch, it's no surprise we start to wonder if we're crazy for not feeling fulfilled, for not feeling like it's ever enough.

### HOW ARE YOU, REALLY?

Have you built your life on a stack of *supposed tos*? Are there areas of your life where you're staying stuck because it's conventional or convenient? Where are you simply going with the flow? What are some life changes you need to make?

So where does this all leave us? Where do we go from here? Listen, you're not wrong for questioning a life that was built on *supposed tos*. You're not crazy for shuffling the stack of status quo and dreaming about what it might look like to play fifty-two card pickup with your life. You're not ungrateful for acknowledging something just isn't working—even if you don't know what it is, or what to do next.

Here's why: when you're navigating an unfulfilled life and you know it, it doesn't just impact *you*. (Even though I want to gently remind you that impacting you would be 100 percent enough.) It shows up in the way you interact with your family, the energy you bring into your work, and the way you experience the world. It pokes its head out in the way you treat the cashier at the pharmacy, the way you speak to your colleagues, and the way you scoff at the neighbor kid who picks a flower out of your landscaped front yard.

The way you show up changes when your external reality doesn't match your internal desire. You don't have to be a chemist to understand the reaction when these two warring notions meet: bitterness. And once you feel that? Once you wake up to that? Well, it's time to make the decision only you can make.

You know that tiny light on your dashboard reminding you to service your engine soon? The one that—if you ignore it too long—brings irreparable damage and a mega-big price to pay? Yours might just be blinking.

# 3

# halfway to a dream:
## GOING AFTER YOUR GOAL

**I've learned that making a "living" is not the same as "making a life."**

**—MAYA ANGELOU**

So, now what? What do we do when we realize we're in the wrong place? What happens when the faint whisper evolves into an undeniable yell? How do we possibly move forward when we realize we're called to make a change, or to pivot, or to scrap it all and start fresh? How do we get from here to there without leaving a path of destruction behind us?

Let's face it; very few of us enjoy veering off course—even from a road we didn't necessarily want to be on. As we adjust our sights to a new path, it can be uncomfortable to confront the difference between what we say we want and what we're actually doing about it. Whether what we want is a small shift like getting bangs, or a massive change like moving to Bangkok, most of us are equipped with two extremes for decision-making: Get over it or get after it! Accept it or make the change. To run toward or run away. Go big or go all the way home!

Heck, sometimes we need the extreme. We need someone to say, "Get on this train right now or you'll be stuck at the station!" We need someone to say, "Last call!" And sometimes we need someone to say, "Ma'am, you're already harnessed into the parachute. It's time to jump out of the plane." But not every decision is an all-or-nothing proposition. Some decisions happen to be a little bit of both.

Honestly, there are a lot of *or*s in most of these scenarios (which is pretty common when it comes to options), but personally, I'm more of an *and* girl. I am that person who would love to have the soup *and* the salad, thank you very much.

That's why, when I was in the thick of my own crossroads, in the midst of figuring out whether I should get over it or get after it, I didn't run here or there like a headless chicken or a Dr. Seuss refrain. In fact, I didn't run anywhere. Instead, I *walked* . . . just a few steps over to my office laminator.

Let me back up a bit to explain. You see, oftentimes, when I was finished filing HR reports or trying to figure out payroll, I'd find myself dreaming about photography. I've always been enamored with photos. I was the kid who would pull out my parents' wedding album and study each image, wondering how they superimposed their heads to be magically floating above the altar. I was also the girl who brought multiple disposable cameras to every prom, who lived for the Walgreens photo center pickup days when you could finally see whose eyes were closed, which shots were too blurry, and which ones were totally frame-worthy. I became the girl who took too many digital pictures in college during the rise of Facebook and shared (somewhat questionable) memories hoping my mom didn't scroll through every single one. I was the girl who didn't want to forget a single minute of life.

So, when this photography fascination poked its head into my adult life, I started to pay attention. At the time, I was planning my own wedding, leaning on professional editorial shoots and the few wedding blogs in existence back then to guide my own decisions. I was looking at wedding photos day in and day out and as the girl who deeply cherished her own parents' wedding—complete with the brown ruffled tuxes and my dad's permed hair!—I wanted to make sure that my wedding story was documented just as beautifully for future generations to enjoy.

We couldn't afford a wedding photographer, so we hired a college student from my church youth group to snap a few engagement photos—in a darling, golden-lit pumpkin patch, of course. From that very first "session," I became more and more curious about photography. I found myself scrolling online ads for a starter camera, something small to play around with. I wanted to document things like my own wedding shower, all the DIY projects I'd do, random sofa cuddles with our dog, fueled entirely by my daydreams about hanging canvases on the wall of our first apartment together. I wanted our lives to be remembered, and I was already imagining the photo albums that would live on for decades. (I'm laughing as I write this, because pretty much every photo still lives as a JPEG on a hard drive!)

And on one random afternoon, I found it: a $300 camera sitting right there on craigslist, in broad daylight, waiting for me. A tiny talisman to set my dream hobby spinning into motion. Practically begging for me to come and claim it. One "Is this still available?" email exchange later, and what started as a spark turned into a blaze.

Now, I know what you might be thinking: *Sure, Jenna, your passion was obvious. You knew what you wanted! What if I can't even figure that part out? What if I don't have a passion? What if I don't know what I want?* Stay tuned, worry not, there's more to come on that. But before we get to the passion piece, we're going to stop to chat about the *plan*.

After I scored my new camera, I felt a tug to not just use it for myself. I brought my camera along to my brother-in-law's wedding in Jamaica and ended up taking a bunch of pictures. Blame it on the reggae and the rum, or the fact that I didn't fully trust the resort photographer to do their story justice, but man, *I felt inspired*. We're talking hanging the dress in a palm tree, styling the rings on a bottle of Red Stripe, the whole nine yards! Once home, I edited the photos with (admittedly terrible) filters and uploaded them to share in a Facebook album titled, "My First Wedding Photography Project." The adventure of it all spurred this idea to really go for it. Who knows, maybe this could be a thing? *My* thing? My *exit strategy*?

A few Facebook "likes" and kind words on that album about my Jamaican photography project and I was *obsessed*. Photography meant I could preserve and *literally zoom in on* life's very magical, intimate, and often private moments—my own and everyone else's. Weddings. Births. Engagements. Ceremonies and celebrations of all kinds. I wanted that skill. I wanted that magic. *I wanted that life.*

Every time I thought about being anywhere but here, my mind drifted to all those scenes I imagined happened in the life of a photographer on the regular: coffee-shop editing; laughing in a field with two people in love; living life behind a lens as a "life documenter." I'd imagine hearing the *click* of the shutter button and holding my breath as I caught something in my lens I knew someone would treasure forever.

I started to get little requests here and there asking if I could bring my camera along to engagement parties, wedding showers, and other important moments in my friends' lives. I decided to play around with this idea of a photography side hustle. Could I really do it? And could I be paid to do something I actually loved? I wanted to find out.

To kick-start the dream, I wanted to create an actual, real-life collage of my all-time favorite wedding images—ones I'd been saving from all over the Internet and that had been cluttering up my computer's desktop. (Obviously, these were the days before Pinterest existed, so my only option was going full DIY.) I'd already built up quite the collection of inspiration photos to piece together the vision for my own wedding with Drew. I could see myself as the bride in each and every one—here, with a birdcage veil; there, with berries in my bouquet. But now, with this big dream in my brain, I started seeing myself not as the bride, but as the one photographing her.

The idea of studying each image and imagining being the one behind the lens, directing moments like the ones I saw in magazines just felt *right* to me. The notion of being able to capture the beginning of someone's love story would be an honor that I was so ready to show up for. I picked up a clearance lunchbox, the squishy, fabric kind, from an endcap in Target to use as my camera bag, and I began to envision all the places I'd take it. I decided I wanted this little collage to live in my makeshift camera bag, because who knew? Maybe someday it would become not just a vision board of my dream but a source for on-the-go posing inspiration! Regardless, until then, it would be a signal for me to stay awake to the dream.

I know what you might be thinking . . . a vision board *is* a little woo-woo, or arts and craftsy, but trust me, I've learned that when you mix the woo with the work, magic can happen. So, on a particularly late night in a particularly empty office, I printed out my collage on the fancy office color printer, tiptoed to the copy room, and pressed start on the office laminator. Slowly, surely, I watched my vision become fully realized, right before my eyes. *Grooms in cornfields! Ring bearers in bow ties! A bride in pearls!*

And then, I heard a terrible, horrible noise. The laminator jammed.

I pushed and pulled on the paper, stared at the machine for ten long seconds . . . and then I panicked. You see, no one at my corporate job even knew about my secret dream of becoming a photographer. I hadn't ever breathed a word, partially to protect my position in the company but also because I was terrified to tell them (or anyone else, for that matter) that my dream life wasn't waiting for me between the layers of my payroll paperwork.

Then, I snapped back to reality. The laminator was entirely jammed with my inspiration board stuck inside of it. I had no idea how I was going to weasel my way out of this one without having to share *why* I was late-night crafting using the company's goods, or *why* there was a paper filled with happy couples in romantic poses with *my name* in a scripty font on the top of it.

I tried everything I could to fix the laminator, but even Google results just shrugged at me: "Please see the troubleshooting manual." (Like that hadn't been thrown away years ago? Thanks, Google.) Eventually I decided to call it a night and went home defeated and sweaty from wrestling with the industrial-sized monster.

The next day, I brought up the laminator situation to our office manager, Cathy, and murmured some awkward excuse about how I ended up breaking it. But as the words fell out of my mouth, I knew the truth was bigger than any bulky office equipment: I was living a double life and I was caught in the act.

Maybe not at the *Mr. & Mrs. Smith* level, but I was straddling the corporate ladder and my unbridled passion; riding two Clydesdale horses going in different directions. And while Cathy helped me pry the laminator's claws away from my makeshift collage, I was getting a palpable push to prepare myself for the choice I needed to make sooner rather than later.

As Cathy reached into the mangled mouth of the laminator and pulled out the scraps of my collage with a puzzled expression, I blurted out, "Outside of the office, I've been trying to figure out how to become a wedding photographer. I'm actually really excited about it, and I know I shouldn't have used the office laminator, but I had this creative idea . . ."

I caught my breath and paused, saying a silent prayer she wouldn't tell my boss and get me fired. But Cathy's eyes lit up in a way I now recognize as a side effect of witnessing honest passion—*it's contagious.* In the buzzy fluorescence of that gray copier room, she watched me come alive. Then like a game of tag where Cathy was suddenly "It," she glanced around the office to make sure no one was listening as she whispered, "Oh, you're speaking my language! I totally get it. I'm a scrapbooker!" (Truly, I ought to have guessed given the ornate beauty that was her bulletin board.)

Passion isn't just something that spontaneously happens in us. It can spark up even when we watch other humans step out of their comfort zone and into their daring future right in front of us. In coming alive to our passions, we invite others to do the same. It's this undeniable energy that transfers from human to human, growing as it's celebrated. In sharing our dreams with someone else, we take the first step of many: admitting we have something pulling at our curiosities, and we just might be courageous enough to pursue that thing. And in that tiniest admission of courage, our to-dream list becomes our to-do list.

It's time for you to breathe life into your dreams. Naming your dream out loud—whether to your Cathy or to the mirror—is an act of courage. Cathy happened to be the first Not-Drew person I told about this dream of mine to become a wedding photographer. Up until that point, I had held that vision close to my heart, afraid to share it with anyone, because I knew if I put it out into the world, I had a responsibility to live up to it.

This first, shaky step is where our confidence grows. This is where the "magic happens." This is how dreams become reality. When we speak the words in our heart, even when we're not sure what's going to come out. Chances are, those words, those ideas, those verbal expressions of passion won't come out perfectly, especially if they're new to being acknowledged. But when we speak our ideas and passions and desires out loud—either a piece at a time or all at once—we're not only declaring an intention, we're practicing using our voice to express what we want. We're telling the people closest to us what we like, what we hope for, what we envision. And we're hearing it, over and over, for ourselves. As we repeat these words like a mantra, we get familiar with them. We refine them. We pick up that dream and we bring it out into the world.

## HOW ARE YOU, REALLY?

What are you dreaming about today? Speak it out loud, even if it's just one of a few that you carry. Write your dream down every chance you get. Then, tell someone else about it. The first person you think of: your neighbor, an Internet friend, your office manager. Pay attention to what begins to happen.

If I really wanted to escape that windowless office, laminated collages certainly weren't going to be the bread crumbs leading me out. More than inspiration, I needed a *plan*. I had to figure out what was necessary for me to learn, create, or get help with in order to turn this idea into a real, paying job. A job that could, hopefully, make me feel more alive. A job that didn't leave me with a pit of dread in my stomach. A job that made me feel like I was riding the right Clydesdale into the sunset. At the very least, a job where I was both getting paid *and* enjoying myself. What a concept, huh?

While the vision was strong, making it happen would require a lot from me. I knew one thing—success isn't like chia seed pudding; it doesn't gel overnight. So I got to work using every scrap of time I could dig out of the margins of my week. I watched countless YouTube tutorials, I researched well-known photographers' blogs for inspiration, and I took endless notes whenever my brain said, *This! Remember this, Jenna! No clue why, but this feels important!*

This was *my* process. It was then, and it still sometimes is today! My anxiety about feeling like I was trying to catch up to a new kind of life was quelled when I sat and studied in this way. I couldn't make up for a lack of a four-year degree in photography, but I could place my butt in the seat of a student, committed to mastering a craft. I knew that just because I didn't know exactly what to do with all the water, I still needed to be a sponge.

I took the visions in my head and started to write them down, seeing if my dream could actually become something more. I analyzed what my time and growing talent could be worth. I ran the numbers and created a budget. I started a Facebook page. I hired an accountant before I had made a single dollar, and I took out an ad, believing in my vision enough to put my hard-earned money where my mouth was. All of my spare dollars went into paying off student loans and any money I made from my first few photo shoots went right back into starting the business.

While most fiancées snuggle up on the couch to watch movies together, Drew never once minded that I spent most nights and weekends behind my computer screen. At my side, he fiercely supported the belief I had in myself to turn my camera into something more. And yes, once we were married, we *both* committed to eating a lot of instant ramen until our budget allowed us to journey into other parts of the food pyramid.

For a full year, I was halfway to my dream. One foot in, one foot out, trying to shift my weight around just to stay upright. Ever been there?

What I want to tell you about goal-digging is this: you don't have to quit everything, hand in your two weeks' notice tomorrow, and up-end your whole life in order to live out your passion. (Likely, that's not a viable option anyway.) Perhaps burning it all down *is* the right move for you, but the odds are that, like a game of chess, you're going to have to make many of your moves slowly, with calculation. You're going to have to walk slowly in the direction of yourself, one small step at a time.

In fact, science backs up this slow-but-steady strategy. According to B. J. Fogg, a behavior scientist, the director of the Stanford Behavior Design Lab, and author of *Tiny Habits: The Small Changes That Change Everything*, big dreams happen by going small. "You must first simplify the behavior," he says. "Make it tiny, even ridiculous. A good tiny behavior is easy to do—and fast."[1]

You know the drill: Lace up the running sneakers. Set the alarm only five minutes earlier. Drink just eight more ounces of water. Leave the Post-it note where you can see it every day. You don't have to scrap everything. You don't have to upend your entire life in an attempt to fast-track your way to success. You don't have to do that thing so many of us do—make a major shift all at once, get overwhelmed, then give up because your ambition is way too big to chew.

Instead, start small. Think tiny (or, as Fogg says, ridiculously tiny). When we think tiny, we're putting ourselves in a place of action *right where we are*. We're skipping past the point of observation, or distraction, or excuses, knowing that, in this moment, we're already at the starting line. We're ready to go.

If you want to be some*where*, some*thing*, or some*one*, but the process of getting there looks a thousand miles long, just get as close as you can. Want to start a fashion label? Borrow your grandmother's sewing machine and make one cool caftan out of old curtains. Want to run a coffee shop? Become a barista. Want to craft your own cheese? Watch YouTube videos to learn how to salt brine and wash some feta.

The gist is this: intentionally place yourself in the proximity of what you'd like to try. Grab coffee with someone who has some experience or advice they're willing to gift you. Search for a little extra time in the margins of your existing responsibilities and "moonlight" in your next adventure. Open up a savings account that you drip small amounts into whenever you can. Over time, these collective actions— *stating* the passion, *simplifying* the plan, and *starting* the process—are what lead to massive change in the direction of your dreams.

Change happens when the woo meets the work. I run a podcast called *The Goal Digger* podcast so obviously I'm a big fan of setting goals, but the biggest issue I come across is that it usually stops there. Sure, goal-setting is great. But that's kind of the easy part. Don't we want goal-*getting*, too? Both will require us to get comfortable with goal-*digging*: doing the work of uncovering every barrier that's in the way of discovering your next steps.

When it comes to moving through step one, step two, and beyond, it's easy to lose steam and decommission ourselves before we ever really get going. We bog ourselves down by thinking of all the things that could go wrong but never allow ourselves to imagine what could go right.

I get it. The thought of starting over or changing paths can be terrifying. How do we trust ourselves to choose the right one? How do we trust in our ability to architect something better? How do we know we'll be on the right track this time? The truth is, we will never know for sure what's ahead, or that it will be exactly as we imagine it on our vision boards. But here's the secret: *none of that matters.*

You don't have to predict the future in order to play big in the present. There's inherent risk in doing anything new, even if it's just a risk to your ego, because learning something new can be a big ol' challenge to your confidence. It's about having faith that—if you fall—the fall won't kill you. Because *falling down is so much better than never rising up.*

The gift of *beginning* is one you must grant yourself. Once you get started, you'll start to see breakthroughs where you used to see roadblocks. You'll observe where you lack in resources and where you can switch on your own resourcefulness. You'll get playful. You'll make it fun. You'll stop freaking out about what success *should* look like and when you're going to get there and how much work it's going to take, and instead, you'll decide to call this whole thing what it is: an experiment in living, the ultimate adventure.

Soon, you'll be surprised to find yourself halfway to a dream. It'll take grit and discipline. You may have to get creative with your spare time, quitting a few tempting distractions—a year without Netflix, anyone?—and commit yourself to taking micro actions that will help you learn and grow. There might be a season where you're admittedly burning the candle on both ends. But chances are, if you're doing something you've always hoped to do, you'll probably love every second of it. You'll probably come alive. In fact, I know you will, because I did.

This story isn't one that happened in the course of one night or even one month. It took me an entire year of long desktop days and late laptop nights. A year of photographing weddings on weekends, filling out corporate spreadsheets on weekdays, and editing, learning, and growing in every moment between. But I did it. On a bright Friday afternoon, I stood up from my desk chair, walked over to my office door, and removed the nameplate. I packed up my office, kicked my dust bunnies, and exited that building for the last time. I like to think my girl Cathy cheered me on the whole way to the parking lot.

Something very significant happens once you decide to step out of your comfort zone and walk toward something new. When you decide to turn to the amorphous dream and give it a shape, say it out loud. Admit to yourself you want something different. Say you're ready for a change. Say it to someone who loves you! Write it in Sharpie on your planner or in your journal.

Wherever or however you speak it—declare that you're willing to work for a truer life, whatever it takes. That slapdash, faraway dream? Name it, *because it's about to be born.*

# 4

# the cozy corner:

## HOW TO HEAR YOURSELF
## (AGAIN)

**Don't try to comprehend with your mind. Your minds
are very limited. Use your intuition.**

**—MADELEINE L'ENGLE**

"Help! This decluttering experiment is a TOTAL FAIL."

Sarah's text came through just as I was headed out the door for errands, but in girl code, an SOS text always warrants an immediate response. I typed, "TELL ME EVERYTHING!" and her voice memo came through faster than I could find my keys.

She'd been working her way through this new, flashy book she'd heard everyone raving about. It was designed to rid your house of any excess, to declutter every bad decision and impulse purchase and extra spatula you've kept hidden in your kitchen drawer for way too long. Sarah followed the experiment *relentlessly*. For weeks, she went through every single step. She packed bags and bags of excess clothing and dropped them off at Goodwill. She even begged her husband to install that pretty open shelving she saw the author recommend, because it's important to have "a place for everything and everything in its place!"

The book's premise was simple: declutter your life and feel less overwhelmed. But Sarah felt more overwhelmed than ever before.

My response was quick: *What's your gut telling you?*

Let's pause for a sec to talk about intuition. You know, that fancy, mysterious word in a quote you see on Instagram or pinned to a Pinterest board. That vague feeling we all reference when we're not sure why we know something but we just deep-down-in-our-fiery-bellies know? Some call it a punch to the gut. Others call it a gentle nudge. A knowing. A hunch. It's been called a light bulb, or a third eye, or even a lightning bolt.

Whatever you call it, it's there. I've got mine, you've got yours—we've all got this custom, built-in GPS system guiding us toward a life that is wholly *ours,* a life ready to teach us exactly what we need to learn when we're ready to learn it.

Whenever I think of intuition, that built-in GPS system guides me straight down a winding road, right to my grandparents' home. As a kid, I remember knowing a long weekend likely meant we'd be loading up the car and heading to my grandparents' farm deep in the country in rural Minnesota. The house is set at the end of a long dirt driveway, lined with tall pine trees my grandpa planted with his own two hands decades earlier. When our car tires would rumble down the lane, a herd of cows peeked over their vast fence line to greet us upon arrival. With views overlooking their lake with the scraggy, little paddleboat that we'd take out to the middle of it before diving into the murky water, it was exactly what you'd imagine when you think of a Minnesota farm. Quintessentially cozy. A second home of childhood dreams.

It was here, in this charming setting, that I first remember encountering my own intuition.

Whenever we went to stay with my grandparents, after a long day filled with pancake-eating contests and fresh air and epic games of hide-and-seek in the barn, we'd pop in a movie and snuggle together on the living room floor. Like kids do, we'd usually fall asleep before the movie ended and get magically transported to our beds. (I wish this still happened as an adult; why does no one transport me to bed anymore?) When I was lucky, I'd end up in a spot called "the Cozy Corner," which was essentially a square plush rug tucked in the corner of my grandparents' bedroom that all of us kids vied for.

I know what you're thinking: You *wanted* to sleep on a rug on the floor? We actually didn't even think twice about the fact we were on a rug with a pile of blankets and without a mattress. We just wanted to be in our grandparents' room. That comforting closeness was what we wanted whether we knew it or not.

A recipe-card-turned-placard hung above that little area with that very name scrolled across it in my grandma's perfect, old-fashioned cursive. Waking up in the Cozy Corner gave us the excuse to climb into bed with my grandparents once the sun had risen over the lake. We'd peek up and over Grandma's side of the bed next to a small stack of half-read books and *Reader's Digest* issues on her nightstand to squeak out our first good mornings.

One such morning, I bounced into bed between my grandparents and as I looked at them with my chin resting in my hands, my grandma asked me, "Jenna, why are you so beautiful?" I turned to her very matter-of-factly, without pause, and said, "Because that's how God made me." Even as a little girl, I believed I was uniquely created. I believed *all of us* were.

There was always an unexplainable, unapologetic confidence within me. It's something my parents chuckle about, even to this day. I was the little girl who spent her Minnesota winters at the hockey rink skating up to strangers on my double-bladed unicorn skates saying, "Hi, I'm Jenna, *J-E-N-N-A*, wanna be my friend?" I became the kindergartner who sat with the fifth grader on the bus, sharing popcorn and giggles. I grew into the little girl belting out the words and enthusiastically doing all the hand motions at the winter choir concert. That was just the little person I was: confident, not *too* cool, and sure she was made to be just the way she was.

Looking back, I was fortunate enough to be raised in a family where confidence wasn't something to shy away from. My opinion—like that of anyone else—was welcomed around the dinner table. I was often encouraged to stand up for what I believed in—even if that meant conflict, or confusion, or contradiction. And I was always, always taught to check in with myself. To listen to that still wildly confident five-year-old voice. To ask: *How am I, really?*

But I recognize plainly that this isn't true for many of us, especially women.

Maybe you were similar in many ways. Confident in your own skin, assured in your own beliefs, rooted in your own values, until . . . something else happened. Maybe you lost your inner confidence all at once in a memory you still can't shake. Or maybe, like me, it was a slower process. As the years stretched longer and the pancakes stacked higher, your little five-year-old self grew into a kid who started to take notice of the world. And maybe as time passed, the message you received from this world is that your confidence and how well you think you know yourself simply can't be trusted. That your opinion about yourself is flawed, and always will be. That you need to rely on the world's opinion of you, because they're the ones that greenlight all your opportunities, right? That, at some point, you need to take your rose-colored glasses off because, *Honey, if you don't, life is gonna eat you alive!*

It's no surprise our instincts begin to fade or we find ourselves questioning our own intuition. From the early days of elementary school, we're conditioned to sit still, to quiet down, and to rarely, if ever, question authority. We're told to trust the experts because they know "best." We're taught to follow the rules and march in a single-file line, heaven forbid we have our own ideas about where we're headed.

Now, rules and boundaries are certainly necessary, and both are essential to keep our world from utter chaos. But when we're young and impressionable, many of these "marching orders" can feel limiting, impacting our abilities to listen to ourselves. As we internalize too many of these messages, we grow up questioning whether or not we really, truly have our own best interests at heart. (Reminder: we *do*.) We wonder if we're wrong to listen to our gut. We second-guess ourselves. We doubt our own knowledge. We stop listening to that five-year-old voice. We drown out our inner confidence and we leave major decisions about our future, our health, our relationships, and our careers in the hands of experts. We take the pill the guy in the white lab coat gives us without doing our own research. We follow the number-one guru's advice on the Internet without checking in with ourselves first. We accept whatever advice anyone offers us as if it's an absolute truth: *Wake up earlier if you want to be successful! Stay up late if you want to get stuff done! Slam more coffee if you're too tired to do it all!*

Over and over again, we listen to everyone but ourselves.

And here's the thing about life: There's no shortage of advice, is there? From the youngest of ages, we're offered constant direction from voices who—with great and noble aim—might be unknowingly guiding us further away from ourselves. The aunt pressuring you to join the family business, the teacher insisting you're ready to take another AP class, the mother who has been dressing you in her alma mater colors since before you graduated from diapers—all in good faith, all purely innocent. As we grow, the list of influence expands with our access to other social circles—both online and off. Our horizons grow exponentially as we're introduced to more and more unofficial mentors.

In our quest for the "best," we learn to keep picking up more advice, probably more than we were ever meant to. The best becomes a line defined by everyone else or people with influence and power. In our weariness for the right path, we grab hold of whatever blueprint or compass is closest. We become information-gatherers, rather than intuition-seekers.

Like my friend Sarah, we buy the decluttering book (or the meal plan, or the gym membership, or the skin-care system) without ever considering whether or not it will work in the context of our lives. We don't pause to ask ourselves how someone else's advice will translate into the rhythms of our day, or the long-term goals for our future.

We must question how incoming information aligns with our own intuition. We must ask ourselves: *Does this feel true to me? Does this method or path align with my goals? How is my gut responding to this information? How am I, really?*

My friend Sarah didn't stop to consider if this author's perspective matched her own. Here she was, with six kids, a dog, and a husband who owned way too many sneakers, trying to follow the decluttering plan of an author who lived alone with various houseplants and a disposable income. Here she was, coercing her family to get rid of all their extra stuff so her house would look like the ones in her Instagram feed. Here she was, trying to justify whether or not to keep the ugly plastic cash register her kids loved but didn't look "pretty" or "styled" or "decorative" on that new open shelving. Here she was, trying to fit an overwhelming project into small pockets of her day *so she would feel less overwhelmed.*

Now, I'm not saying to ignore outside information entirely. I don't believe the *only* voice we need to listen to is our own. The truth is, to make our best decisions, we need both information *and* intuition. We can learn from those on similar paths as we forge our own. And we live in a wildly beautiful time where we have the capability and the access to learn anything—at any hour!—from our pajamas, no less. But we must be vigilant about which voices we allow to guide us.

When we start to pay closer attention to how what we consume makes us feel, we are invited to create boundaries around what we will let in. This doesn't mean that life should become one massive echo chamber or that you simply click unfollow the moment you disagree with someone, but this does mean you have full permission to be the gatekeeper of what comes into your life.

Not only is this permissible, but it's vital. According to *Harvard Business Review*, current research suggests that "the surging volume of available information adversely affects not only personal well-being but also decision-making, innovation, *and* productivity." In short? We're paralyzing ourselves with other people's opinions.[1]

That's *exactly* what happened to me. Fast-forward a few decades from my own cozy corner, and there I was, having left a job I didn't love in order to create a career I did . . . still marching to the relentless beat of other people's opinions. I went from having an impressive-sounding title that made me feel secure to a title I made up myself, one that, at the time, sounded like a hobby to most people. I wanted people to take me seriously, and I wanted to take *myself* seriously. So I searched nonstop for "the formula" to success. I read all the advice. I clicked on all the articles. I listened to every voice around me, offering their own personal brand of what it meant to be successful: *Work for free! Charge more! No, charge less!*

I tried it all. When those voices said, *Hustle,* I asked, "How hard?"

But those guiding voices, endless tips, and "must-try" strategies slowly began to tune out that audacious and confident intuition I had as a five-year-old. The voice—*my own*—that was bold enough to leap toward a more passionate career was being stifled and silenced by everyone else's ideas. I was etching other entrepreneur's definitions of success and placing them in the part of my brain that told me there was one path to winning, one path to becoming "the best."

I worked hard, then I worked even harder. I took on more clients, more work, more weddings. I went on to be named the top wedding photographer in Wisconsin for four years running. As in my previous work, I was on another rapid upward trajectory. An all-out sprint, actually. Instead of sitting in an office mapping out my promotion strategy, I was working from the couch and climbing a ladder I was unknowingly building for myself in this hunt to feel successful. I had quit the job, but I hadn't quit the game.

I had unintentionally created a life that was on the fast track to robbing me of my values, again: the ability to do the things I loved with the people I loved. I'd become an entrepreneur to gain back my time, to reclaim my life, to make more memories. I had visions of afternoon coffee dates and working from bed after sleeping in, waking up rested (with glorious bedhead to boot). I had believed I was going to experience true freedom but instead I felt trapped with commitments.

In reality, I quit my nine-to-five only to end up working 24–7. Don't get me wrong, I was happier than I had been punching someone else's time clock, but that happiness was coupled with exhaustion. I was so wildly passionate and so curious about learning new techniques that I'd tell myself, *I'll stay up just one more hour. I'll take that break when things slow down. I'll sneak in an episode of* The Bachelor *once I plow through this to-do list first.* But the to-do list kept growing, with no end in sight.

There was no CLOSED sign on the Internet, after all. I'd read about a new editing filter I should try, and then I'd spend my evenings playing around with it. I'd come across a really cool website template and spend all weekend learning how to code and tweaking my WordPress site. I'd join the new social platforms and figure out how best to market my work there, and here, and everywhere—whatever could keep me more connected, more inspired, going and going like the Energizer Bunny with a sunny disposition and a Nikon strapped to her chest.

My values got lost as my work became more important than my life. I missed friends' weddings, weekends with Drew, time at the family cabin, and farmers market afternoons strolling through aisles of Wisconsin cheese curds and lavender soap. And I realized, this might *look* like success. But this does not *feel* like success. I finally got really honest with myself and acknowledged that even with all I had built and the ways I had succeeded, it didn't *feel* like I had expected it to.

Want to get clear on what success can look like specifically for you? Let me lead you through an exercise my business coach taught me at

WWW.JENNAKUTCHER.COM/MORE

I had envisioned that version of success feeling different, being different. I envisioned free time and enough money to splurge on that new dress from Anthropologie, but I found myself working so hard I wasn't even enjoying the fruits of my labor in my dog hair–covered yoga pants.

And that's when that little voice whispered to me again, telling me it was time to take a step back. To listen up. To check in with myself. To ask, *How am I, really?* And to get quiet enough to hear the answer.

### HOW ARE YOU, REALLY?

Picture your five-year-old, knobby-kneed, maybe freckled self. What do you love? What do you want? What do you need today? What are they whispering to you right now?

Many times in my life, my grandma recounted that early moment on her bed—my five-year-old, uncontested confidence, my belief that who and how and where I was was exactly how I was intended to be. I'm now convinced she wasn't simply strolling down memory lane when she'd mention that. She was reminding me to hear my own voice, she was attempting to return me to myself, to big dreams and cinnamon-sugar pancakes and my unwavering individuality. That's what the best voices do. They don't always show you the way forward. Sometimes, they show you the way *home.*

My grandma makes sure I never forget my childhood spirit. Her constant reminders of my strangely confident self and my firm inner truth have guided me through many crossroads I've encountered since. When I spend my time thick in the fog of overwhelm, wishing I had a map or cheat sheet, that story from my childhood flashes a floodlight on my next best choice. It was such a small, seemingly insignificant moment, but when I wield that "knowing," that confidence, I feel stronger.

It's been said our intuition is a whisper, but for me, it's just a little blond girl on a Minnesota farm. Matter-of-fact, without pause, zero intentions to play it cool, and keen to tell it like it is. If my intuition sounds like a five-year-old with confidence, I know I'm on the right track.

Tuning into our intuition requires that we first be willing to get quiet. To be still. To ask *ourselves* for advice before we ask someone else. And to learn to trust the answer we hear. Once we practice the fine art of hearing ourselves, we can create our own set of unique, God-given truths while also leaning into some of the teachings of those who have gone before us or even those wise ones next to us.

Francis Cholle, author of *The Intuitive Compass*, puts it this way: "We don't have to reject scientific logic in order to benefit from instinct. We can honor and call upon all of these gifts, and we can seek balance. And by seeking this balance we will finally bring all of the resources of our brain into action."[2]

*It's in the science* and *the self.*
*The work* and *the woo.*
*The Google* and *the gut.*

When we invite that balance, we can begin to recognize the differences between our own voice and the voices around us. We start to find peace about whether or not we're *doing the right thing.* We can start to hear our own voice again, loud and clear, above any other noise. It sounds different for each of us, but it's there and it's impossible to describe because it's not just within us, it *is* us. It speaks our language, and you'll know it when you hear it. And also? You'll know it when you *don't.* (My friend swears she can always tell when she's letting another voice drown out her intuition because her intuitive voice—her native tongue—never uses the word "should.")

My method of listening to the rules, processing them, and asking myself which ones I can break is a strategy I have stitched directly into my character. As the muscles of my intuition become stronger, it becomes easier to know how to sift through outside advice and take what's meant for me, letting the rest go without apology.

It will take time to gain enough courage to fire your favorite guru and replace it with your intuition. But as soon as you do, you'll realize that what you once believed to be absolute truths are truly mere suggestions. You'll know that the best path for you is one you can stand firm on. And more often than not, you hold the directions yourself.

I visited my friend Sarah a few weeks ago and smiled when I saw that her beautiful open shelving proudly displayed the kids' favorite cash register. As we sipped coffee on well-worn sofas surrounded by well-loved stuff, I couldn't help but think how welcoming her home felt. It was wholly Sarah. Perfectly lived in. Warm and vibrant, with just a few improvements left over from her decluttering experiment: a new plush rug, a happy little plant, and a shoe bin for all those sneakers.

It looked like the coziest corner of all.

# 5

# mothers studying mandarin:

## HOW TO HAVE SOME FUN AGAIN

**Creativity itself doesn't care at all about results—the only thing it craves is the process.**

**—ELIZABETH GILBERT**

"I'm so stressed out. Everything feels hard right now. The baby won't sleep and the house feels so tense all the time and work has just been . . . insane. I mean, I know it's just a phase. I know I shouldn't complain. But I'm totally burned out." That was where the text message ended. At first I paused, not totally sure how to respond. Do I encourage her to stick it out with work? Drop off muffins? Take the baby so she can nap/shower/cry?

In the end, I settled on all of the above. But also, I sent this: "When's the last time you felt joy?"

Remember the spring of 2020? When the whole world broke wide open? When a global pandemic redefined what it meant to be a human being walking this planet? Stay-at-home orders circled families together as they problem-solved what a new normal might look like under their roof. Office employees became remote workers overnight. A whole generation of homeschoolers cropped up out of necessity. As essential workers bravely showed up to carry us through the confusion and fear, we all had to find new ways to ask for help, connect with our friends, and see our family. (I had to personally come to terms with just how often I touch doorknobs.)

It was hard, wasn't it? Achingly hard, and it left us all with a profound sense of gratitude for frontline workers, educators, and the simple things that once brought us joy. Maybe what you missed most was splitting a burger at your favorite local restaurant, or aimlessly browsing the aisles at the co-op picking out your favorite brick of cheese. Maybe it was hugging. Just hugging.

In the absence of normalcy, of "life as we knew it," many of us played around with things that might trickle the joy back in. With the time saved on commutes and traffic, a lawyer I know joined free ballet classes on Zoom. I heard of mothers studying Mandarin alongside their seventh-grade kids. My friend, on furlough, fiddled around with a ukulele he hadn't picked up in over twenty years. Maybe it was because we had more time, maybe it was to save us from boredom, and maybe it was to get the heck away from everybody else in our house. Or maybe we were all just looking for ways to drown out the existential dread we collectively faced as a world.

No matter the reason, people of all walks of life found pockets of time—some deeper than we'd ever wished for. In my own small family, we took up hiking and biking, and our dining room table became cluttered with tiny puzzle pieces. We bought an espresso machine and learned how to steam oat milk to craft a perfect latte. We kept our cars parked outside in the cold Midwestern winter so Drew could do burpees in a makeshift garage gym. I pulled out the slow cooker and perfected the recipe of my now infamous "street corn soup."

The pandemic was a collective burnout-to-breakthrough moment if we were one of the lucky ones. We were tired. We were confused. We were scared. And what saved us, as researchers like clinical psychologist Dr. Jeff Gardere suggests, surprised us all: *our hobbies*. "In time[s] of uncertainty and instability . . . people need an anchor to familiarity and what once brought them comfort, stability, safety, and happiness," Gardere said.[1]

I don't want to gloss over the fact that there were many people who were not able to slow down long enough to find that anchor. There were kids underfoot who could no longer attend school, aging parents left without caretakers or visits or companions. There were many who could not pivot how they worked week in and week out, who had no time or need to add a single thing to overstuffed routines. But there were also many of us, who, for the first time in most of our adult lives, sandwiched between work and childcare and mounting responsibilities, filled any spare time they could muster with hobbies, passions, curiosities, and creative pursuits. To keep from burning out, they ignited the flame of play.

Play might actually feel counterintuitive when you're falling head-long down the slope of burnout. I mean, the things we do for fun got flagged as a waste of time once we started punching the clock years ago. But play is what helps us slow down just long enough to remember who we used to be and how we want to feel. Together, play and work ignite a spirit that is innately human. We crave both enjoyment and fulfillment. That combo is the *right* kind of fire we're looking for.

Tell me: Are you on the verge of burnout and don't know what to do about it? Maybe you're reading this and you're not sure your breakthrough will ever arrive. Maybe circumstances are forcing you to stay right where you are and you feel just as stuck as you did for the better part of 2020. The truth is, we can't always change our circumstances. But we can always put down an anchor in the midst of the crazy. We can *always* pause to check in with ourselves. And we can, just like Dr. Gardere recommends, revisit something that once brought us comfort, stability, safety, and happiness. We can get really quiet, and really brave, and ask, *How am I, really? When's the last time I felt joy?*

When I encountered my own burnout moment years ago, it was this question that pulled me right into a breakthrough, in a major way.

Here's what you might not know about wedding photography: Since the Midwest wedding season is condensed due to our merciless winters, it's a hard-and-fast grind for six months straight. I worked every single weekend, traveling hours to weddings, shooting all day (which is one of the most exhausting things to do—*period*), only to come home wrecked and smelly, but still needing to slip into my office chair and back up each image onto my hard drive while editing a couple of sneak-peek photos to share before I even entertained the thought of sleep.

Now, don't get me wrong. There are few things as special as being invited into the most intimate parts of someone's life. I was a fly on the wall as a mom zipped her daughter's wedding dress with tears in her eyes. I was the Kleenex keeper when a father witnessed, in disbelief, his baby girl as a bride. I was there for the first whispered vows until the final "Sweet Caroline" chord, and for a day in my life, I was a welcomed part of someone's family . . . like an honorary bridesmaid with a camera.

Being responsible for documenting future family heirlooms was a heavy responsibility but one I showed up to fulfill with a smile and supportive Dr. Scholl's shoes. There was this undeniable high that would come as I left every wedding, hugging all my new friends, sensing their anticipation to see my work, feeling like the girl of the hour. I would slam a 5-hour ENERGY shot and plop down in my car to head home while reliving the reverberations of a celebration that wasn't even for me!

But as much as I loved my job, there were many signs a burnout was on the horizon. My computer traveled with me *everywhere*. I was always plugged in, my phone was basically a cacophony of dings and pings and rings, and my clients would often text me questions at all hours of the day: "Are stripes too much? What about plaid?" "It's okay if we bring the dog, right? Can you hold the leash while you shoot?" "Aunt Mildred says it's too hot, can we switch to a cooler location?" "Hey, I know it's only been twenty-four hours lol . . . any chance I could see more photos yet?" It was like I had jumped on a roller coaster and forgotten to get off.

It's no surprise I started to feel the effects of being "on" all of the time. When we're passionate about what we do, it's easy to take on all that we can, to serve at the highest level. But the highest level is way the heck up there, and the constant climb can be exhausting. It's easy to want to give up. Don't we all have days where we just want to throw our phone down into the Grand Canyon and walk away from it all? That's where I suddenly found myself. I didn't know if my burnout was a phase, or a feeling that would take up permanent residency, but I needed to find out. Did I need to change careers again or just take a nap? I didn't know. But once those grueling six months slowed, I went looking for the answer.

One weekend, while visiting Drew's parents during my off-season, my mother-in-law and I ventured down into their basement, which had become a vast archive of all her creative ideas and endeavors. She was an elementary school art teacher, which meant there was no shortage of pipe cleaners, crayon boxes, heaps of fabric scraps, and every size, texture, and color of paper imaginable.

Lined floor to ceiling with art supplies, that basement was a crafter's heaven. Even though the whole family joked about "the puff paint room," I found myself giving thanks to my mother-in-law's tendency to hold on to things. Looking around the room, we both thought a hobby might offer me a welcome respite for my tired eyes and overworked soul. Something creative to cling to while I rested from my busiest wedding season yet and geared up for next year's (even fuller) calendar. As I dug through her boxes searching for a just-for-fun creative outlet, my fingers grazed against a watercolor palette.

This was the time when watercolor art was *everywhere*. The logo I had designed for my business was watercolor, watercolor calligraphy quotes were blowing up on Instagram, and watercolor wedding invites were the gold standard. You couldn't log into Pinterest without seeing watercolor work popping up under almost any search you'd sling.

I loved the idea that a fun activity I tried as a kid could become something meaningful with a little paint, a dash of water, and the right weight of paper. My mother-in-law, of course, was game to support my latest curiosity. She dug out tubes of watercolor paint, a handful of brushes, and equipped me with every tool I could need to get started. I wanted to experiment and relearn how to watercolor, fully expecting to complete somewhere between four to five sad-looking flowers before discovering I had the talent of the back half of an earthworm.

Once home, I dumped all my gifted art supplies onto the dining room table, and thus my painting station was christened. For twenty minutes a day, I committed to sitting my butt down at that table and painting whatever came to mind. Overlooking the Wisconsin corn-field that was our backyard, seated in an uncomfortable chair I got on clearance at Target, I shut my laptop and grabbed a brush, wait-ing for inspiration to strike. Slowly, each page took shape with words, flowers, abstract designs, my dog, and my coffee cup. Some days were easier than others, but I slowly started to look forward to my water-color breaks. My creativity was slowly trickling back in.

A few weeks later, I was with my mother-in-law in a huge, beauti-ful auditorium waiting to see the play *Wicked*. While the room was still buzzing with people finding their seats, I opened up my camera roll to show her what her art supplies were turning into. I was pretty shocked by her reaction . . . she loved them!

She notched her glasses down to the tip of her nose to see them up close and turned to smile big at me. "Jenna, these are lovely. Have you shown anyone else?" Truth was, I hadn't. I wasn't painting for anyone other than myself, my feeble attempt (that was working) to feel creative again. She encouraged me to post a picture of my paintings online and stop keeping them all to myself, to let people into what I was doing in the same way I had brought my coworker Cathy into my photography dream. She passed the phone back to me, and I felt the tiniest prickling of nerves.

This wasn't my first rodeo of exposing my imperfect art to the world, but she was right. I'd already been in the habit of sharing every-thing from my morning toast to my throw pillows on social media, so what was the deal with my watercolors? Maybe it *did* actually mean a lot to me. Maybe that's why I was keeping it close. I was staring down at a picture of me holding one of my paintings that Drew had taken, a floral wreath with the words "Let's be adventurers" written in the center (long before that phrase was, shall we say, overdone). Just before the lights in the theater went down, I decided to go for it. I posted it on Instagram, immediately slipped my phone into airplane mode, and sat back for (arguably) one of the best Broadway performances I've ever seen in my life.

During intermission, out of habit I pulled out my phone, turned service back on, and saw the notifications flood the screen. There were comments like, "Wait, can I buy that?" and "Please tell me you'll sell this! I want it!" I quickly shut my phone off completely, not knowing what to make of those questions because, frankly, I hadn't even considered such a notion. Plus, we were next in line for the bathroom, and I've got the smallest bladder on earth.

Later as I was responding to the comments on the post, totally floored with gratitude, I started to think about what this hobby could mean in a larger sense: Was my art worth something? Would someone really pay for these creative explorations? I had originally turned to watercolor painting as an outlet for me to detach from my business and all its pressure. Nothing more, nothing less. But what if this creative spark might actually turn into something more? What if I sold that painting? What if I sold more paintings—enough to splurge on a date night with Drew? What if I sold enough paintings to take a weekend off in the middle of my next wedding season? Heck, what if I sold enough paintings to sustain me during the entire off-season of weddings, those lean six months I experienced every year?

In the months to come, I'd pull up to my painting station and churn out a growing variety of sentiments, quotes, and floral arrangements, slowly building up my inventory of watercolor designs. With a little research, I discovered a site where I could run my own little printshop and all I had to do was upload the art and they'd take care of the rest! My prints could be put on things like mugs, pillow covers, phone cases, T-shirts, you name it. Within a month, my digital print-shop had launched.

A few hundred dollars the first month turned into a thousand dollars the next, and pretty soon my watercolor hobby was paying the monthly mortgage on our house. I was going over my latest sales numbers from the week and took a sip of coffee out of a mug with my own art on it when my phone chimed at me. Another handful of sales had rolled in. I thought, *Wow, am I really doing this? Is it actually working?* The watercolor paint stains on my shirt responded, "Yep."

When I initially picked up a paintbrush, I didn't have plans or ambitions, or even the insight to think that it could become a business. That was never the goal, or the why. But those little pansies and peonies I was painting had other ideas! As the sales in my printshop grew, my newly found passive income meant I could book fewer weddings and watch more reality TV on the weekends with Drew. As my overworked body and mind regained their vitality, I learned this invaluable lesson: short-term play reaps long-term rewards.

The reward is in the process itself, that flow you can reach when you lose yourself in a state of momentary, outcome-free bliss. "One way to think about play is an action you do that brings you a significant amount of joy without offering a specific result," writes Jeff Harry, a positive play coach. "A lot of us do everything hoping for a result. It's always, 'What am I getting out of this?' Play has no result."[2]

The lesson here isn't to turn your watercolors into your work. It's to turn your work into watercolors. It's to take the hard edges of your day, or your commitments, or your responsibilities, and make the decision to soften them into something playful. Inviting joy, wherever you can. Inviting play, whenever you can. Inviting creativity, however you can.

Maybe "creative" isn't a word you'd use to classify yourself or a title you'd claim. But creative is more often an adjective or adverb, rather than something you do. Whether you're a mother attempting to meal-plan for a decidedly picky kiddo, a newlywed trying to make ends meet, or an accountant swiveling in the chair of a cramped cubicle, I believe we all are creative beings. But time and time again, we lose the title or claim of creator. We forget that these hands were once covered in finger paint.

Maybe you lost your creativity the way I did—on a fast track to burnout. Or it vanished when you began to learn how to "color within the lines" in order to collect grades in art class. Or maybe you've quieted the creative voice inside you with a digital pacifier, spending hours scrolling through the creative passions and dreams of a perfect stranger rather than scraping together your own.

Perhaps your most playful muscles have grown atrophied from leaning on the guide books, the how-tos, and the proven methods so much that you've started to doubt your ability to return to the posture of creating just for fun.

However you think you've lost it, the good news is this: It's still there. It's always been there. It's in you. Creativity is inherent, ready to be unearthed in any given moment. It doesn't require a basement full of watercolor supplies, a supportive mother-in-law, or even a moment of career burnout. It just needs an outlet. A *reason*. An invitation.

The truth is, even five minutes a day of play can inspire, enlighten, and encourage you. Doing something with the sole purpose of fun and enjoyment will remind you that you're worthy of those two things in their purest sense! How would you fill those minutes if you gave yourself time? If you treated time as a precious currency? If you didn't wait for the burnout to arrive, but instead, scheduled in time to play, be creative, test your abilities, chase your cravings? As my grandfather used to tell me, "Time flies, but you're the pilot."

What can you do in five minutes just for *you*? What is a thing that once sparked your curiosity and joy that you've pushed aside in the busyness of your life? How can you bring it back?

Time is tricky, isn't it? We never feel like we have enough, even when it comes to adding more fun and joy to our lives. If you need a real wake-up call, the next time you find yourself saying you simply don't have time for something fun, for a little playing in your life, for trying something new, shift your words and say, "Creativity is not a priority for me right now" and see how that feels. Kind of an ouch moment, yeah? There's no denying that spare time is a privilege, a novelty, but when we keep putting off the true desires of our hearts and exchange them for things like mindless phone scrolling or online shopping, we're showing what our priorities are through our actions.

I won't pretend it's easy. I know that you're busy. I know that once the juggling begins, it's hard to stop. I know you're wearing many hats and playing many roles. But what will it take to get creative within the roles you're already playing? Saint Francis de Sales once said, "Every one of us needs half an hour of prayer a day, except when we are busy—then we need an hour."

Swap the word "prayer" for whatever makes your heart sing, or what makes your soul recalibrate, or what helps your heartbeat return to you, and you may have just unearthed the secret magic of creativity: that it doesn't exist to fill up our *time*. Creativity exists to become a respite from all the other ways we fill up our time. And in doing so, it fills up our *self*.

I have a friend who was itching to make her way back to the violin, but as a preschool director and part-time caretaker of her mother, she had limited practice time. So now, every Friday, she leads a student assembly at her school, where she and a few other teachers play music for the kids during their snack break.

Another friend of mine was dying to learn how to knit but couldn't find a window of time where she wouldn't be interrupted by one of her three kids under four. So, she joined the local YMCA. While other parents use the free childcare perk to hit the treadmills, she waves goodbye to her littles, finds a quiet corner, and busts out her knitting needles.

Another young, single friend of mine spends her days as a barista in a craft coffee shop (and loves it), but decided to trade in some of her savings for a kiln and wheel to keep on the two acres she shares with an old farmer couple a few towns over. Now she makes, uses, and sells her ceramics at the coffee shop, weaving her two loves together little by little, or as she says, "pulling shots and throwing pots."

If you need a place to start weaving a little more joy into your life, pay attention to your curiosities: the things you Google, the forums you could read for hours, the thoughts that nag you, the YouTube videos you watch, the visions you hold for a *someday* version of you. The things you are curious about or are aching to do are not random, they just might signal an area where you can try, play, experiment, and expand.

Do you want to learn how to whittle? Memorize a poem by Emerson? Learn to tango? Want to figure out how to make your own gelato? Dig for geodes? Knit a mitten or two? It doesn't matter what *thing* you choose. The benefits arrive, no matter the medium. The pausing. The intense concentration. The full-on engagement of learning (or relearning) a task. The mental flow state we get from engaging in play is the absolute antidote to a distracted, passionless life. Trust me. I speak from experience.

"The best moments in our lives are not the passive, receptive, relaxing times. . . . The best moments usually occur when a person's body or mind is stretched to its limits in a voluntary effort to accomplish something difficult and worthwhile," says positive psychologist Mihaly Csikszentmihalyi. "If the activity at hand happens to be something we enjoy and we're good at, we achieve a flow mental state—and it can leave us feeling ecstatic, motivated and fulfilled."[3]

My own foray into the watercolor shop left me feeling all of those things, and more. I went on to run it for a few years, operating as both play and profit, until I decided to shift into a new season of endeavors and explorations. But I didn't shelve the paints for good. Nowadays, you can find me at a just-as-rugged table, crafting side by side with my girls, brushes in hand as I model for my daughters what it means to commit to play—no matter what.

For many of us, finding our way back to creativity requires the bravery to regain what might have been lost in the hustle, lost in the grind, lost to the sea of expectations handed to us the moment we started forming full sentences. It requires anchoring ourselves to the *now*. It requires the commitment to explore, to slow down, to get messy, to become students again. It's in these small moments of curiosity where we find our childlike wonder. Where we claim our liberty to loosen up, to let go. Where we receive permission to meander on or off the page, to color outside of the lines, to move wherever we fancy.

Yep, I'm saying all you have to do is give yourself the time, even a little bit. Time to put down an anchor. Time to find your joy. And all else will follow.

Here, take a brush. Your carte blanche awaits.

# 6

# rumble and quake:

## HOW TO CHANGE YOUR MIND

**The changes we dread most may
contain our salvation.**

**—BARBARA KINGSOLVER**

Remember when "You rock, don't ever change!" was scrawled in our high school yearbooks, sandwiched between "LYLAS" and "Go Bulldogs!"? (While you're at it, remember high school yearbooks?) We meant those lines as a compliment, of course. Even as kids, the implication was as clear as the bubbly fonts and Sharpie underlines: *I like you as you are. Please stay the same. You're cool now. But will you still be cool if you're different? Will you still like me if you become . . . cool?*

As adults, we still do this. We still wish for everything in our lives to stay exactly the same, even though we know they won't. We outgrow friendships. We move states. We change hairstyles, wardrobes, our taste in music. We meet new people, have new conversations, and continually build out our vocabulary for understanding and responding to the world. As we soak up new information, new ideas are formed. Slowly, as we bump and dig and interact, the shape of who we are changes.

While we witness our own changes, we can't help but see it in the people around us. And when the people we love most change? That can be the most staggering shift of all. It's like how a friend struggling in her marriage recently described her spouse to me: "He's just not the same person I married."

And most of the time we say this as if it's a *bad* thing. As if the goal is for us all to forever stay as we once were, with our own enduring interests and desires and safe bets, cryogenically frozen in time for the convenience of everyone around us. I mean, I don't know about you but I'm personally glad I evolved beyond who I was when I was eighteen. And although my nineties tiny eyebrows in the shape of upside-down Nike swooshes were iconic, I'm not exactly that person anymore, and I'm not mad about it.

Change is inevitable. It's as imminent as the moon and the tide and the seasonal Starbucks menu. It's a rite of passage for all of us. Transformation is power, energy, momentum. It keeps us moving forward. It's the one given in life—that everything will change, that all will be made new, that evolution is just around the corner for us all.

And while it can be jarring as hell, I'm here to tell you this: It's okay to change your mind. (It's also okay not to.) It's okay to have different dreams as you grow and age, to transform who you are and who you want to become. We don't yet know everything there is to know. We haven't yet gone through all the experiences in our lives. We aren't finished learning. All of this means we can't lock ourselves into a commitment to never change our minds, unless we commit to never changing our lives. And even then, good luck, because change comes for us all.

I know many of us are raised to fight hard for our beliefs and to stand firm in them. We're encouraged to draw a line in the sand and to set hard boundaries for what we will and won't do. We all know the saying "Stand for something, or you'll fall for anything!" But as new information shakes us, old beliefs form cracks. (Heads up: that's not a bad thing.) People come into our lives breaking molds and gifting us the opportunity to rewrite any outdated ideals we no longer need. Changing our minds means we can be agile and flexible as the ground quakes beneath us. It means letting each new revelation bring about the opportunity for new evolution.

Here is the good news! While change can feel scary and while we're prone to avoiding it, changing who you are is beautiful. Changing your mind isn't failure. Changing what you believe signifies growth. I know it can feel like we're betraying an identity or breaking something that was supposed to be unbreakable. But your identity is *supposed* to shift and transform as you grow.

I can't choose to live a life where I'm predictably consistent in every belief, forever and ever, amen. We all would if that were possible! But instead, we have to say, "I've changed. I'm not who I once was." In fact, the world would be a better place if more of us were willing to speak those words more often.

Here, I'll go first. I definitely whiplashed my friends, family, and everyone I loved when I changed my mind on something pretty major years ago. If I had photographed your wedding, you would have witnessed me cooing at babies, clowning around with toddlers, laughing at dad jokes—heck, dishing out a few of my own. You likely would have stood back and thought, *Now there's a girl who can't wait to start a family.* But had you been able to read my mind? Well, my thoughts might've surprised you.

The truth is, I've always loved kids. I was a certified babysitter at the ripe age of twelve (shout-out, Claudia Kishi!) and was a nanny for a few summers. I even dressed up as a mom of twins one year for Halloween. As I grew older, motherhood was something I pondered at great length. The question *Will-they-won't-they?* tends to come up at some point for every young married couple, either via family culture, peers, or straight-up societal norms. I somehow simultaneously held my own *Will-I-won't-I?* at arm's length for years (which as a woman isn't super easy to do when you already have the ticking biological clock reminding you to make up your mind sooner than later). I heard many friends throughout my adult years say, "I always knew I wanted to be a mom." But me? I just didn't know.

Drew and I were happily married; it was just us two (plus our two unruly rescue pups). We had freedom, a rhythm that left room for spontaneity, full nights of sleep. We felt a level of contentment we didn't necessarily want to challenge. We liked our simple little life without the responsibilities of diapers and middle of the night cry-fests. Like, why *couldn't* it be just the two of us? What was wrong with that? There's a reason Reese's Peanut Butter Cups come in pairs!

So, for the first five years of our marriage, we told our parents we would never have children. Yeah, we used the forbidden "never" word. And whenever anyone asked us about kids (which, let's be honest, happened moments after we said "I do" at the altar, if not before) we just kind of brushed off the thought and assured them we were good and content and had zero plans for kids in our immediate future. Their response was the same time and again: "Oh, you'll change your mind!" Even now, that phrase makes me cringe. I will, of course, change my mind about things, but you and I both certainly have no business in predicting the specifics for each other.

The doubt I carried surrounding parenthood wasn't really based on becoming a mother, but more on the fear of giving up the life and identity I had worked so hard to create. I worried I would lose the freedom I was slowly earning in my tireless pursuit of success as an entrepreneur. I worried I'd ruin my career momentum. I worried about it all. With every ponder of my future, my list of fears and nonnegotiables seemed to just keep growing. I couldn't yet look at motherhood in a way that would show me what I might gain. I was too focused on what I would lose in the exchange.

My list of fears and nonnegotiables kept growing as time went by: I wanted Drew all to myself; I didn't want to "ruin" my body; I required ten hours of sleep a night; I was afraid to push a baby out of my *you-know-where* . . .

But after years of flat-out certainty that a desire to become a mother simply wasn't there, something did change. *I changed.* I could feel my heart starting to crack open and new desires for my life began spilling out. Or maybe it was pouring in; I'm honestly not sure which. For me personally, time was absolutely a factor. We had been married for five full years, traveled together, got our career footing, and bought our first house. We watched as our brothers became dads; we held our tiny nephews in our arms and felt the undeniable connection that comes from bonding with another mini human.

We migrated from receiving invites to friends' weddings to receiving invites to baby showers, sweet little parties with the tiniest diapers and Boppys and Bumbos and all the other weird-named things they make for babies. I watched my friends' bellies expand as the baby inside them grew to the size of an avocado, a mango, a melon. I photographed one of my best friend's births and witnessed moments even more beautiful than the ones that happen at the end of an aisle with quiet vows. I literally watched them meet a human they loved the second they laid their eyes on her.

As we began to entertain the idea of starting a family, we started to realize we had already done a lot of the things we had dreamed of doing together. We were running out of reasons why parenthood wouldn't work or why it wasn't for us. We noticed that the lives we found ourselves living felt like ones we could welcome a child into. I mean, we didn't go out much, we loved going to bed early, and takeout was way more our jam than a fancy night at a restaurant.

Slowly, my vision for my future started to evolve. In the ultimate I-told-you-so moment (joke's on me!), I began to feel those longings deep within me that maybe Drew and I *were* supposed to have kids after all. I started imagining my own home filled with Boppys and Bumbos, a serene nursery with a rocking chair. The desire began to bud its little roots deep into the corners of my heart. The shift in my mind was noticeable. Loud. Banging. Clear.

As I settled into the possibility of a changed mind, I realized that my thoughts around motherhood shifted from what I would lose to all I might gain in becoming a mother. As soon as I removed the fear, I saw the desire to be a mother *was,* in fact, there in me. I saw that I could change my mind, and my changed mind could, in fact, be an invitation to something else just as beautiful.

Ask any human if they love welcoming change with open arms and you'll likely notice resistance. I know how awkward it can be to flip the script on anything that might threaten to shift your life and your identity, even one small part of it. It's like entering uncharted territory, an entire scenario you may have carefully avoided confronting for many years. (Up until this point, I had spent some decent time, energy, and dollars trying to *not* get pregnant, so considering the exact opposite felt like switching hands to write or driving on the other side of the road. Possible, but absolutely wonky at the start.) While not every change comes with a side of identity crisis, it can be easy to look back and see only the life-altering shifts. The hardest pivots. The scariest changes that upended more than we wanted them to.

Is that where you are right now? Are you finding yourself in the middle of a changing mind? Are you feeling resistant to what that means for your life or your future? Maybe you need to change your circumstance, or maybe you just need to change your mind *about* your circumstance. But whether your heartbeat is leading you to baby booties or Bora-Bora, something scary happens when we finally claim, "This *is* what I want for my life." Especially when that thing requires us to step into a new identity and step away from what we've known or what we're known for.

Cognitive scientist Dr. Maya Shankar once shared with me this idea of "identity foreclosure." It's this notion that we often commit ourselves to one identity, a very specific one, without having explored all the options out there, and in labeling ourselves or claiming a specific identity, it can make us feel fixed or stuck.

Want to dive deeper into the idea of identity foreclosure and how it might be showing up in your life? Head to

WWW.JENNAKUTCHER.COM/MORE

to learn more from Dr. Maya Shankar.

Hmmm . . . "fixed" or "stuck," words a lot of us would likely use to describe our current reality. However, getting stuck is one thing, but *staying* stuck is something entirely different. Take it from Ina, who was in her twenties and working in nuclear energy policy, management, and budget for the White House when she thought, *There's got to be something more fun than this!* So she kept her eyes peeled for something that would be just that: *fun.* After spotting an ad for a specialty-food store for sale in Westhampton, Long Island, she made a crazy low offer on a whim. That crazy low offer was accepted. "That's when I said to myself, 'Oh, shoot. Now I have to run a specialty-food store,'" she later told *Time* magazine.[1]

And that was the beginning of Ina Garten's life-altering career trajectory toward becoming the Barefoot Contessa, and, lucky for us, the catalyst for the creation that became known as Beatty's chocolate cake.

It's easy to brush this off as an unrelatable example or a one-in-a-million crapshoot. But isn't Ina's decision the same crossroads we all encounter when on the precipice of change? To leap or not to? To go or stay? To dare or play it safe? To change course or . . . not?

The truth is that change can often create chaos. Sometimes chaos shows up uninvited, and sometimes we know we're the ones who have to put it on the guest list. It can rumble our life as we know it and shake a foundation that once felt firm while we attempt to find our footing again. Change can make us second-guess, well, pretty much *everything.*

"There's this insight in cognitive science called the sunk cost fallacy,"[2] Dr. Shankar says. "[It leads] us to irrationally cling to things that we put a lot of time and effort into because we don't want to experience the costs of departing." That's why so many of us worry that abandoning something we once loved will cost us *someday*, and in doing so, we disregard what living a life that is unfulfilled is costing us *today*.

Sunk cost fallacy is exactly why our closets are stuffed with clothes that no longer fit but we hold on to because we spent so much money on them years ago. It's why we push through and finish the four-year degree we don't really want because we're already halfway there, and wouldn't it be a shame to have wasted all that time? It's why we stay in jobs, relationships, houses, cities, and identities that no longer work for us. We keep and cling and stay, hoping that it will all be worth it, or because we don't want everything we've invested to have been for nothing.

But this is what it means to be human, walking around with a changed mind and expanding heart. Our nameplates get removed and replaced with new titles that better reflect our current passions, interests, or skills. Our Spotify playlists shuffle from Rage Against the Machine to Raffi and back again. We stock our fridge with cheese sticks where the fancy gouda used to be. We replace our lacy thongs with compression socks. With every season of life, our calendars and checkbooks display vastly different priorities. They *have to*. Because with every season of life, we grow into vastly different people.

I know I have. During my own first baby steps into motherhood, I started out as *that mom* who promised herself her kid would only eat organic everything and never have GMOs. But once the idea smashed up against reality? Pouches, Goldfish, and Yogis can be found in every bag, purse, and compartment in my car. File that one under: things I didn't understand until I learned them myself #192,384. File that one under: ways I have *evolved*.

I've promised myself a lot of things throughout my lifetime. *I'll invest in a 401(k)! I'll have a corner office and wear high heels! I'll have perfectly tailored power suits! I'll never be an annoying partner to Drew! I'll gracefully juggle being a mom and a boss! I'll be the hardest worker in the building! I'll find a way to make a difference on this planet every chance I get!* And while some of these promises and goals were beautiful and valid, let's just say I should've known better than proclaiming things in absolutes. I was not wise to make so many promises to myself, just like way, way back in the Blockbuster days when I would let my DVD rentals sit on my coffee table for two weeks, gathering dust and racking up late fees.

While some of the visions I once held for myself ring true, most of them aren't all that enticing to me anymore. And that's okay! Sometimes being open to having your mind changed, to being challenged, means that in the midst of transition, you might feel like a walking contradiction. The most powerful people—both the ones in your daily life and the ones on your daily feed—who have fought for changed minds went through their own transformations. The former Silicon Valley exec now feels convinced to unplug. The style blogger decides to stop promoting fast fashion. The author apologizes for publishing a problematic book twenty years ago. They've overcome or triumphed, they've contradicted themselves, failed publicly, or awakened to a new truth. Or all of the above.

As we examine and explore what it feels like to evolve as a human, we have to keep coming back to our *why*: Why does this matter? Why is this worth the work? Why is this chaos necessary to take me from who I am to who I want to become?

Chances are, if you google "origin story" with anyone who's making or has made a difference in the world, from Oprah to Lizzo, there's likely a story of overcoming or transforming, of using their changed minds to fuel a changed world. They've found themselves in identity crises time and time again and yet they continue to evolve, unfold, and shift as they grow. They recognize that the journey isn't about avoiding change; it's actually all about change. Not resisting it but inviting it. They know there is no shame in changing. I mean, call it silly, but I know this from experience as the girl who used to publicly proclaim her undying love for mac and cheese, and now, ten years later, is solidly gluten-free.

My identity—and yours—will forever be shifting. Maybe little by little, or maybe in big, cracking, sweeping motions. So the big question remains: How can we invite an ever-changing identity? How do we welcome new dreams and honor new ideas? How do we allow change, and even be excited by it?

### HOW ARE YOU, REALLY?

Get really still. What longings are rising to the surface? Which identities are shifting for you? What long-held beliefs are being rearranged, deconstructed, made new? Can you allow space for them to create a bit of chaos? Can you let them rumble and quake?

Maybe that's right where you are today. Maybe you're on the precipice of a changed mind you worry could be wildly inconvenient for the ones you love. Maybe you're feeling nervous about revealing a new side of yourself to the people around you. Maybe you want to get sober but your roommate still wants to split the cabernet tab. You're in the thick of deconstructing your faith but your father is the pastor of your local church. You want to try for another baby but your husband isn't on board. You want to homeschool but your mother-in-law worries about socialization. You want to hang a Pride flag on the front porch but your neighbor says she'll call the HOA. You want to unfold and explore a part of yourself but others have told you to stay quiet. Or maybe you're silencing yourself because you worry a changed identity means you'll no longer belong.

I know I've been tempted on that last one. When I was pregnant with my first daughter, I went on a girls' trip with two wildly successful women, and as most driven women do, we were talking about our goals, all the kinds of things we wanted to achieve, what we were committed to working toward so that the next time we saw one another we could proudly report on all we had done. This idea of showing up to our next adventure and being able to rattle off our accomplishments was undeniably enticing to us as achievers.

But the funny thing was, as I sat there, my hands on my bulging belly, my baby moving around, I couldn't connect with their enthusiasm to conquer the world in the next 365 days. My visions looked a lot simpler. As they shared revenue targets, stages they would speak on, launches they would complete, the promise I made to them (and to myself) was, "Next time you see me, I'll want to report that I have loved on my baby, kept us both alive, and learned how to clothe myself in the identity of being a mama. That's it, that's really all I can commit to." I wanted to not only become a mom . . . but I wanted to let that be my focus, my goal, my sole mission.

After that trip, I spent a lot of time wondering if maybe I was broken because I didn't share the drive I once had, or if my impending motherhood was stealing my ambition. I questioned if I'd ever get my mojo back or regain that desire to conquer the world. And while I felt the friction of a shifting identity, one in transition, I also knew I was as ready as I could be for motherhood to crack me open. To reveal itself to me. For so long I had feared having a child would show me that all the work I had done, the significance I had found in that work, didn't hold a candle to this brand-new soul, and as my stomach rippled and my little one kicked, I prayed that would now be the case.

Truth is, I didn't just live up to those promises that first year, I embodied them. I let the experience of shifting who I was transform me. It felt like I was introduced to an entirely new person as each day passed. Frankly, I've changed in ways I would've never seen coming. Who I am now is nowhere near what I perceived I would even *want* to be ten years ago. And ten years from now, I hope I have grace for the person I am today and the current visions I hold for myself.

Change means we get to let go of who we thought we were or who we've been told we are to become something different. It *also* means we get to allow the people around us to go through that same process, and we get to love them the whole way through, all the way to the other side.

If I could go back and write something different in all of those yearbooks I signed, I think I'd say something like "I can't wait to see who you become. Keep on changin'!" (Although I'd still have a very cool signature with some kind of swirl underneath it.) But I'd love to be able to embrace what I know to be the truest thing about every single human: we're going to change. It's going to be hard, awkward, and challenging to exist in a world that, for some reason, values some changes and resists others. It's brutal to keep transforming, opening up about who we are, and making space for one another, but I hope we never stop.

You're already in the midst of it. Whether you're in an upswing, downswing, or in some swirly middle, I hope you never stop. I hope you begin to see how miraculous it is that you and I *get* to change. As we grow, we're continually accessing more and more of our truest self. You're greeting yourself piece by piece!

I hope we all learn how to accept change as a process of being alive. Because when you do, you'll stop feeling that urge to run in the opposite direction when it comes.

And oh, how it will.

# 7

# a battlefield of cuts:

## HOW TO LISTEN TO YOUR BODY

**The body knows. When your heart sinks.
When you feel sick to your gut. When something
blossoms in your chest. When your brain
gloriously pops. That's your body telling you the
One True Thing. Listen to it.**

**—CHERYL STRAYED**

You know what is absolutely, positively unfair about this wild ride of a life? Once you finally change your mind, you assume the rest of your life will magically fall into place in the direction of your dreams, right? Ever been there? You finally get up the nerve to start that Zumba class and, just two weeks in, you twist your ankle. Or you convince yourself to be a more adventurous eater, order the oysters, and break out in hives with a shellfish allergy. Or you and your family muster the courage to move across the country to pursue a better life and your moving company loses every last box on the way there. Sometimes, our minds jump into gear a little faster than our bodies, and our fumbling feet take awhile to catch up. At least that's how it happened for me.

Once Drew and I decided we'd start trying to have a baby, we splurged for one last hurrah. Hawaii had always been a *someday* trip for us, a place I would sometimes find myself in my dreams. We figured now was better than someday, so we pinched pennies and frugally planned our dream vacation. On an extra-cold Wisconsin morning, I rolled a suitcase packed with sunscreen and sandals as we set off for the clear waters and cloudless skies of Maui.

As luck would have it, my childhood best friend, Mollie, was honeymooning just down the beach from us, and she, at the time, happened to be pregnant. We were sitting in chairs poolside eating nachos and talking about my period (which was apparently lost at sea) when she randomly blurted out, "Jen, I think you're pregnant." She had quickly become an authority on pregnancy, being pregnant herself, and her senses were pointing to a possibility I naively hadn't even considered. I had chalked up my lateness to stress, getting off birth control after a decade of being on it, or something funky with the moon and the tides.

Once Mollie dropped that thought into my head, I couldn't shake it. That night on our way to a luau where mai tais would be served aplenty, our crew swooped into a Hawaiian convenience store to get a pregnancy test. Next stop: public restroom. Before I could even finish saying the words "two double lines," Mollie had kicked in the door of my stall and started screaming. Drew was standing outside, and I'm fairly certain he was frightened over the commotion. But Mollie's intuition was right . . . I *was* pregnant!

After we exited the bathroom and simultaneously told Drew and Mollie's husband the news, we had just a minute to compose ourselves before we were given our table assignments for the feast we were about to enjoy. We quickly ran to the beach, put our toes in the sand, and took photos, looking shocked and holding the positive pregnancy test I had just peed on. Me in my floral wrap with tears in my eyes, Drew with a look that can only be described as excited surprise . . . it was these moments of unconscious bliss that still bring me back to that day, a feeling I will never forget.

That night we celebrated (I'll take a mai tai, make it a virgin), and I slowly started to process what this news meant. While the dancers swayed on the stage and shared their Polynesian culture and history with eager onlookers, my mind couldn't help but wander. A baby was coming. I looked down. It was already here. Right there, inches away from my fingers that were touching my belly. I remember thinking that if this night was just a dream, it was a really good one.

We crawled out of the hotel bed the next day with an "Is this actually happening?" hangover. I took another pregnancy test just to be extra sure I wasn't dreaming and sure enough, I was still pregnant. I called my parents, then my sister, and as I was telling my sister the happy news, my brain took an unexpected turn mid-thought. Perhaps it was morbid honesty, perhaps fear. I said to her, "If we lose this baby, if something goes wrong, I want to share it with the world. It's important that this little life means something."

Even now, my sister remembers being caught off guard by that remark in what should have been a high-key, full-of-giggles-and-awe, celebratory time. For me, that first seed of doubt might have been a hint I did, in fact, have a maternal instinct after all. While I calculated the due date and signed up for all the apps, I also had a keen awareness that not every pregnancy leads to a baby.

We returned from Hawaii in a state of bliss. In every direction I looked I was pulled to thoughts of motherhood. I watched a young family at the airport and looked at them longingly, imagining our life just one year from then. My eyes lingered on the tacky onesies in the souvenir shops, smiling at how tiny they were. I told the woman sitting next to me on the plane that I was pregnant and a little nauseous, just proud to utter the words "I am pregnant."

It's hard to describe if you've never experienced it, but the second I saw those two lines, my life changed. I'd heard it before, but experiencing it really sealed the deal. In my heart, I immediately became a mother, my needs secondary to the poppy seed–sized life I was growing. I became the kind of pregnant person who stopped eating tuna on the spot and went for the organic smoothie. The mother who opted out of the hot tub and steam room, and the one who wouldn't dare take a sip of wine no matter what the Internet says is okay. I wanted to make sure I was doing everything right, by the book.

I dove headfirst into the visions of motherhood, starting a Pinterest board for our future nursery, downloading a baby name app, and signing up for all of the things that tell you a play-by-play of every day as a pregnant person. *My baby is a pinto bean now, and I can't wait for it to be a grapefruit, but not super stoked on the melon-sized part.* My brain was occupied with thoughts of the future, my life expanding for the first time beyond my own existence.

And as much as I want to keep unfurling this first-time pregnancy experience for you, I can't. The rest of this particular story is mostly just the hard parts. Numerous doctors' visits, blood tests, an ultrasound where Drew fainted and then . . . bad news. I heard the words "I'm sorry, there is no heartbeat." There was a surgery that left me feeling emptier than I ever knew possible. There was a devastation that is hard to understand unless you've experienced it for yourself.

We had lost our baby.

The aftermath ravaged me in ways I could have never guessed. I was angry. I was disappointed. I was confused. I lost the will to hold tight to a vision that had consumed me, and I buried myself in anything that could drown out my desires. There were days when I didn't get out of bed. There were days I spent stuck in some kind of no-shower, lots-of-Netflix time warp. Weeks where I felt hatred for my body, feeling that it had failed me, that it had ultimately betrayed me.

> If you or someone you love is grieving a miscarriage, find support at
>
> WWW.JENNAKUTCHER.COM/MORE

I wondered: Who are we if our bodies aren't doing what we want them to do? Or what we think they *should* be able to do? We cannot *be* without a body; they're intrinsically a part of existence. And when they're not okay, we're not okay. The whole of me is *not okay*. So what does it mean to walk around this world in a body we hate, feel disconnected from, or utterly betrayed by?

Honestly, it wasn't the first time I'd felt this feeling and asked these questions about my body. It was the *millionth* time. If I trace this feeling back far enough, I find myself as an eight-year-old, wishing there was a way to separate my body from the rest of me. It's an innocent memory from years ago, and it's one that I still loosen from the depths of my brain when I question how I experience my body as a woman in the world today.

*I am in third grade on a school bus, headed for a field trip to the zoo. The sunlight is glowing through the windows, hitting my legs just right so they glisten. The breeze tangles my ponytail. I feel warm, hopeful, ready for adventure and monkey sightings. But there is a boy, pointing out the hair on my shin, laughing.*

That's my moment. That's the one. The first time I felt disappointed to be living life in my own skin. We all have that moment, don't we? That tiny realization that other people have opinions about our hair, our laugh, our smile? Do you remember yours? And if you do, do you remember what happened next? The path that would likely take us years to understand, and even later, if we're lucky, unlearn?

I went home that night, a whirlwind of emotions, and begged my mom to let me shave my legs. "You're only eight," she'd said. "That's too young." So, I vowed to wear pants for the rest of the school year to hide my hairy legs—no matter the temperature.

But as the spring months grew warmer and pants became unbearable, I decided to take matters into my own hands and rid myself of that embarrassing leg hair—to heck with permission! My parents simply couldn't understand how mortified I felt. Smooth legs were, at the very least, invisible legs, especially to mean little boys on the bus.

I jumped in the shower and borrowed my dad's razor and, well, you can guess what happened next. A few days after my great "experiment," I'd fallen asleep on the couch between my parents—head in my mom's lap, legs reaching over my dad's—only to wake up the next day to one of those we-need-to-talk conversations about the fact that I had gone against their wishes. Disappointment was etched into their faces. After the scolding and my urgent pleas for a razor of my own, my mom, understanding what it meant to move through this world as a girl, gave me a lesson in how to shave without creating a battlefield of cuts. Looking back, she more than likely knew I'd crossed a threshold I couldn't really back away from.

The truth is, we live in a world that created that threshold (and a million others) by offering us tons of messages, most of them false, whether subliminally or spelled out in neon letters. We live in a world that eats with its eyes first, that profits off reminding us our bodies don't measure up. And we march right up to the line on a battlefield of cuts.

Philosopher Simone de Beauvoir wrote of a woman's experience walking that line, saying, "Through compliments and admonishments, through images and words, she discovers the meaning of the words 'pretty' and 'ugly' . . . she tries to resemble an image, she disguises herself, she looks at herself in the mirror, she compares."[1]

Those words were written more than seventy years ago, but even today, disguising and comparing ourselves is an instinct that is still undeniably alive for most of us. While negative body image is still very much the current reality for most women, I'd be remiss to ignore the fact that we're making strides, and we're inviting the generations that come after to follow suit. I am so grateful that women are working to change the age-old definition of beauty to extend far beyond what we once considered alluring. From #nofilter publications to Photoshop-free ads to greater representation in skin color and shape and ability, many powers are at work dismantling the idea that there should be a standard at all. We're waking to the truth that our bodies—these glorious vessels—don't exist to be seen under the gaze of others; they exist to be heard over the whispers of the world.

### HOW ARE YOU, REALLY?

Look at your body today. What is it showing you?
What is it saying to you? What is one uniquely
beautiful thing you're noticing?
What do you love about what you see?

Our bodies beg for us to listen. They want our attention. But sometimes, when we perceive our bodies have failed us, we dissociate. We separate our minds and our souls from our bodies. We let our minds be angered by or become obsessed with our imperfect bodies. We let our souls marinate in disappointment of the many ways in which our bodies don't meet our expectations—from how they look to how they perform to how they age. And we feel unwelcome in our sturdy thighs, our wild hair, our soft bellies, and our smile lines.

So how the heck do we put ourselves back together after decades of believing we're broken, of separating our bodies from our souls? How do we take steps toward connecting our head with our heart and our limbs with our lives? How do we walk our bodies toward glorious wholeness—both today and as we age through tomorrow?

My friend who is a clinical therapist working primarily in the research field of body positivity once handed me a question to ponder that truly shook me: "Jenna, what if you're not just *in* your body? What if you *are* your body?"

Now, wherever you stand on Plato or philosophy or embodiment theories, hear me out. Do you remember that incredible feeling you got as a child, swinging high above the treetops with the sun on your shoulders and the breeze in your hair, when everything was beautiful and perfect and right with the world? You closed your eyes and felt the physical sensations of all of that, in your soul, didn't you? The peace arrived from a depth undiscovered—it was far more than skin-deep. It wasn't just you, thinking or feeling. It wasn't just you, thinking about how you should be feeling. It was you, full stop. Experiencing. Living. *Being.*

Where the heck did that feeling come from? And what would it take to get it back again? To move forward into older age by paying attention to how we *feel* in our bodies, more than how they *look*. To experience gratitude for the smooth satin of our favorite pajamas on bare legs without peeking at the label's size first. To feel the relief of letting our hair down after a long day without criticizing its split ends. To see ourselves, wholly, when we look in the mirror, and not just the ever-changing texture of our faces. To run headlong into the breaking crest of ocean waves and feel cool refreshment over every inch of our dimpled cellulite. To love our sharp angles, or curves, or weak muscles or our bulging ones.

We will have many moments of getting this right, of feeling present and lovely and here, fully alive, as a human being. And we will have many moments of getting this not-so-right, too. Time and time again, I've questioned myself and my worth by the curves and bumps of my meatsuit, the me-shaped-shell that holds my soul, my shimmering personality's Tupperware.

Until one day, years after that first miscarriage, I didn't.

I was standing in an elevator at the corporate office of one of the biggest clothing conglomerates in America, riding to the top floor with two other women. I was twenty weeks pregnant, fresh-faced and in my pajamas. When those women candidly asked me why I was headed to the top floor, I laughed and said, "I know it's hard to believe a thirty-year-old pregnant lady is the model for today's underwear shoot, but here I am." I'm pretty sure I did an awkward pose or dance move as I proudly claimed my role and the elevator doors opened.

From the moment I walked into the studio, I was met with massive editorial photos of beautiful models, a gorgeous receptionist directing traffic, and cushy chairs in the waiting area. Let me tell you this—showing up as the talent for a photo shoot in your pajamas, barefaced with your melasma showing, and your baby belly poking out from under your T-shirt is definitely a "look."

But on my journey to finally get to a place where motherhood would happen for me, I had dropped all the things that had once worried me—the broken-out skin, the weight gain, the stretch marks—and saw them all as signs of my miracle. Ask anyone waiting for a child, fighting for their health, or healing from a traumatic journey, and I think they'd tell you they'd take any and all of the scars, reshaping, and indentations if it meant receiving their own miracle.

Those women in the elevator had no clue of all the things that had led me to that long ride up to the top floor. It would have been easy for me to disqualify myself from that moment, from that entire experience, just as easy as anyone watching would've raised an eyebrow. But I stood there, feet planted, with the feeling that I 100 percent belonged in that moment. A feeling that all of the things that had led up to that day, the things they couldn't see with the naked eye, had prepared me to stand on set, a hand resting on my baby bump, a leaf blower giving my hair that perfect windblown look, wearing a cute ribbed underwear set—with pride. It didn't matter if anyone else saw the miracle in motion: I had lived it and I felt it.

And yet here we are, staring at that body in the mirror and wondering when we'll feel proud of it. We're all grown up and missing opportunities left and right because we don't like how we appear when we show up. We feel disconnected from the person we see in our reflection, our photos, and the voices coming out of our mouths. We're uncomfortable with being seen as we are, especially when we can slap a filter on it or hide behind a digital screen. We still daydream about trading bodies, even entire lives, with someone else. Wasting precious time wishing and waiting to become someone we're not means we're missing what's right in front of us.

*You* are your own miracle in motion. No matter what you've gone through, take a moment to stop and pause on that preposition "through." We've all heard that line that everyone is going *through* something. "Through" is a powerful word, because it means you didn't stop at the front door, the starting line, the opening scene. You went through, beyond, and forward to whatever came next. And your body came with you. It carries the same stories you do; in fact, it's how you moved *through* it all. The sweat, the tears, the muscles in your legs helping you pull yourself up off the floor. The mind that says, *No matter how I am feeling, I will also keep pumping blood to all the right spots.* Your fifth-grade science teacher wasn't kidding. Your body works hard for you. I'd even go so far as to say it loves you, so it matters that we work hard to love it right back.

We all want to experience the wholeness of life, but so many of us refuse to accept the wholeness of *ourselves.* Sometimes, when I get caught up in the spin cycle of ignoring or belittling my body, I try a trick my friend recommends: calling my body by name. I know that sounds a little too simple (and probably a lot too "spiritual earth mama"), but it helps to cross the mental bridge of looking at my body as this thing I'm stuck with that's part of me, and instead realizing it's this thing that *is* me.

*It's Jenna, and I'm Jenna. The Jenna that winces from the bite of a lemon, that laughs loudly at a toddler's knock-knock joke, that cries during the insurance commercial (you know the one), that always carries a set of tweezers to pluck away that stray chin hair. We're the same. We're one. We're in this thing together.*

Whether it was messaging that hit you as a little girl, a marketing campaign targeting the things you desperately want to change, or the seemingly innocuous habit of letting every Instagram story play out like it's a reel of reality . . . our lives are filled with reminders that we are *too much* and *not enough*. Something tells me we don't need the world to remind us of the things we think about on repeat each day, but it does.

Chances are, if you're a living, breathing human being, at some point in time, you've felt disappointed in your body, too. Maybe you didn't experience a miscarriage; maybe the shame, hatred, or guilt slipped into your life in a different way. Through your perceived flaws or imperfections, through the added weight or the stretch marks or the aging elbows, through the stray hairs or bumpy skin, whatever it is for *you,* I know I'm not the only one who has felt uncomfortable, unacceptable, or misunderstood in my body.

Our bodies aren't personality Tupperware, waiting to be shoved and stacked and squeezed into smaller spaces. Our bodies are soft, uniquely shaped, hairy-legged beings that need wide, vast space to birth dreams. To live long, to leave legacies. To do the work that ignites us in any and every way. To rest and enjoy what we've earned. To heal. And our job is to listen to what our body is telling us.

The problem is that most of the conversations we have with our bodies are simply us telling them what we want them to do, what we wish was different about them, or why they're not good enough. When you think about these conversations, they aren't really conversations at all; they are one-sided monologues rooted mainly in what we want things to *look* like.

Instead, ask yourself things like*: How do I feel? How can I move in a way that celebrates my body? Where am I lacking? What am I craving? How can I be one with my body?* When we can stop dictating and start conversing with our body like a trusted friend and ally, not just speaking at it, *but asking it to speak to us,* we can start to lean into the cues, signals, and requests it is begging us to notice as we move through our busy lives.

If we truly want to live a life of enrichment, of fully loving ourselves, others, and this world—we have to know ourselves. And to know ourselves, we have to know our bodies—how they feel, how they move, how they wander and leap and change and age in such gloriously unexpected ways.

What does your body want to do? What is it itching to try? Do you want to climb Kilimanjaro? Be a surrogate? Build a tiny house? Learn to cook stracciatella? What are your taste buds yearning for, today, right this very moment? What are your hands asking for you to let go of, to pick back up, to carry for a friend? Where do your legs want to take you?

Your body knows. *You* know. And it's time to listen.

# 8

# married to mr. six-pack:

## HOW TO SPEAK TO YOURSELF

**What I know for sure is that speaking your truth is the most powerful tool we all have.**

**—OPRAH WINFREY**

Here's what I want to tell you about self-love. After tuning your ears to what your body is offering up and closing your eyes to what the world thinks of your good-and-gilded shell, the real challenge awaits. When it comes to loving our bodies, we can't stop at just *listening* to them. That's only the beginning! What completes the work is when we *stand up for them*.

During my season of healing from that miscarriage, I soaked up every ounce of time I could with the women with whom I had formed a sisterhood. On one particular night, we planned to meet at the local Irish pub, and I was doing that thing where you sit in the car until you see your first friend arrive so you don't have to sit in the corner booth alone. As I passed the time, scrolling on my phone, I realized I hadn't posted anything on Instagram that day. I opened my camera roll, gave it a few thumb scrolls, and landed on a photo from Hawaii. Drew and

I, standing, smiling in our bathing suits. I was feeling a little spicy that night, and quickly typed up a caption that was essentially a response to a troll comment I'd received earlier in my direct messages, wondering how I, a "curvy" woman, had managed to "land" a guy like Drew. Her words, not mine. I'm using a heavy coating of mental quotation marks here because these seemingly harmless words often carry connotations that aren't so empowering.

For reference, if you've never seen him, Drew is a knockout. He's chiseled and tan with a megawatt smile. You can literally feel his warmth just by staring at him. He also has a six-pack. And I . . . *don't*. In the troll's eyes, we didn't add up. We were mismatched.

Trust me, I was no stranger to criticism. Over the years, I expanded from only sharing my photography or my work to letting people into more than just the results of my professional life. I wanted my feed to be real, not solely a highlight reel like we were all too tired of seeing anyway. So, I opened up about my struggles with my body, I shared about my miscarriage, I talked about the challenges of running a business, and I posted about throw pillows. I told myself that I could share the things that delighted me, that were honest about my life. Even if the topics weren't screaming with inspiration or positivity. My feed was an extension and an expression of my life. And since I didn't post just the good stuff, I opened myself up for feedback and thus, criticism, too. I had gotten good at ignoring it, but that night, in my rush, I typed unapologetically what I had really wanted to say about my worth, my body, and my marriage. I hit publish before I had the chance to censor my thoughts. The photo might have had a filter, but my words definitely did not:

*Someone once slid into my DMs and told me they couldn't believe I had managed to land a guy as good-looking as Drew. I'll be honest that I was taken aback. Part of my insecurity with my body has stemmed around being married to Mr. 6-Pack himself. Why should I, a curvy girl, get him? I feel unworthy and I write narratives in my head that because I am not thin, I don't deserve him. This man has embraced every curve, every dimple, pound and pimple for the last ten years and has always reminded me that I'm beautiful even when my inner dialogue doesn't match. So yes, my thighs kiss, my arms are big, and my bum is bumpy but there is just more of me for him to love and I chose a man that could handle alllll that (and so much more). I am so much more than my body, so is he, and so are you.*

I hit post and dropped my phone into the abyss of my purse before enjoying some sweet potato fries and conversation in the corner booth at the pub with my gals. Once home, I checked my feed once more before brushing my teeth and falling into bed. I could tell the post was resonating with my community, but didn't yet realize just how much further it would spread.

By the next morning I had emails from Yahoo!, *Daily Mail,* and other news media outlets requesting interviews and information. I checked my Instagram messages, and it's like my phone had sprung a full-blown notification leak. The likes and comments (both positive and not so positive) flew in at a faster rate than I'd ever seen on anything I shared before. All of a sudden, there was my photo on the front page of People.com under the headline: "'Curvy' Blogger Reveals She Was Body-Shamed for Being Married to 'Mr. 6-Pack.'" I fielded calls from the *Ellen DeGeneres Show* and emailed with editors of the *New York Post*. One by one, the comments poured in: *Some guys like insecure fat chicks. A "curvy" girl? LOL. Don't make it sound sexy and sweet. Fat is fat. Tell it like it is.*

While there were so many uplifting, encouraging words from women who were sharing just how much my caption had resonated with them, there were dozens of negative comments like these. In a season where my relationship with my body was still majorly healing, the world's criticism felt like opening a fresh wound. Suddenly my body was the center of attention for thousands of people, mainly strangers, to discuss. There I was, caught in the windstorm, totally unprepared. The truth about going viral is that it's uncontrollable by nature. Rapidly spreading. A contagious force. It can't be stopped. In fact, it's possible that the more you try to contain it, the more viral it becomes.

Even if you've never experienced that level of judgment, I know that your words to yourself can be just as viral and carry just as much vitriol. Whether or not you've been on the front page of People.com, you've likely found yourself spinning in your own criticism cyclone: "I hate the way my eyes wrinkle." "My nose is crooked; it's all I see when I look in the mirror." "My arms jiggle when I wave. Have we invented a new way to wave yet? Maybe I'm a winker now?"

Criticism is contagious. Have you ever sat at a table and like a domino, one person mentions something about their body and all of a sudden the entire conversation is a symphony of trying to combat someone else's self-criticism by queuing up the things we hate about ourselves? Talk about fighting fire with gasoline.

That same fire can spread just as destructively inside, too, unless we work to tame it with our inner narrative. So how do we do that? How do we course correct the thoughts that consume us? Changing the negative voice that constantly dribbles out at all of us from the world's speakers—and most importantly our own—is a sort of revolution. That means the first step is one we make with our own two feet. It starts at home, between the real you and those versions of yourself you've been trying to squeeze into over the years. Between the mouth speaking the words and the heart that wants to start believing them.

If you want to heal, you must look in the mirror each day and make a choice. How you rise up to your battles is linked to the kind of warrior you believe you are. Out of every battle you will face, I can promise you that how you respond to the challenge is affected by *how you view yourself*. Yes, the leading role of your life is meant only for you, but you have to be willing to accept the part. You have to believe it belongs to you and only you. You have to suit up, *your way,* day after day and own it with confidence.

You have to ask yourself, Who *am I, really?*

In the midst of my own viral moment, as soon as I asked myself that question, I knew what to do next. I kicked my positive self-talk into high gear. I stopped reading the comments (lesson number one, *always and forever*) and I went on a walk to think through my next move. I wanted to normalize that such a love or conquering of insecurity could ever exist. I wanted to put my peace out into the world as a radical response to the ones who doubted that two people could love each other regardless of how they look. I understand the doubt. I am painfully familiar with it. I live with it. And while I knew I'd be speaking from within a body that isn't the highest on the marginalized bodies list, *not by a long shot,* I felt hope that maybe there was a message in this for us all.

After pausing to consider what I most wanted to share, it occurred to me that so many of the upsetting comments were reflections of the commenters' own doubts about their value, their worthiness to be loved, appreciated, accepted, adored, wanted, celebrated, *believed*. I couldn't possibly respond to all of these humans, and I knew I didn't actually need to do that. I needed to respond for *myself*. And for anyone else who might be looking for the truth, so they could see me owning it, even in the face of people whose minds I might not ever be able to change.

My fingers flew across the keyboard as fast as possible and I hit send on something short, honest, and in the moment:

> *We've spent the last few days reeling at the fact that society believes that seeing two people (who happen to have different body types) in love is newsworthy . . . I am not defined by titles like "curvy" or plus size, Drew is not defined by "Mr. Six-Pack." Our story has held ups and downs, love and loss and we've chosen to show up and turn the mess into our message. Because we believe the world is hungry for REAL and going viral has proven that.*

In my own way, and truly for myself, I stepped up to the plate and swung. I reclaimed the narrative. I'd forgiven my body for many things I'd once framed as betrayals—whether hairy legs or irregular ovulation cycles—and it was time for my words and actions to reflect that. I wanted to completely transform not just how I thought about my body, but how I utilized it, strengthened it, and celebrated it unashamedly. Out loud. No more blame. No more "If only this were different." No more tsk-tsks in the mirror—or anywhere else, for that matter.

Body acceptance was daily, brutal work, work I had been invested in thankfully before this viral moment. It involved a lot of paying attention to and redirecting my thoughts as I explored the way I spoke *to* myself—and the way I spoke *about* myself. But over time, that work became evident in my words, my thought processes, my decisions— and now, to the world.

In a season full of transition and loss, in a time we were trying to conceive the child we had longed for, reframing my words and percep- tions about myself was the only thing that carried me through. Com- ing to terms with things I couldn't control—from fertility to Internet feedback—meant fighting every lie with a hard-fought truth. Cleaning up my self-talk saved me. Having this gentleness with myself still saves me often and swiftly. I invite you to try it.

Science does, too. Psychologists have been gushing for ages about how powerful our own words are to our self-worth, our healing, our joy, and our coping. Research suggests that positive self-talk can help you approach challenges and stressful situations with a more open and optimistic mindset. The more optimistic our words become, the more optimistic our *minds become.*

Elaine Mead from *Positive Psychology* has this to say about it: "It isn't about . . . thinking you're amazing; it's simply about reframing how you view things, removing negative bias, and approaching life with the idea that you can tackle things—and even if it doesn't go perfectly—you'll learn from it for next time."[1]

Reframing how you view yourself isn't a one-and-done. Insecuri- ties like to get a long-term foothold, working their way into our minds and sounding a lot like truth. It's easy to mistake that voice of negativ- ity for our own, sounding like our inner mean girl. My inner mean girl sounds a lot like, *If only you were thinner. Eww, look at that cellulite. You should really cover up more. Your skin is so bumpy. What thirty-year-old has acne? Your lack of self-control is showing. People would like you more if you were prettier.*

*They are really going to see how you've let yourself go. A size twelve, really? Remember when you wore a six? That extra baby weight is going to stay there forever. Your body is ruined. You're always the "fat" friend.*

Insecurity via the comparison trap tempts us to keep our heads down, focused on the shape of the shadow our bodies cast on the ground. It took a long time before I learned to look up from the ground, from the shape of my shadow, from the endless scroll through comparison land . . . because it's the well-deserved spotlight on us that is casting the shadows in the first place.

If we really look at it, the inner dialogue we've adopted over time can sound a lot like the headlines that target us to lose fat, stay young, be beautiful, and yet, it is also a voice harsher than the harshest of critics. While some of your thoughts and reflections might inspire you into positive action, most of the time, the inner critic only exists to cut us down, to deflate us, to reflect all the messages we've internalized.

So do we have to stay stuck with these thoughts on repeat for the rest of our days? I don't think so. To change your inner narrative, you first have to be willing to pay attention, to notice. When I notice a thought that isn't productive nor is it motivating, I've learned to pause and redirect. I first stop the cycle and ask myself, *Where did I learn this?*, in an effort to uncover where the hopeless belief came from. And then I reframe it in the same way I'd correct someone I love when they share an unkind thought about themselves. I literally pause and ask myself, *What do I know to be true? Sure, my arms don't always fit in blazer sleeves, but they can overhead press a hundred pounds. Yeah, my legs have cellulite on them, but they carry me through my days and allow me to climb up mountains. (Literally and figuratively!) Do the bumps on my booty stop me from dancing? No, no, they don't.*

Instead of gaslighting your own feelings, or punishing yourself for having a negative thought in the first place, your challenge is to redirect that energy back to what you have learned is true about you. Think of this as thought shepherding! Every gentle nudge back to truth, back to what you know is good about yourself, helps your brain learn new boundaries. In your practice of consistent redirection, your mental dialogue will begin to change the tone of its voice. You're literally rewiring the connections of your brain!

I don't look in the mirror and think, *I am perfect.* That's not me! It's not who I want or expect myself to be. That's still projecting a societal expectation of who I *ought* to be in order to deserve love, happiness, recognition, and all the other good things.

I don't even look in the mirror and think, *Well . . . Drew thinks I'm hot.* I'm not validated or valued simply because of someone else's approval (even though, yes, he does think I'm liquid hot magma).

I look in the mirror and think a variety of wonderful things. Like, *There she is.* Or, *Girl, I know you're tired, yesterday was rough. What do you need today? I'm proud of your strength.*

Adjusting my thoughts in the throes of a negative spiral really doesn't take a ton of time. But it does take a lot of patience. You'd be shocked at how long we've had those same thoughts running through our brains, almost becoming unnoticeable because they are just a part of our existing! But, once you rewrite the story enough times, that new story slowly becomes the leading narrative for your thoughts.

Let me be clear: not all of us have a negative storyline surrounding our bodies. Maybe your inner narrative is different from mine. Our brains don't discriminate from any source of insecurity, whether stemming from a perceived lack in beauty, brains, or brilliance. None of us are immune to the many ways in which the mind quickly spirals from what is true to what is *not*.

But I've also encountered something mind-blowing in my quest to change my dialogue: most of us don't talk about our bodies or our looks in the same way we might talk about other aspects of our life— particularly our work, our accomplishments, or our productivity. It's so much easier to sing our own praises when it comes to external successes over speaking about our own bodies or the successes we have *within* them.

Why? Because the narratives we give ourselves in all facets of life can be impacted by the messages we've received over time. We're taught that we should celebrate accomplishments like grades on a report card, that one office presentation, or our dissertation, or to hype ourselves up in the new Facebook group we joined. We accept praise in the forms of accolades or work milestones but on the flip side, we deflect when someone gives us a compliment on an outfit or comments on our beauty.

As little girls, people commented often on our appearance, but as we grew into adults, we started dropping the "cute" and "pretty" and started leaning on titles, diplomas, or achievements that show our worth beyond what meets the eye. It's like on our quest to prove we have brains over our beauty, we forgot that these two are not at odds with each other. We can be both brilliant and beautiful—and a million things in between.

Despite our wide spectrum of beauty *and* brilliance, we're taught that it's vain to speak about the way we look in a positive light. We're encouraged to belittle ourselves or point out our flaws to never risk making someone else feel insecure or less than, but in doing so, we forfeit our own security in our skin and lose the chance to give someone else the invitation to own who they are. We're supposed to *look* confident but not *speak* confidently about our looks. I mean, heaven forbid we ever reference something we love about ourselves . . . isn't that the cardinal sin of womanhood?

Think about it. How many times did you watch your mother deflect a compliment growing up? Or how many times have you heard a friend belittle herself after receiving encouragement? How many times do we quickly change the subject after someone says something nice about us or the way we look? Why is it that we default to diversion when it comes to accepting kind words about ourselves but we could host an hour-long seminar on what's wrong with the way we look?

I vividly remember the day that my grandma shooed away my camera lens when I told her I wanted to take a picture of her. I made her stand in front of a garage door as I snapped away while she proclaimed, "Now Jenna, that's enough." In her seventy-six years of living on this earth, she still didn't feel like she had a right to take up space or be worthy of a beautiful photo of her beautiful self. I remember thinking, *Wait, so this feeling never goes away? This feeling of unworthiness follows us each decade of life? You mean that I have the rest of my days to spend worrying about, hating, or wanting to change my body?* The utter thought of it exhausted and deflated me.

My grandma knew what I know now: that the thing about self-love is that we will never "arrive." We don't just wake up one day and stop poking and prodding at our bodies, zooming in on what's wrong with us without celebrating all that is right. Self-love is not a destination but a choice, a daily (and sometimes hourly) decision to see, love, acknowledge, and respect our true home—the only one we've got. Choosing to love the part of us that is "the body" requires a conscious tension of choosing joy and contentment in the shell that moves us through our days without growing complacent about the fact that we need to honor it in whatever ways we know how.

My grandma was still learning this delicate balance when that same photo of a beautiful, beaming woman, a woman I loved, standing in front of a garage door, became a lasting memory. Almost exactly three years later, that photo was printed next to her obituary, a portrait of her vibrance that everyone could see, even when she couldn't. I only wish she'd known a fragment of the radiance I saw then, and still do.

### HOW ARE YOU, REALLY?

If the words you said to yourself—and about yourself—were audible for the world to hear, would you be proud of them? How can you challenge yourself to be kinder and gentler with your whole self—including your words? What are five ways you can compliment your body today?

Digging into the beliefs we carry about our bodies that hold us back, trip us up, and weigh us down doesn't mean being blind to who we are. Relearning how to accept yourself doesn't mean we can't seek self-improvement, as long as it's fueled by self, as in, *our own*. The heartbeat of accepting, embracing, and utilizing who we are means reframing our perceptions.

As sure as the sun rises, there will always be thoughts that pop into your head. But as much as our brain waves have the capacity to focus on the things we hate, we also have the capacity to refocus them right onto the things we love.

If you're not sure where to start, I've got good news. Psychologists insist that accepting yourself is something you can (and must) learn at any age.[2] So, in the interest of practicality, I want to leave you with one magic word that changes everything about the way you speak to yourself. It's a tiny dose of kindness—the proverbial spoonful of sugar—and you can sprinkle it onto every sentence you utter, today and tomorrow and for the rest of your life. One word, one million possibilities. Are you ready to hear it?

It's "yet."

I can't run that marathon *yet*. I can't control my temper *yet*. I don't have the guts to try that thing in the bedroom *yet*. I don't like my freckles *yet*. I don't love what I see in the mirror *yet*. I don't know how to truly believe I am worthy, enough, glorious, and powerful . . . *yet*.

You get it, right? You see how transformative that word is? How much of a game-changer your life can be when you put an ellipsis where the period once was? How every slapdash, bone-chilling, head-swimming dream can feel within your reach after just three bold letters and a believing mind?

Try it. Shout it out loud. Right this sec.

*Yet* after it.

# 9

# vision fulfilled:

## HOW TO MAKE (NO, LET) YOUR DREAMS COME TRUE

**The vision is always for the appointed time. Be patient, prayerful, and wait for the fulfillment of your visions.**

**—LAILAH GIFTY AKITA**

If you've been paying attention to the words in this book, you'll have realized something profound: dreams expand. Not only do they themselves expand, but they influence other parts of your life to do the same. I'd even say that dreams help expand *everything*. Nothing goes untouched. They expand our hopes for our future. They expand our creative ventures. They expand our passion and our empathy and our intuition.

And, as much as I'd love to tell you otherwise, we both know the truth: they also expand our fear.

It was in Hawaii (once again and one year later) that I learned of my second pregnancy. Even though I ran to Target and picked up a cute baby outfit so we could take pictures the day we discovered I was pregnant, it would take the rest of our trip for me to feel anything other than cautious, to accept any future other than a guarded one. I was no longer afraid of the unknown, the unseen. The known and seen was *precisely* what I was afraid of.

This was the first time in my life when I had to ask myself the question, *Will I be okay if history repeats itself, if we encounter another loss, if this doesn't happen for me?* Every moment the answer was different. I googled "chances of repeat miscarriage" on a daily basis, and then I'd catch myself and chuck my phone off to the side, where I'd inevitably reach for it later.

As I ran through my own cycles of doubt and hope, I took to wearing the word "surrender" on a gold chain around my neck, knowing I needed the reminder that I couldn't control the outcome of this one. Most days I didn't want to see that word dangling around my neck. I didn't want to *have* to surrender anything.

We arrived home from Hawaii and scheduled a doctor's appointment right away. As I sat down on the vinyl exam table, scratchy white paper sticking to my vacation-tanned legs, I vowed to stay hopeful. To want and pray and plead for the best. And to feel it all no matter what. If bad news was coming, I was ready to face it.

I laid back, closed my eyes, and whispered a prayer. Then, I heard the most glorious sound in the entire world. *Thump-thump, thump-thump.* It was my tiny baby's heartbeat. It sounded exactly like hope, like love, like a drumbeat guiding us all forward.

We called our family right away. "There's a heartbeat! We listened to it! We saw the baby!" The odds were now in our favor! Trust me, I looked them up. Daily, hope grew stronger as we rearranged long-term plans and bedrooms, and researched the best nursery rocking chair. To swaddle or not to swaddle? What about pacifiers? Sleep training? I googled my brains out once again—this time, with a very different emotion guiding me. My hope was stronger than I thought it could be.

By the time my next ultrasound rolled around, I was making small talk with my ob-gyn. We chatted about work and the weather, and I was fully prepared to start diving deep into asking her for a breast pump recommendation—Medela or Spectra?—when time began to slow. She started the ultrasound, I looked up with expectant eyes. I watched her hand hover over the keyboard, eyes searching the monitor. I felt the wand stop moving as she turned to look at me.

"I'm sorry" is what I heard next.

They say that anger is the second stage of grief. But if this is your second round of grief? Hell, anger comes first.

I had no questions. I had no words. I just felt rage. With tears streaming down my face, I got dressed and ran out of the building, not even waiting to hear what the next steps would be—I knew them already, I had already done them before. I just needed to get out of that place and scream. *Why was my body broken? Why was I dumb enough to hope? And why didn't anyone talk about how hard this was?* With every honest doubt and cry and question, I felt propelled to find answers I could accept.

The season that came next was one of discovery, one that felt wildly new and different from our last loss. After the pain of my first miscarriage, I threw myself into anything that would distract from the despair and disappointment I felt in this body that had betrayed me. Now? Well, I'd made a vow to sit with anger this time around—no matter what. I laid in the fetal position with my dog for a while before I let myself stand up and face decision-making. Over and over, I checked in with my feelings. Over and over, I asked myself, *How am I, really?* And one day, I answered with absolute confidence, this inner assurance: *I'm ready to heal.*

I met with holistic doctors and naturopaths. I gave vials of blood in search of answers. I experimented with dietary changes, shelving my beloved grilled cheese sandwiches for a warm gluten-free bowl of mac and cheese (not a bad trade-off, BTW). I kicked my five-times-a-week CrossFit habit and traded it for long walks listening to meditation music and slow flow yoga. I raided my cabinets for any items containing chemicals that could disrupt my hormones. I created massive boundaries around screen time and sleep and left my phone charging downstairs every night. I launched a massive vitamin regimen to the point where I had to buy a pillbox the size of my grandparents'. And I even started cutting back on caffeine (which was, and still is, in my opinion, a superhuman feat of willpower).

Through each of these changes, one thing stayed the same: I kept dreaming.

Even in the face of uncertainty, anger, and defeat, I stuck to the promise I made myself. I kept placing myself as the lead character of my own story. I had fallen in love with a new idea for my future. I was supposed to become a mother. I felt it in my bones. That was the love story I was hooked on, the one I saw myself in, and I stared at the blinking cursor in my life story praying a happy ending would still be written.

I started to dream about what it would look like to show up as the kind of mother I wanted to be: a present mom, a joyful mom, an engaged mom. I asked myself the hard questions: Could I maintain the current hours I was working with a newborn in tow? Was the business

I built enough to sustain a family? Could I make this work fit into a life with kids?

When I got quiet enough to be honest, truthfully, I didn't love the answers. In theory, I knew a baby would fit beautifully into my life with Drew. But theory and reality are very different things. Looking at my life and my career, I couldn't envision juggling a baby with the long weekends away, being booked a year in advance (sometimes two), or the late-night editing sessions, all things I was doing as a wedding photographer.

While I struggled to imagine bringing a baby into the world at my current pace, I found myself dreaming up the kind of work I could do while I waited for the motherhood chapter of my story to finally unfold. While it looked entirely different from what I had been doing, I wasn't afraid to try something new. And I knew *exactly* what it would be.

For years, in comment sections and in conference rooms, people had taken to asking me how I found success so quickly. In a short time, I had worked my way from a shutter-happy gal with a side gig to being named the top wedding photographer in the state. My earnings jumped from zero to six figures in three years flat—and people other than my banker took notice.

Coming from a business background and having retained a ton of information from those college marketing courses I took, I made it a priority to understand the strategy behind my craft just as much as I understood the craft itself. But I sometimes wondered if my left-brain-meets-right-brain approach would work for other people, or if I was just lucky. I decided to test out my marketing strategies and announced online I was going to offer mentoring sessions for other photographers.

My plan wasn't foolproof, but I was feeling bold. Minutes later, with the *ping* of a notification, someone booked. Then another, then another. Turns out other photographers wanted to try to do things like I did. Maybe there *was* something valuable to my systems, something I could share.

I remember those mentoring sessions like they were yesterday. Local photographers would come to our house and we'd sit at the dining table together while I walked them through exactly how I built a successful photography business from scratch.

I started to notice themes around the questions I was asked, and I found myself repeating the same strategies over and over again. From my email templates to my pricing guides, I handed over every part of my process, and after dozens of sessions, it became obvious that the demand would soon be too great. I knew I had to find a new way to get this information out into the world! But I didn't want to create another business trading time for money. I knew there had to be a better way to serve others who were looking for sound strategies in an easy-to-follow format.

Looking back, those mentor sessions were a catalyst for me. They sprouted roots in multiple creative directions, and I watched one little idea branch off into another . . . into ventures I had no idea could ever be mine. Ventures like starting a podcast. Launching an online course (and then another, and another) on how to market your work as an entrepreneur, from Instagram strategy to the power of Pinterest to growing an email list. I created a new business around work I could do from anywhere, work I could fit in between burping and feeding and changing an infant. Work that could work for me. Work that could run while I rested. *Work that could work for us.*

It wasn't all easy, developing a new rhythm of work and pivoting my passion toward the unknown. I was brand new again, at another starting line. Halfway to a dream, shooting weddings on weekends and hosting live webinars during the week. I was back to burning the candle on both ends: juggling the success of my photography career with this new side hustle. It took time (as it usually does!) for success to materialize, for this new idea to be a viable career option. But the vision I clung to, this notion that I could create something once and serve many, that I could build a business that wouldn't stop the moment I did? It kept me going.

No matter what your dream is, you may be tempted to give up on it when the going gets tough. And when I say "tough," you know I'm not referring to some vague kind of toughness they talk about in truck commercials. I'm talking about the experiences that make you think you were born to fail. Your doubt will likely tell you that your present challenges feel impossible to bear, so how could you possibly work toward a future dream? Your grief will try to tell you that the buck stops with that loss and moving forward isn't an option anymore. Your trauma will insidiously try to steal your future joy. Human instinct just wants the pain to stop; that's our survival mode kicking in. So, imagine how resistant to instinct it would be to walk headlong into the possibility of more unknown, more failure, more ambiguity?

Bad days? I had a lot of them. But my bad days created a tough love (or as I like to call it, "strong love") for myself that still calls me up and out of sitting too long in my anger or sadness, simply waiting for things to change. Because we all do that, don't we? We cloak our doubts in a word called "waiting." We fall back on what's practical. We crave an identity shift, but we refuse to fully believe we are capable of newness. We stop our footsteps from inching closer to change. We even trick ourselves into thinking that "someday" will be so different from our "today" but do nothing to make the difference occur. And we find ourselves dreaming about an improved life without actively working toward it.

So what do you do when your deepest dream for yourself feels entirely beyond your capacity, or control, or comfort? I know what *not* to do: don't wait.

Merely waiting for fear to go away will steal all the time you've been given right now. I'm not telling you to move *on* from your pain and fear and grief. I'm telling you to pick it up and move *with it*. Because if your only choice is to take what you've got with you, everything you are *right now*, then take it with you to where you're going next. Your grief and fear can come with you on the ride, and maybe along the way, they'll look out the passenger window and see the only way through it is to go through it together.

Your pain can expand your deep well of empathy. Your fear can heighten your desire for change. Your grief may prove to be a strength to open up the experiences that await you, making them richer. Pain, fear, and grief are not weaknesses. They're your companions for your transformation. We're only in danger of losing time when we simply wait for them to go away.

I want you to pause for a minute and breathe these words over yourself. You've been given a very magical gift: today. Your life that you're living right now. And the hardest, most beautiful truth is that *right now* is the only time you can be sure to have. That bright future? I want it, and I want you to have it! But creating it starts right now—and it starts in your mind.

HOW ARE YOU, REALLY?

What is the future you see for yourself? Does it scare you? What makes that vision scary? What needs to happen next to make it real? What's one thing you can do to move you closer to your future—today?

Building your future begins with visualizing yourself going through the motions of what it takes to succeed—whatever that looks like for you. Psychotherapist Amy Morin writes, "The way you think is important—it affects how you feel and how you behave . . . [but] positive thinking only works when it's combined with positive action."[1]

Belief pairs well with a glass of behavior. Which means that whoever first told you "practice makes perfect" definitely meant well but misspoke. I think practice makes *power*, meaning the action of stepping into the patterns of a life you *want* is the only way to create it.

Set aside the patterns of the life you *have* and focus on the patterns of the life you *want*. Let's say you want to revitalize a particular relationship. What choices would the revitalized version of yourself make? What rhythms would *already* be part of your life if the relationship were *already* at its most vibrant and connected state?

Leaving love notes on the dashboard? Splurging for concert tickets to see the band you both love? Clearing your afternoon to bake a favorite dessert? Sending an encouraging voice text in the middle of the day? By living as if you've already established these habits—these small rhythms and daily choices—you're moving that far-off goal into a real-life action today. You're pulling the dream closer to yourself, instead of pushing yourself closer to the dream. Can you see how different that feels?

Sometimes, we can take on this change all by ourselves. But other times, we need help. I know I did. I desperately needed someone other than myself who I could rely on to shoulder the burden of unpacking my grief. Someone to be a vessel that I wouldn't feel sorry for pouring out my feelings into. In the throes of getting honest about my fertility struggles and open about my experiences, I received a message from a stranger who had also been through similar miscarriages. "I want to help," she said. "Can we meet virtually for six weeks?" Her name was Erin Treloar and her own experience with loss had fueled a passion for helping women cope and heal in healthier ways.

Week after week, we'd connect. Each call had a different goal, whether it was reconnecting with my body, facing my healing head-on, or learning how to dream again. Over the phone, Erin would walk me through as I performed a body scan, prompting me to describe my grief—what it felt like, where it lived, where I was carrying it. Over and over, we'd uncover lies that had taken root, beliefs that felt limiting, thoughts surrounding my life that no longer served me. Each week, though tempted to skip the hard work, I'd take a deep breath and answer her call when it came, and at the end of the hour I'd wipe my tearstained cheeks and get back to work.

During one of our sessions, she led me through a transformative visualization exercise. You know those instances where you know your life was just changed? The kind of experiences that create a chasm where you can clearly see a before and after? Well, this was one of those.

I remember sitting in my blue armchair, her voice inviting me to turn up my intuition, like a dial on the radio. I remember her telling me to imagine a life that was different, a life where my vision was fulfilled. I remember closing my eyes, letting myself go there, even though it was painful. I remember the silence over the line as the exercise ended, needing a few minutes to sit with everything I saw for myself and for my life.

When I finally felt ready to continue the session, she asked me to describe my most vibrant version of myself. "Close your eyes," she'd said. "Tell me everything you see."

> Tune in as Erin guides you through the
> same exercise that changed my life at
> WWW.JENNAKUTCHER.COM/MORE

I was smiling, wearing a white linen top and Madewell jeans. I was barefoot standing on a Persian rug at the kitchen sink washing a spatula and in the background I could hear a little girl giggling as she and her daddy shared pancakes off the same plate. The dogs were begging underneath her chair, waiting for a crumb (or an entire pancake) to drop. There was faint, happy music playing in the background.

I felt the tears trickle from my cheeks down my neck as I shared this vision. I sat in silence, not wanting to lose a vision that felt so pure, so joyful, so incredibly different from the life I was currently living.

I kept trying to correct this vision, to place it in our current home on the river and to imagine this scene happening in the space I was currently in, but it just kept going somewhere else. Like when you're dreaming and also half awake, trying to control the story racing through your brain to no avail.

I loved our old Craftsman house. It was quirky and beautiful, but the four walls had held a lot of heartache. When we first moved in, after Drew and I had decided to start a family, we christened one of the rooms the nursery. That room sat empty for years. Stuffed in the closet were the baby items I had purchased in excitement during my fleeting pregnancies, things unused that I couldn't yet let go of.

I finished telling her about each little detail of the vision I held. And then I said the words . . . "I think we need to move."

You know when you have this vision, this idea, and you just want to hold it close to your heart so that no one bursts your bubble? Yeah, I've had those, too, but this wasn't one of those. This vision was so crystal clear, I had to share it. It was like I could *hear* the baby giggles in the other room.

That night when Drew got home from work, I told him about the call with Erin, the vision I had, and his brown eyes lit up. I mean, who wouldn't love the notion of pancakes and baby giggles and pretty Persian rugs? (Well, I'm pretty sure he couldn't care less about a rug, but whatever.) As it turns out, I wasn't the only one who felt stuck in our house, a space where we were reminded of our unfulfilled vision every time we walked through the hallway. The lives we found ourselves living didn't reflect the vision we had for our future. And frankly, the thought of something different and new was more than appealing—to both of us.

At this stage of our relationship, it was hard to surprise Drew. We were pretty comfortable taking risks and making leaps, so nothing really felt off-limits or shocking, even the idea of moving to a new house. And as crazy as it sounded, I just couldn't shake the idea that if I wanted this vision to come alive, I needed to be an active participant in its creation. I didn't want to spend any more time shoving away the visions of a life that truly made me happy. I wanted that future. I wanted the pancakes and the slow mornings. I wanted the little giggling *girl*. But my life didn't look anything like that vision . . . yet.

*Maybe I could start with the Madewell jeans,* I thought. *A house would be too crazy, right?*

But one evening, while Drew was on a run, I scrolled Zillow, typed in areas near my family in Minnesota, and I saw it. I quickly shot off a text to our daily family text thread with a link to the real estate listing in Duluth, just miles away from my family. "Maybe this should be the future Kutcher Craftsman?" I sent with a wink.

By the time he returned, all sweaty from his run, my entire family had sent responses with exclamation points and all caps and cheer emojis galore. My grandpa even filmed himself chanting, "Do it, do it, come home!"

"Did you see the listing?" I asked Drew.

"What listing?" he said, still out of breath. "And what the heck is happening in the family text thread? My phone kept buzzing on my run."

I cracked open my computer and pulled up pictures of the house. I pointed to the long farm table. Room for everyone, room for pancakes. "This! This resembles that vision I had with pancakes and a baby girl!"

Just a few days later, we found ourselves caulking windows, cleaning baseboards, pulling weeds, readying our beloved restored home to hit the market. We weren't moving because of my vision, exactly, but we weren't *not* moving because of it, either.

Hear me loud and clear: You don't have to pick up your life and move zip codes away to step into a new dream. Start where you can, when you can. You don't need to go big, but you need to *go*.

That life? It's happening right now. It's unfolding as your eyes scan this page. When your alarm clock went off this morning, you got another day of it. This is it, your one beautiful life. Kick off your covers. Get up. Forward is forward and slow progress is *still progress*.

Soon enough for us, our progress looked like packed boxes and a scheduled moving truck. We were heading back to my beginning, to my roots, to a fresh start. To wide, open spaces and Minnesota accents. I was going home.

I think often about what would have happened if I'd allowed doubt, negativity, and despair to cloud my vision for the future. If I'd let myself get stuck in the overwhelming logistics of boxing up our entire lives and moving to another state. If I'd have looked around at my reality, shrugged my shoulders, and given up. Would I have found myself on moving day, just a few short months later, unrolling a Persian runner into the kitchen of our new-to-us Minnesota house? Would I have found myself suddenly nauseous, unwrapping a pregnancy test, calling for Drew to find a roll of toilet paper in one of the boxes stacked by the front door?

Would I have shimmied back into those Madewell jeans, emerged from the bathroom, and gleefully held up two pink lines for Mr. Six-Pack to see?

Her name is Conley Kate, also known as Coco. She has ten fingers and ten toes and furrows her brow at bedtime. She's everything we dreamed of, our third-time's-the-charm, our firstborn rainbow. Her name means hero. When I look at her, I understand the truth: she saved us all.

Two back-to-back losses and a three-year period with a lot of suffering passed us by before the day came when I stopped holding my breath. The day we held our wiggly little miracle in our arms. The day I understood the most profound lesson of all: the season of waiting was just as important as what we were waiting for. I felt the profound, inexplicable weight of those words that day and every day since.

Sometimes, I close my eyes and remember that first pregnancy. I remember Drew and I sitting by the poolside restaurant at the hotel in Hawaii trying to figure out how we would make it all work. How were we going to rearrange our lives to make way for something so . . . massive? Parenthood felt impossibly huge. Like trying to park a boat in a bathtub.

Our vision wasn't aligned with our reality, with the logistics of our lives. Drew was working a nine-to-five. I was a full-time, busy photographer working far too many hours. We hardly ever saw family. We ate way too much takeout. We talked about navigating the busy wedding seasons with a newborn, the shifting of client work to accommodate a semblance of a maternity leave. While our hearts were aligned with the vision of our future, the reality of where we were when the test said "pregnant" didn't accommodate the opportunity for us to be the kind of parents we wanted to be.

I often look back on that time—the one of waiting, of questioning, of holding on for dear life. The one where we stayed steadfast with hope and continued to plant the seeds even when we knew the harvest was certainly never promised. Those years in our lives are a critical piece of our story. Each shift and slight evolution of our lives equipped us to be able to enjoy our greatest adventure and gift yet.

The pain was worth it. The path held purpose. I can see it now, it was all aligned.

Today, we roll out of bed, Drew makes himself a coffee, puts on the kettle for my daily lemon water, and warms up a little milk for Coco. I smile while gazing into the monitor, watching our babbling little miracle wake. I wish I could tell you that I meditate daily or that I get in a five-mile run before the sun even rises, but I prefer a morning sans shin splints.

He hands me my hot lemon water and I smile because, to me, these little gestures are love. We spend a ton of time together: Drew, me, and that sweet little girl who we're about to get out of her crib.

We're not in any rush for anything. Our calendar is like The Chicks song "Wide Open Spaces." We sleep hard and rest well, tangling up our hands or our legs, and fall back asleep to the sound of white noise on the baby monitor. We live our lives from a place of believing that very few things are urgent, a pace that I've come to love and need.

Oh, and if you're wondering: Yes, there's a long dining table with room for everyone. Yes, there are white linen tops (rarely ironed). Yes, there is quiet music. And yes, most certainly, there are pancakes.

I pick up my phone, scrolling while I sip, and as I do, a memory pops up in my Facebook timeline: a picture of my corporate office door with my nameplate and title. It read: JENNA KUTCHER, EXECUTIVE LEADER OF HUMAN RESOURCES. It certainly was a lot easier to describe who I was and what I did when I had a title that I didn't self-appoint. You know, the one that sounded important.

But I know the truth: I miss nothing about that office, that role, or that title. That nameplate is shoved in some closet in a box labeled "Random Things" that will probably get tossed someday. And seeing it again recently reminded me not only of how far I've come but what my life would have looked like had I continued to climb the ladder someone else had built in order to feel understood, valuable, and successful.

The thing is, our plans never play out *exactly* the way we expect them to. I've allowed myself to change in ways I could have never imagined, ways I would've never seen coming. I look around me—a sticky high chair, a mug of hot lemon water, a free weekend ahead—and I feel like I'm still trying to take it all in. I'm still processing the last three years, let alone the last three decades, of being alive.

I used to think I was supposed to build a life where I would have to hustle first so I could rest later. But I can see now how my visions fulfilled—of career, of family, of wholeness—have each, slowly and surely, invited me toward a different pace of life, a new way of living.

I never dreamed I'd get to spend my days with my husband and my daughter here at home together. Living, working, and playing under the same roof. I couldn't have known my work would revolve around nap times, or that I'd make it a rule to always say yes when I'm asked to go for a walk in the middle of the afternoon. I didn't think success for me would be found in putting my baby to bed every night and being there to wake her up every morning. I never knew that asking myself that one, singular question—*How are you, really?*—would kick off such a wild, unscripted journey.

Sometimes, answering that question will invite you to stand still right where you are. But other times, your answer will mean moving to where you're not yet: just the smallest step in the direction of your dreams. It will feel like the tiniest amount of progress, but trust me; the expansiveness that will arrive when your path and purpose begin to align will offer a different kind of pace. The *sustainable* kind. The big-picture peace that comes from knowing you're building a life you don't need to run away from. A life that fills you, not depletes you. A life that welcomes you home to yourself. A life you don't have to pretend to enjoy.

One weekend, I asked a few of my friends what they would do with their life if they could do or be anything at all—if money wasn't a factor. My friend who works in a lab said he'd become a middle-school shop teacher. Another friend who works as an event planner admitted she'd love to be a bartender. And my dietitian friend who helps patients with diabetes revealed she'd love to open a bakery.

And now I want to ask you that same question. Without pushing away your gut response, without explaining away the answer: What would you do with your life if money wasn't a factor? What dream would you chase? What legacy would you create? What vision would you fulfill?

I can't tell you who you'll be in five years, but I can tell you—without a doubt—that if you're brave enough to answer this question, you're brave enough to take one step to go after it. Trust me.

Today, as I strap Coco into her stroller for a morning walk, it hits me: *This is it.* This is the vision. This is, for me, what was on the other side of yes. This is the dream I longed for, the one I hoped for, the life I worked for. All of it. There are tantrums and triumphs. There are tears from both laughing and crying. There are moments of healing from the past. Grief still exists. While my path thus far has brought hardship, it's also brought surprise and delight. (And snacks, lots of snacks.)

As we walk down the sidewalk together, a friendly neighbor waves us over to say hello. We stop at her house just as Coco reaches her hands high into the sky, shouting "Gooooood moooooooorning!"

"How are you?" My neighbor laughs.

There it is again. That simple question. That eye-opening, heart-bursting, life-changing ask. I look down at my daughter, at her messy tendrils and her dimpled cheeks, and I wait for her to piece together her own words.

I know it will take years for her to learn how to answer that question honestly. So for today, I whisper my truest answer for the both of us: *profoundly, astoundingly grateful.*

# who
# you have
# (and who
# has you)

as we form and shape our belief that we have something to offer, we now have to understand how that purpose plays out in our lives, and how we can go about turning ideas into action. the best part? We need not go it alone. Now is the time to process who is in your life, who leads you, where you lead others, and the hand you have in building your own structure of support and change. With you in your lane and me in mine, tiny actions will add up to real movement, and as we gain momentum with glee, we'll question why we waited so long to simply start.

And we're off,

*Jenna*

# 10

## the cribbage board:

### HOW TO SHARE A DREAM

**Love doesn't just sit there, like a stone, it has to be made, like bread; remade all the time, made new.**

—URSULA K. LE GUIN

I'm gonna be *real* honest with you. This is the point in the book where you might feel tempted to fling these words far across your bedroom onto the floor (or, if you're reading poolside, straight into the deep end). Because here's what you might be thinking: *Jenna, this all sounds great. Follow my heart! Dream the dream! Show up authentically! Be me, 100 percent!*

But what about the people around me or the one I pledged my whole entire life to? What about my partnership, my marriage? What about fairness? What about following through with my vows, my commitment, my word? What happens if I show up fully, tell the truth, and my dream gets ignored—*or worse*, rejected? What then?

The good news is you don't need to worry about that_yet. While our brains like to run fast with the what-ifs, let's drop those for a bit. Focus first on the fact that as you shift and evolve as a human, as you clothe yourself in a new identity time and time again, love and acceptance always has to start with you. Don't worry about walking through life feeling like Jason Bourne. Don't worry about alienating your spouse. Don't worry about the potential side-eye from your roommate or best friend.

As you become more outwardly passionate, as you lean into your vision, as you come more alive, you invite everyone else in your life to do the same—even the people closest to you.

Yes, I'm about to talk about my marriage, but try not to stop reading here if you don't have a partner or spouse, or if you don't really want to talk about your romantic situation, or if you simply don't care to venture into this kind of conversation! For one, you might not know where this conversation is about to go (a bad habit I tend to have in many other kinds of conversations: assuming the trajectory). But also? We don't have to walk in another's shoes *literally* in order to learn from them. Empathy is a gift that crosses deep rivers on our behalf. Come with me and trust that I'm not telling you *who* to be, but asking you *who you are* by showing you a little more of who I am.

Back when I was a newlywed, if you were to ask me what makes for a successful partnership, I'd have spouted off the familiar maxims I learned from my parents: *Never go to bed angry! Marriage comes first! Fight clean! Communication is key!* Each of these are helpful in their own right. But now, over a decade into our journey as husband and wife, I know the truth: what makes Drew the man of my dreams is that he's never afraid to chase one.

This dream chasing thing? It's—quite literally—written into the very foundation of our relationship. Over a decade ago, wrapped up in French lace and wearing a birdcage veil, my vows were simple: *I will always encourage you to chase your dreams because through them your soul shines.*

If I could add to those vows today, I'd probably say this: *And if something we're chasing makes your soul dim? Babe, I don't want it for a second.*

Drew and I met in college—in the back row of a communications class, and again in the cardio center at the gym, then later, outside my dorm. We just kept running into each other. He was everywhere I was, and we soon realized we shared the same areas of study in business and communications.

Over time, we became the best of friends. We swapped stories and sorrows, traded flashcards and fast-food bills. We saved seats for each other at every lecture. We even gave each other keys to our apartments in case of emergency (and I swear, nothing else). When I say "friends," I mean that in the most underlined, boldest font. I would have loved to give him a key to more than my apartment (i.e., my heart), but I was scared and the timing was never right. Everyone around me told me to hold on to that "good thing" we had as friends and not ruin it. And I couldn't imagine not having Drew in my life. But to be honest, I was willing to risk ruining it to see what could happen.

Three years into our friendship, the lines had officially started to blur. Once, while I was home for Christmas break, my mom asked me, "Are you sure this guy's just a friend?"

I wasn't.

We weren't just friends, not really, and I knew it all at once.

We had crossed over somewhere along the way.

Later, we'd watch the movie *Home Alone* together, and I'd surprise him with a kiss.

A week after graduation, he'd surprise me with a ring.

It was all working out, the timing, the relationship, the preserved friendship-turned-love story . . . but then, ten days before our wedding, I got a call at the office. Remember, that windowless, suffocating one with the bowl of M&M's? Someone over the loudspeaker paged me to grab my office phone and, in an instant, my heart sank. No one ever called the office unless it was an emergency. I knew it had to be important. I grabbed the phone and heard Drew's shaky voice on the other line as he told me, "Babe, I just got let go."

It took me a minute to realize what he was telling me. *Like, from your job?* Once the shock settled, it hit me: I was going to start my new-lywed life riding off into the sunset as the sole provider, the bill payer, the student loan financer—with no idea where we were headed next.

I thought of all the bills due, the honeymoon we planned up the north shore, and the fact that we were in charge of funding our wedding, *oh, next weekend.* My brain went straight to the wedding budget, thinking of anything we could scrap last minute. We weren't really the extravagant types, so the budget sort of shrugged at me. There were no extras, no corners to be cut. I mean, we were serving pizza and sheet cake at our reception, so eliminating major money-suckers just didn't seem like a possibility. There were none. Thinking about every check I'd written during all the months of wedding prep and all the bills about to be due, I couldn't pull my mind back into work for the rest of the day.

That night, I drove home in the dark after another grueling ten hours. My brain was in overdrive. I couldn't get Drew's sad voice out of my head. Even though my primary feeling was fear, I could feel another current under the waves. I trusted Drew. And I trusted myself. We would figure this out; we always did.

After the wedding cake had been sliced and diced, the flower arrangements had wilted, and the pizza gobbled up, save for a few stray crusts, we drove a few hours up the shore of Lake Superior to steal a few days away and to celebrate, regardless of the circumstances. We split a few meals and passed on dessert in the name of pinching pennies, but we still had a wonderful time and saved the worries for when we returned home.

Over the next two months I would kiss him goodbye and head to work, praying that day would be the day he got an interview. He responded to job postings, updated his résumé, and reached out to contacts. Dead end after dead end. He'd nail the first interview, and sometimes get a second. But without a long history of past, specialized experience, the hiring manager would inevitably go in a different direction. Drew was frustrated, I was stressed, and we both felt worried that the weight of earning an income was entirely on my shoulders.

Fast-forward a few months, Drew finally got a lead, then an interview, and a second interview. It was with a company that sold wine and while he'd be a glorified shelf stocker for a while, it felt promising. We didn't care about the retail hours or the fact that the holidays were the busy season. We just needed security, and this was our chance.

Here's the thing about Drew—he can do *it all*. He had already extended his abilities into many different industries—a stint at a law firm where he was the coffee fetcher and copy master; that time where he passed the exams to become licensed to sell insurance; his job selling cell phones; his gig selling billboards. While his path was far from linear, there was definitely a theme in there that helped him as he tried to figure out what his passion was—the man can sell anything. (Trust me, those soft, brown eyes are *really* hard to turn down.)

He got the wine job and over the next few years he worked his way up from a stocker to one of the top sellers in the company. His work ethic gave us the security needed for me to eventually be able to make my own scary leap from the corporate world to being a full-time photographer—a baton being passed off for me to take, and run with.

We had found a rhythm, we had adjusted to the fact that he only got ten vacation days every year, and we had carefully planned our one trip to Hawaii. (Yes, *that* trip.) So, there we sat, positive pregnancy test in hand, still processing all the change, watching the Polynesian dancers, and calculating my likely due date, when his face fell. The baby was due right in the middle of his busy season, the season where you literally couldn't take a day off. The reality hit us that I'd likely be on my own, navigating newborn motherhood, while he ran from grocery store to grocery store stocking wine for the holidays.

Was this what we had worked so hard for? As we sat poolside talking about what parenthood could look like for us, and what it could mean for the paths we had chosen, he said something that still surprises me to this day: "If I could do anything in the world, I would want to be a stay-at-home dad." It almost felt like a whispered confession. I took a sip of my virgin piña colada and stared at him for a moment. *What? Where was this coming from? Was he sure about that statement? Could we actually make it happen?* While I did not expect those words, when he said them, I knew he meant them.

Truth be told, those words were slightly shocking since we had only just opened our minds to the idea of having children. Growing up in the Midwest, as in many other places, specific gender roles were ingrained in us since the days of playing "house" in kindergarten, where the girls would stay in the Little Tikes house while the boys went to work. Could we get past the expectations others held for a traditional marriage? And would he *really* feel fulfilled with his hands in Play-Doh all day? What if he resented me every day I snuck out to get work done? I mean, there are a lot of people who say they'd like to be stay-at-home parents, but not everyone thrives in that role.

But here's the thing about visions and callings: it's not anyone else's job to understand yours. It's no one else's responsibility to know it before you do, give it to you, or figure it out for you. Others can and will help. But the source must be you.

And Drew and I committed to keep sharing our visions with one another so that as we learned more about ourselves, we could knit our dreams together to create a single, shared vision. One we were always working toward. One we were chasing together.

We knew others might not understand or relate to where we were headed. If someone else didn't see it or get it, it's because they weren't close enough to it, and that was okay. A "calling" or "way you want to live your life" is rarely as big and loud as a billboard. It's not always easy to find the right, succinct words to announce or share it. And usually that's because it's something we're still figuring out little by little. Most of us only work that kind of thing out in the arms of intimacy. Where we can whisper those confessions. Where we can ask the questions. Where we can say, "Can I show you another part of me?"

Once I started imagining this future life where we would all be together, where Drew would fully step into his days with a kid on his hip as I continued to build my business, I couldn't shake it. He was a *natural* with kids. I had watched as he transformed from a human who had never held a baby to a man who wasn't afraid to admit that baby shoes were really cute, especially the tiny Nike ones. And he was *so good* at being our "domestic engineer"; we had long ago submitted to the fact that he was a way better cook and better at vacuuming than I'd ever be! (Ahhh, carpet lines!) As soon as he spoke those words, it's like someone hit play on a movie in my mind. I could see him, happy, at peace, fulfilled. And as soon as he handed that little dream over to me, I knew it was now mine, too. A shared goal. Love is so cool.

As someone who had been chasing her own dreams for the last few years, I knew what came next. I felt a responsibility, a calling, a commitment. Now that I knew his dream, it was my turn to pass the baton and let him run with it. But there was one small catch, a detail that was missing . . . being a stay-at-home parent requires a child. With each loss we endured, I feared he would resent me for ripping his dream away again. His dream had become our dream, but with the particular dream of starting a family, I was, of course, *innately involved.* It wasn't like the times when Drew would run a race and I would get to be the squealing person with a sign on the sidelines shouting some version of "WOOO, YOU GOT THIS, BABE!" I played a pretty big role in this dream coming to literal life. And while I struggled with loss and the betrayal of my body, Drew's struggle was just as deep—a dream deferred. An identity left unfulfilled.

This is a story about Drew and me, of course, but it's everyone's story, too. The story of how love ties up a bit of our identity with someone else's. The story of what loss looks like when more than one set of hands are holding the ashes. The story of how after holding on to hope, we need to be the ones that are held. Love, loss, faith—this is about all of us, saddling up with whomever we have chosen and riding off into a someday sunset that we can't possibly yet see.

But sharing a life with someone is not always sunsets and champagne. There will be times where your partner will bear the brunt of life's burdens, and there will be times when you will. There will be times your souls feel dim, either one of you, or worse, both. There will be times when you get to chase your dream and times when your partner gets to chase theirs. It won't always be equal, it won't always be even, and it won't always be convenient. But here's what I've learned: a wild, expansive love is rarely those things.

I know "wild" and "expansive" feel like vague words, like descriptions you'd see slapped on a coffee mug or a peony print. But Drew showed me that this kind of love isn't just a phrase you'd find on an Etsy tee. And, more importantly, he showed me what it looks like instead.

Drew was stuck in this limbo for three years, doing one thing but yearning for another. I knew *exactly* what that limbo felt like because of my own career path. I had lived it before. Once a dream sticks, there's usually no going back. But instead of complaining or comparing, instead of losing hope or giving up, Drew stocked the hell out of that wine. While, at times, it would have been easy to grovel or pout, he stayed on the path he was on, celebrating the small stuff, showing up day in and day out, and clinging tight to the vision that like all things, this, too, was temporary. That our dream *would* happen. That our time would come.

I recognize this season now as one of dual grief: the grief of lost babies but also lost dreams. And if there's one thing I've learned about grief, it's that it can look different from person to person, season to season. For us, in our marriage, we approached our grief from separate ends of the spectrum, meeting somewhere in the middle. Drew wanted to fix things and to make everything better. I wanted to curl in the fetal position and cry.

Oftentimes, women are born to cast visions and role-play bright futures, like we did when we were five and wore lace tablecloths as wedding veils. So, the moment that pregnancy test alerted me we'd be expanding our family, I started to dream forward at hyperspeed. And when we lost our baby, our dream, I grieved the shattered vision of our future family. But Drew, even though he shared that same grief, well, he was more concerned about *me*. And he let that concern and care guide him to do the simplest thing, and the hardest thing: show up for me and show up at work, all while I couldn't show up for much of anything at all.

Showing up for each other—whether as spouses, partners, collaborators, family members, neighbors, or teammates—looks a lot like that sometimes. Like swallowing your pride and slinging pinot. It looks like helping your partner carry sadness, frustration, and anger while you're already dragging your own. It looks like taking turns and chasing goals, both separately and together, knowing the finish line is wherever love happens to land.

Maybe you're in a place where it feels impossible to walk each other forward, to shift the weight of the burden and inch your way through it together. Can I share with you what worked for me? Every time the present left me feeling stuck, I reminded myself of the truth— that there was a shared vision on the horizon. There was a compelling future around the corner. That good things were coming.

When I couldn't see it, Drew could. When Drew couldn't see it, I could. And when we both couldn't see it? We'd say it. We'd pause, because there was no "getting there" if we weren't going together. There will be times when you'll need to approach your partner with unflinching honesty. You'll need to say, "This feels too hard. Remind me why we're doing this. Show me what we're working toward. Paint me the picture. Tell me how beautiful the view is going to be."

And there will be times your partner will need you to do the same. The trick is to not give up on each other simply because the vision is changing or the timing is uncertain. The trick is to say the truth out loud, over and over, as many times as you must. Scrawl your shared dream on every baseboard in your home. Write it down in marker and tape it to your fridge. Make it your computer password, whether it's *debt-free* or *Dubai*.

Trust me, those daily reminders *work*. Take it from researchers and clinical psychologists John and Julie Gottman, who cite "shared common meaning" as the highest level of the Gottman Institute's training model for successful marriages. "When couples have that shared dream, the inevitable ups and downs of marriage are less bothersome. Creating a larger context of meaning in life can help couples to avoid focusing only on the little stuff that happens and to keep their eyes on the big picture."[1] According to Dr. John Gottman, couples who talk about their hopes and dreams with one another openly are more likely to be happy and less likely to be struggling.

---

### HOW ARE YOU, REALLY?

Take a close look at your most significant relationship. Can you get creative and carve out a scenario that adds value to you both? What is your shared vision? What's a dream that might allow you *and* your partner to come to life? What steps can you take together to make that happen?

---

In the culture of our home, talking about our dreams has become an important thread. We don't "take turns" doing the dirty work. We don't divvy spending money fifty-fifty down the middle. We don't split the laundry mountain into his and hers piles. We're not after balancing our relational checkbook of equality; we're after equanimity. We're constantly asking, "How can I add value to your day? How can I encourage you? What do you need?"

Even when Coco came into our world and life felt both fuller and messier than ever, that shared vision kept us committed to tag-teaming the workload. I mean, what does a stay-at-home dad do when the baby is attached to my boob at all hours of the day? How could Drew fully take on his dream role when I had to nurse Coco to sleep or she just wanted me in the middle of the night? Up until I finally weaned, it would have been easy to feel tension that he wasn't living out his role fully, not because he didn't want to but because he wasn't personally lactating! But I knew the truth: we were working toward the same goal.

So, every time he'd bring in a crying Coco while I was on a conference call or recording a podcast episode, I'd pause, mute, nurse her—and then get back to work. Drew and I both recognized the value of a teammate in those moments, and we both made sure a day didn't go by without a sincere thank-you for each other, and for the life we'd built. Even on the most chaotic of days. Even when things were tough. Even when we both felt like we didn't have an extra ounce of energy, love, or affection to give.

Most of us are all too familiar with those days. As the years stretch on and responsibilities grow, it's easy to feel spiteful, bitter, or resentful when we don't feel valued in the ways we deserve. When we don't get the help we need, or we don't feel the support we crave. But part of working toward a shared vision means wanting wholeness for *both* parties. Whenever I start to feel unvalued in any relationship, I pause to ask myself: Am I looking for this person to offer a value I can offer myself? Is this an area I've been neglecting in my own life? Is this a circumstance where I feel unfulfilled but am hoping for someone *else* to satisfy?

Once, my friend found herself in the middle of an argument with her spouse. She felt like his hobby took up all his free time and she was becoming less of a priority in his life. He listened and nodded and asked, "Would you like me to take a break from the league?" Yes, she answered.

But a few weeks later, after his weekends were wide open and they had plenty of time for each other and their family, she realized his soccer league wasn't the problem. Soccer made him come alive. He loved it! And she wanted that for him. But watching him live out his passion only made her realize she didn't have one of her own. In the end, she realized she wanted him to keep his hobby. She just wanted one for herself, too.

How many times does that happen in our relationships? We project our unfulfilled desires onto the ones closest to us. We claim their circumstances are keeping us from our unmet needs, and we crush those under our own roof with bricks of expectation and resentment.

This is when we have to get really honest, both with ourselves and our partners. This is when we have to ask, "How are you, really?" and listen hard for the truest answer. This is when we have to understand that relationships are a beautiful blend of expectations and needs and wants, some voiced and some left unspoken, and it's our job to bring them all into the light.

This honesty has carried us through all of our shifting identities—both Drew's and mine—and every second of dreams deferred. Our shared vision includes both of us working to meet our own needs *while also* working to meet the needs of the ones we love. It's the reason he greets me with hot lemon water in the morning. It's the reason I surprise him with triathlon gear so he can pursue what he loves, too.

Most of life's work is done without an audience, without "likes" or emoji-riddled comments, without gold stars telling us someone noticed our hard work. As we walk through life and do our work whether it's inside or outside of the home, as we push past the exhaustion, the days we feel unseen or unnoticed, we need to tether ourselves to our visions of the future. Each day is one step closer. And if we're lucky, hopefully there's someone right alongside us holding the candle to that vision when the world feels too dark to see it for ourselves.

Years ago, during premarital counseling, we told our pastor that Drew and I played cribbage with each other, and we mentioned we kept track of who had won more games on the back of the board. And while I don't remember everything about the blur of our wedding ceremony (minus that unfortunate moment when a fan blew out our unity candle) I do remember our pastor's words about cribbage: "You're not competitors. You need not keep score or tally your wins and losses. You are now a team, fighting for the same goal."

How beautiful of a realization is it that we aren't competitors, that we aren't opponents with anyone else on this journey of life. That we aren't called to keep score or tally up our wins, but that we're meant to cheer, support, and come alongside one another as teammates on this journey of being alive day in and day out. But mostly, how lucky we are that we have a partner next to us, naming and chasing dreams on the same side of the cribbage board.

Life isn't a game. There are crazy mornings and distracted dinners, and harsh words can be lobbed faster than you can call a muggins (shout out, cribbage fans!). But every night when Drew and I fall into bed, we remind ourselves to look at our lives in pure amazement, in absolute wonder of what we've been given. As we fall asleep, we take turns spouting off a few things we're grateful for—how cute Coco sounds when she mispronounces "banana," how incredible the weather was for an afternoon walk, or how perfectly in-season the raspberries are.

Sure, we're nonconformists in terms of gender roles. Once strangers find out that I work while he does the lion's share of cooking, parenting, meal-planning, and cleaning (truthfully, I've never met a man who loved a vacuum more than my husband), I usually brace myself for the inevitable question to come: *Then what the heck does Jenna do?*

I chase my dreams so Drew can chase his.

Drew chases his so I can chase mine.

# 11

## tacos and truth:

### HOW TO CREATE YOUR AUTHENTIC COMMUNITY

**Each friend represents a world in us, a world possibly not born until they arrive, and it is only by this meeting that a new world is born.**

**—ANAÏS NIN**

"I'm beginning to doubt that having long-term friendships is even a possibility anymore," my friend Brittany said, as she sipped her margarita. I reminded her we had been friends for fifteen years—and she said, "But that's different." I heard the meaning behind the words: finding true friends in each stage of life, the kind that will stick around, isn't an easy process.

I'm guessing you feel this, too. As busy people, we find ourselves squeezing playdates and dinners and birthday celebrations into already full calendars. We send emoji check-ins to that new colleague who seems cool, hoping it might turn into a someday friendship. We try to reconnect with old friends over the noise of toddler tantrums or airport layovers. But life gets in the way, and things fizzle out, and sometimes, we're left wondering why.

How do we keep a friendship alive? What does community look like as we age and evolve and let our identities transform? How can we feasibly foster the types of relationships we can bring our full selves to when we're so damn busy all the time?

As we grow through each decade, it feels like there's a fork in the road that reveals how the paths we take and the decisions we make can begin to divide us. Things like careers, relationships, children, health, geographic distance, and plain ol' convenience all impact the vitality of our friendships, and our ability to create or keep the closeness we crave. Year after year, it becomes harder to create the kind of community that transcends the life stage we currently find ourselves in.

Remember when it was easy? Remember when our only criteria for friendship was whether or not we shared the same enthusiasm for Lisa Frank erasers or Twinkies or *Full House*? When did it all get so complicated? As grown-ups, the stakes seem so much higher. *Do we share similar values? Does she hang out at places I can't afford? Are we in the same season of life? What the heck happens if our kids or spouses can't stand each other?*

So, I get why we would want to try to blame our lack of close, intimate friends on honorable things. Like grueling workloads, or changing dynamics of parenthood, or moving cities for a new job, or the ever vague but well-meaning, "I'm just doin' me for a little while." It's easy to wish for the kind of instant friendships that don't require any clutter clearing, where we can jump right in as relative strangers and slip straight into the BFF zone where we're loved openly and unconditionally. So many of us dream of the girls' nights out when we spill the reality of our world and laugh endlessly over martinis, and yet most of our relationships are watered down to pleasantries or a random text message every other month saying, "We've got to get together soon!" The kind of soon that never seems to come.

Maintaining rich and vibrant relationships takes work, commitment, and shared expectations. It isn't a fast track. It's the slow route of showing up in the small moments, knowing that's the only way we learn how to show up for one another in the big ones. It's investing in one another throughout the years, scooching over to sit down in the front-row seat of one another's lives. It's a friend asking, "How are you, *really?*" when you've been dying for someone to notice how much you need to talk.

But challenging ourselves to dig deeper with the people in our daily lives is the only way we can learn, over time, to see through one another's defenses. This is how we become people that know *exactly how* to bring support in big or small ways. We learn, in a series of tiny and consistent interactions, when to offer tough love and when to shut up. We know the food she's going to crave after her C-section. We know to tell the new people in her life that she does *not* like surprise parties. We know what kind of flowers to send the minute her dog dies. (We know the minute her dog dies.)

Sure, we'll mess up at times. We'll have conflicts and misunderstandings and miscommunications. We'll have to apologize even more than we ever thought we could, simply because we know when we need to. We'll fail to show up where and when we're needed most. So will our friends! A trusted circle of relationships is filled with varying challenges, push back, emotions, and distractions, and a willingness to talk about them, even the uglier parts. That's the beauty of it.

But how do we get there? How do we transform our everyday interactions into deeper relationships? How do we grab a casual latte and tell a new friend we hate our job or our marriage is failing or we struggle to contain our temper with our kids, knowing we won't be judged? Honestly, who even has time for a casual latte these days, anyway?

It will take work. It will take intention. And it will take patience. But most of all, it will take honesty. Why? Because it's only possible to find true friends when we're intent on being true people. Being up-front about who we are can be an awkward journey, especially if we're used to hiding behind walls, masking various personality quirks, or changing ourselves in order to be accepted. But much like a fifth-grade teacher would tell you, when you make friends *that* way, they were never *truly* your friends at all. Changing my approach to friendship so that I could go to bed at night knowing I'm utterly, gloriously *me* in my relationships? Well, I'll never tell you it was an easy journey.

Growing up, I was undoubtedly one of the kids who liked to follow the rules. I said no to drugs, I always made honor roll, and I was never more than five minutes late for curfew. I didn't even *try* alcohol until I went to college.

One of the reasons I chose the college I did was because I had been recruited as a diver to join the swim team. While we were ranked one of the top Division III schools in the country, the team also happened to be known for what they did outside of the pool: partying, drinking, and sometimes using those diving skills to go from roof to backyard pool (never a good choice).

Away from my childhood nest of safety, I felt a new sense of curiosity. I wanted to be cool and was drawn to the excitement of rule-bending after all of those rule-following years. Sure, I filled up a red Solo cup with foamy keg beer and said yes to whatever was on offer. That first semester, *I lived it up.* I made friends in the dorm with others who loved to party, and we would sit around an IKEA table next to the futon and pregame before venturing out to one of the college parties. Laughing, experimenting, and making a fool of myself quickly became my definition of fun.

Once, my coach joked, "Are you guys a swimming team with a drinking problem or a drinking team with a swimming problem?" But later that weekend, the weight of my coach's words finally hit me: *I had never needed alcohol to have fun before. What had changed?* Feeling reflective, I made up a lame excuse for why I wasn't going out that night and instead hung in the dorm rooms watching old seasons of *The O.C.* on DVD. Hungry at 10:00 P.M. (which I think is called the classic college "fourth meal"), I wandered over to Taco Bell and ran into my friend Brittany. (Yup, my same friend Brittany from earlier in this chapter!) She was a party friend of mine, but that night, she was totally sober and hungry, just like me. I grabbed my tacos and we sat in a booth to talk.

As we sat, wide-eyed, fully present, and eating an array of fast food (hungry girls exist), we started to talk about who we were before college, why we hadn't gone out that night, and how we both wanted a change. Together, we realized that even though we'd gone out plenty of times wearing our denim miniskirts and our spaghetti-strap tanks, we never really got to know each other. That night, we talked for hours, eventually moving our conversation to the curb outside of our dorm, sharing such similar thoughts and experiences. We were still sitting on the curb when our drunken friends passed by, stumbling their way home together from whatever party they had been to and we gave each other a look that bound us together in what came next.

The entire second semester, I didn't have a sip of alcohol. With Britt by my side, we started joining faith-based organizations. We skipped the Thursday night house parties and joined a Bible study in the dorms. We'd climb on the bus and go to church together on Sunday mornings, and I genuinely loved the feeling of having a show-up friend. The kind that you just know will be there, without wondering, reminding, second-guessing. We found our groove and while it was new, it was *honest*. In our bond, our entire college experience shifted. (Also, that no-hangover thing was nice.) She's still one of my best friends to this day, over fifteen years later, and we often recount how fate led us to Taco Bell that Friday night and we grew the courage to change the path we were on because we had each other.

You've heard it a million times before: if you want to make a friend, be a friend. That's true, but I believe there's more to the old adage. To find your people, you have to be *your* person.

You have to show up as *yourself*. Your full, true, and whole self. Naked while fully clothed. It's one of the hardest, most important things to do, and it's one of the rarest practices in our modern, digitally tethered age. Why? Because we get this wrong over and over again. We scroll through seas of familiar faces every single day. We send Insta likes and emoji affirmations. We rely on social media to keep us, well, *social*. And we assume that, if we're connected 24-7 to nonstop, ever-expanding networks, we'll never run the risk of being lonely.

But can I offer you a gentle truth here? The opposite of loneliness isn't just connection. The opposite of loneliness is being *known*. It's a connection with people who *you know* truly know you.

A recent study cited as many as 80 percent of those under the age of eighteen and 40 percent of adults over sixty-five years of age report being lonely.[1] According to the study, loneliness is *perceived* social isolation, not objective social isolation. Those researchers put it this way: "People can live relatively solitary lives and not feel lonely, and conversely, they can live an ostensibly rich social life and feel lonely nevertheless."

Ever been there? In the back row of a jam-packed church, feeling like you could leave the building at any minute and no one would miss you? In the middle of happy hour drinks, looking around the table at your colleagues, wondering if any of them know when your birthday is? The girl at the brunch everyone overlooks when someone says, "Who should we set the new guy up with?" *Um, hello? Is anyone there? *waves hands around* I'm right here!*

Loneliness comes down to how *known* we feel. And the less we show up as our most honest, authentic self? The less known we actually are.

HOW ARE YOU, REALLY?

Are you showing up fully for the people around you?
If not, what's keeping you from a more authentic
relationship? What's holding you back from
offering your honest self to friends, new and old?
What are you afraid of?

Honest, authentic relationships require just one thing: our honest, authentic selves. Not perfect people, but open people. If we can't fully know and accept ourselves, how can we fully know and accept one another? Posturing is a terribly popular habit. But if we don't learn to set it aside—for ourselves, and for our friends—it can damage every chance we have at brave, true friendship, no matter our age.

All too often, we approach female friendships from a scarcity mindset. There's an undercurrent of judgment beneath the words we say and the choices we make. We question every decision or value we have, like, *What if this new friend thinks I'm super crunchy for bringing my own pureed sweet potatoes to the playgroup?* Or, *When should I tell my colleague I can't meet for happy hour drinks because I'm working toward sobriety?* Or, *How do I explain the complex reasons for why I can't go home for Thanksgiving?*

*What if she thinks I'm too serious? What if she thinks I'll judge her for her choices? What if I'll miss out on a new friendship with her because I'm . . . me? What if . . .*

And while those thoughts can scare us, the thought of presenting a false reality should frighten us a lot more. In the face of whatever judgment or confusion that might come our way, we're better off choosing truth. *Our* truth. With each brave move to reveal our true selves to one another, we're making more space for people to show up just as *they* are. That's what friendship is. That's what communities are. That's what authenticity *does.*

I know how many of us struggle with this. There are barriers between the kind of friendship we crave and the kind we currently feel equipped to give. Trust doesn't come easily for every human. How can we be the realest version of ourselves if trust is a hard thing for us to believe in? Maybe, in addition to all of those external factors like time and distance and dynamics that are beyond our control, there's something else at play here. Maybe we also struggle with maintaining and beginning intimate relationships with other women because we haven't learned the art of acceptance—*a gift that starts with us.*

When I think of accepting ourselves to accept others, a memory instantly floods me. I remember walking into a room with my mom and daughter in tow. To my left, I saw a Tony Award–winning actress, and to my right, an Olympic gold medalist. I was immediately intimidated. There were racks on racks of clothing, a salon of chairs with hairdressers and makeup artists on standby, dressing rooms, and a set for shooting. I'd just arrived at the Aerie Role Model photo shoot in New York City, my first time meeting other influential women from all walks of life, deemed *role models*, no less.

I found a nearby chair to nurse Coco and as I looked around at confident women of all shapes and sizes, ethnicities and backgrounds, I felt totally out of my league. *Why am I here, again?* I was just a small-town Minnesota mom who worked from home and talked into a micro-phone each week (ha, funny how we belittle our life's work so fast)!

We nervously met one another and made small talk as people shuffled us around, trying to get us all fitted and ready for the group photo. The set was bright green, there was a massive sofa, and we all stood by as they placed us one by one into the shot. I watched as (my now friend) Molly Burke and her guide dog, Gallop, sat on the floor. I smiled as Ali Stroker rolled her wheelchair through the rough carpet. I witnessed the poise in Aly Raisman as she settled into her place. I giggled as Tiff McFierce shimmied her way onto set. One by one, we all were placed in the frame.

Want to hear the full stories behind some of the women in the room? Listen at

WWW.JENNAKUTCHER.COM/MORE

And then it hit me. We might have all taken very different paths to arrive on that set that very day in New York City. We might have carried different stories from our past, and we sure as heck were writing different stories onto our futures. But here we were, together. Our paths had crossed for a reason. And each of us had something to learn from the others. And I had something to teach these women myself. Otherwise, I wouldn't be in the room.

I look at those photos today and see strangers who became friends—the kind of friends you call to check in on, send birthday gifts to, and receive their family's Christmas cards. A group of "role models" curated by a brand, a group of women who weren't just leaders but who became students of one another. What started as awkward forced laughs for a camera transformed into rich dinner conversations, text threads, and meetups whenever we were in the same city.

I know what would have happened if I'd kept my guard up. I know what would have happened if I'd resisted the idea of showing up fully as myself, or if I'd let intimidation or assumption keep me from staying open to forging new relationships. I wouldn't be able to call these women my friends, and I would've missed out on something altogether beautiful.

Maybe it's nothing like a New York City photo shoot for you. Maybe it's the carpool lane or the yoga class or the office copy room. Our origin stories, when it comes to relationships, are going to look different for everyone. Some will begin fast and furious, like an instantaneous connection. Some will grow slowly for years and years and years. Some friendships will last forever, and some simply for a spell. However your friendships look today, there is so much beauty to be found when you move forward in the mess of relationships, seeking to learn from it all.

But what I want to tell you most, today, is there is nothing wrong with you if your circle is small. Or even if it is empty. You are not unloved nor unlovable. *There is time.* Time to learn and grow. Time to heal from your past, because it's not your past that needs your wiser self, it's your present. And your future. I mean, *The Golden Girls* didn't even find one another until they were in their sixties and answered a roommate ad from the grocery store bulletin board! How's that for timing?

Studies show that on average people have three to five close relationships in their life, and that's it.[2] That's way more than enough BFFs, right? But it's so easy to wish for more as one quick scroll on Instagram shows us the bride with ten bridesmaids or the bachelorette party with tons of friends in matching swimsuits. We see other people with their inner circle, their ride-or-dies, their Lavernes and Shirleys. It seems like everyone is surrounded by endless support. We wonder, *Why don't I have that? What's wrong with me?*

In our search for silver-screen friendships or Insta-worthy Vegas trips, we find ourselves overlooking the small, daily interactions we are involved in. We're so quick to complicate it all, aren't we? We fail to recognize the people surrounding us right now, today, might have all the makings of our next great friendship tomorrow.

Just this morning, Coco and I took our daily walk before school drop-off and stopped to talk to our neighbors, Howard and Sandy, who brought along a bag of Goldfish crackers for Coco. We chatted with our neighbor Kathy, too, who was waiting with her doodle, Manny, tail wagging, as she held out a pink hydrangea for Coco to put in the basket on her trike. This Saturday, we'll have a coffee date with another set of neighbors, where we'll pull out the lawn chairs and watch the kids play with Tonka trucks on the driveway.

Each of these delightful relationships can be considered friendships. Maybe not the kind shown in sitcoms or social media feeds, but meaningful just the same. We're all wildly different, from various generations and backgrounds and perspectives. And we're sure as hell not hosting a slumber party or Vegas getaway any time soon. (Most of them aren't even on Instagram, so consider the group swimsuit photo a solid *nope*.) But can we rely on one another? Can we check in on one another? Can we learn from one another and grow alongside one another?

Absolutely. It's a different approach to friendship, I'll admit. It's the kind that brings together the whole damn circle—from eight years old to eighty-eight years old. A circle where we are all growing, stretching, giving, and receiving as we walk through life together. Creating this type of authentic community means we can all show up, fully, as our multifaceted selves. It means we bring different gifts to different situations. We can reach out to one friend when we need a good cry. We can reach out to another when we need a kick in the pants. And we can reach out to a third when we keep forgetting the secret ingredient to that slammin' chili recipe (cocoa powder, always).

Friendship isn't a spotlight to be shoved into. It's a floodlight to be *shared*. And once we let that kind of relationship shine, we get to see that, yes, we can vote differently, dress differently, and think differently—and—as impossible as this sounds, we can still love one another wildly and walk one another home.

Dare to go first. Dare to expand your definition of friendship. Dare to believe you'll get back what you give. Dare to take a chance on a new acquaintance that doesn't believe the same things you do. Dare to prioritize getting together when your calendar squares are fuller than full. Dare to choose friendship in a world that celebrates independence.

But mostly, dare to go deeper. Dare to ask the real questions, and dare to answer the hard ones.

Dare to lean over the bistro table, or your front porch, or the Zoom screen and whisper: *How are you, really?*

# 12

## pride's utter chokehold:

### HOW TO ASK FOR HELP

**No matter what accomplishments you make, somebody helped you.**

**—ALTHEA GIBSON**

Almost everything I've ever wanted, I've asked for. When I wanted Drew, I went in for the kiss. When I wanted a gig, a project, or a client, I buttoned up my big-girl pants and pitched like my life depended on it. Just yesterday, when I wanted mashed potato pizza (don't knock it till you try it), you'd better believe I placed that order quicker than you can type "Pizza Luce."

Still, there's a four letter word I've always *hated* asking for: H-E-L-P. My pride is relentless. My desire for control is seemingly insatiable. My independence is a rocket booster ready to blast me into another dimension. What a cocktail, eh?

But all that changed when I heard those words for the second time: "There is no heartbeat." When the doctor whispered that, it felt like my own heart had stopped beating, too. And at the exact moment, a girl named Caitlyn hit send on her fourth email to me.

It was years prior, back in 2016, when Caitlyn sent her first email, then the second email, and then the third email following up. She was a virtual assistant, ready and willing to help me offload some of the weight of running a business solo.

Her stubborn persistence was undeniably powerful, but it was no match for my pride. Each time she reached out, I responded, "Thanks, but no thanks!" Not literally, but basically. I thought I didn't need help. I kept on my way with a shrug and the belief I could do it all alone, just like I always had.

I had never hired anyone before. Not only was I afraid to have someone see just how unkempt and frankly embarrassing all my systems were (I had like fourteen spreadsheets labeled the same exact thing), but I was also afraid of being someone's . . . boss? Being "in charge" of my own business was already a lot of work, but owning the responsibility of actually caring for and providing a paycheck for an employee petrified me. From her emails, I could tell this person was a treasure of a human and would make an incredible virtual assistant. She came across as confident, tenacious, and somehow so very warm all at once. So, what would happen if I brought her in and royally screwed everything up because I just wasn't ready?

I had pondered these thoughts (and many more) in the past, but then, Caitlyn's email arrived. It had been a minute since I'd heard from her, reminding me she was there, ready and willing to help if I ever needed it, and this time, I cried. Right then, I needed help more than I even knew how to express. In the throes of another loss, I was trying to imagine how I could keep things afloat. To this day, I'm convinced that what compelled her to reach out to me one more time despite having been told, more than once, to shove off (nicely!) . . . was something a whole lot more powerful.

To be honest, it was the first time in my life that I couldn't just *push through*. Not this time. Not with this. The waves of grief wrecked me and all I could manage to do was lie in my bed with my little dog Tucker snuggled close to my chest. I didn't care about responding to requests, checking social media felt trivial, and every ounce of schedules, timelines, and productivity was swallowed up in my pain. This time, I had committed to being still. I had promised not to distract myself from my grief with dings and pings and notifications. I had promised to not bury myself in work, but instead to sit with it all, and man, did it *hurt like hell*.

We've all been there before, haven't we? Knocked to our knees, wondering how we can continue on. And while the things that knock us may change through the years, the feeling of defeat while on the ground remains the same. Heartbreak at thirteen and heartbreak at thirty, they may take different forms, but both leave a lasting mark. Both will make you do a double take on your life's path and leave you wondering if you've been walking in circles instead of forward. Is life just some kind of sick, infinite loop of pain? Is heartbreak just another one of life's few guarantees?

And then, sometimes when we least expect it (or don't expect it at all) help shows up and changes everything. Maybe for you, help comes in the form of a doorbell ringing with a warm meal waiting outside, or a friend's offer to drive you to a doctor's appointment. Maybe it comes through a stranger's compliment breathing light into your life on a day filled with darkness, or a person picking up your Starbucks order in the drive-through after a chaotic morning.

I clicked on the reply button to Caitlyn's email and typed a few words before I collapsed backward like a starfish into my bed. The weight falling off my shoulders in that instant was astonishing. Staring at my ceiling, I laughed at how straight to the point I had been with her because I had no room left in me for explanations.

My reply that time consisted of three words I rarely allowed myself to utter. "I need help."

I want to pause here and say that—if you're in this place of struggle now—you needn't say anything other than those three words. You don't need to justify why or explain the series of events that led up to your eventual surrender. Those three words are enough. They're all we need to say. In fact, they're *everything* we need to say. Uttering them just might be the most courageous step you can possibly take today to get you through tomorrow. And when you are on the receiving end of those words, do your best to hear them as enough, too.

As soon as the *whoosh* sound of a sent email played out of my phone, I knew I had turned a page. Pride's utter choke hold on how I ran my life, my exasperating need to fill every single role by myself, my desire to control it all loosened. It had to. I felt the bitter taste in my mouth from years of hurrying through the wilderness and blazing through every obstacle alone just so I could pat myself on the back and say, "You did it. You saved the world single-handedly! Here is your *crown*!"

Dismantling that thinking was tough for me, especially because I was horribly comfortable with being so uncomfortable. The truth was, I was addicted to torturing myself by piling on more work thinking *that* would lead me to some kind of grand prize, even though I had no idea what kind of prize I was really looking for. What was I trying to be the champion of? Nonstop pressure? A gold medal in "Doesn't get enough sleep at night"? A trophy for "Most stress zits"?

Years later, my friend would send me a voice text that said these words: "Am I wrong for wanting to simplify things? To give up on the notion of always growing and just kind of . . . pause for a bit?" This friend? She was an entrepreneur, an achiever, a golden girl, someone who was also sharing and creating and launching new things, but in a season of waiting for her own family to start, she was feeling this urge to slow down and stop the incessant need to build.

I texted back, "Have you ever thought about the fact that you can press the brake without forgetting where the gas pedal is?"

Oftentimes, we keep doing more, chasing more, piling more into our lives, not trusting in our ability to slow down, coast, or, heck, even pause. We don't want to lose momentum and we don't trust ourselves to pick right back up where we left off. So we buy into the lie that constant motivation is a *required* personality trait for all good little worker bees.

We trick ourselves into thinking that every new request that demands more of our time and attention just might be our breakthrough, a chance to have everything we want. We say yes to every invitation because what if your next big break was around the corner or in that email invite or at that networking event? We've heard the stories of that single encounter or opportunity that fanned a spark into a flame and changed someone else's life, so we worry that if we say no to a single thing, we'll be the one to blame for missing our chance. What if it passes us by, whatever "it" is? What if we take a break, unclench our fists, and, like sand in a palm, our hard work starts to slip through the cracks? The what-ifs are endless, so the fear keeps us hitting the accept button on as many of life's RSVPs as possible.

Most of the time when something has felt like it might be *it*—that big break I've been waiting for—I've found myself compromised, stretched too thin, and even executing someone else's vision for something that doesn't fit my own version of success. It's the shiny opportunities that often leave us feeling deflated and dull, mostly because they usually involve us being a pawn in someone else's game. A game we told ourselves we've given up but a game we still find ourselves playing time and time again.

When we operate from that fear-of-missing-opportunity place, we're pouring cement into our boots, weighing ourselves down as we compress into being "yes people" for everyone else but us. When we investigate, we recognize that our yes is *rarely* in reply to ourselves. While "yes" should feel like the trademark word for freedom, it's clear how easily it can be used to bind yourself to a life that does not reflect what you really feel, what you actually want, and who you truly are.

I want to say today what I said to my friend then: you are absolutely not wrong for wanting to simplify, to slow down. In fact, I praise the fact that you are expressing that yearning in a world that feels like a race, one that celebrates busyness with a badge of honor. You don't need permission to slow down or rest.

Here's what we know. We know that starting is the hardest part, but after that? Slowing down takes the silver medal in challenges. We chase our tails and spin our wheels, forgetting that we have been smart and savvy enough to figure things out thus far, and we doubt our ability to recreate success once the momentum slows. But if we don't acknowledge that the same gifts, skills, and talents that got us to where we are today can get us to where we want to go in the future, we belittle the very things that make us uniquely qualified for our own calling.

Hindsight, in its unfailing clarity and kindness, would eventually help me put a very important puzzle together about my own life: this is a habit for me. A common occurrence in the life of Jenna, The Achiever. The independent woman. The control freak. I pine for help but then push away the hands that offer it to me, because what if they find out I don't have it all together? What if they don't do things the way I'd do them? What if they don't care as much as I care?

My pride just kept getting in the way. It wasn't like there was a lack of humans who were willing and able to help. My community includes some of the most serving, generous, helping-hearted humans you'll ever come across. The problem wasn't them; it was me.

My pride existed because I thought my achievements were the only things keeping me, well, alive. Wanted, loved, known—all for my work. And when you live like this, it can take just one little "failure" to make you feel like you've gone from an A-plus to a failing grade. Pride is, in fact, what made me feel like everything I did *had a grade* in the first place. So, I classified having to ask for help as a failure. They felt like the exact same thing to me. "Can you help me with this task? I'm overwhelmed!" sounded a lot like "Looks like I can't succeed at anything! You win, I lose, I can't do this, game over."

Yep, making sure I was doing it all was like a game I was constantly in danger of losing. What did I think I was at risk of losing? My identity. Losing the reason (I thought) that people loved me. The reason that kept people sticking around. The thing that made them want to work with me. The way they trusted me.

And all this time, I needed to learn to trust *them*.

That day, there was no denying the truth: I needed help, without a single doubt, and not only was I ready to receive it when Caitlyn offered, but I was ready to step into a life *full* of accepting help. I was also ready to get really comfortable with asking for it, too.

While that day felt nothing like a celebration at the time, I'd now like to raise a toast to the moment I finally said yes to letting people in, to admitting that I couldn't do it all, to loosening up my white knuckle grip of control in order to open my hands for possibility.

Caitlyn became my first hire, and even from our very first exchanges at a local coffee shop, I finally started to see the light. As we sipped our coffees and ate our scones, I slowly began to let her in. I answered her questions, shared the areas where I was struggling to get by, and cast a vision for where I hoped our relationship would go. By the end of our coffee date, I had nervously given her the password to my email and I told her, "Let's just start super small. Can you help me respond to people? I can't even bear to open my inbox right now." The blood flow returned slowly to my extremities with the tiny release on my grip of control.

The next day, there I was, still in bed, still sad, still numb, but I realized while I had been resting, Caitlyn had already begun serving my clients and keeping things afloat. When I finally logged into my email, I gasped at my number of unread emails. Zero. Already? I dropped into my "sent" folder to see kind, efficient communication in every single message. That tiny check-in gave me a feeling I hadn't yet experienced as an entrepreneur: freedom. I checked in with Caitlyn to make sure she was okay, and she replied with a gleeful, "Doing A-okay, J!" There I sat with my bedhead hair all over the place . . . nodding like, *Ohhhh, I get it.* I get it!

I now had the capacity to not just do but to *feel.* It's like I could hear the bells chiming in the cathedral, like I could hear the angels singing! Rejoicing, I made myself a cup of coffee and thought about how to make the most of my handful of extra hours I would have that week. Hours where I could just be. Where I could grieve my latest loss. Where I could sleep and heal and log the hell out.

By the end of week one, I gave her my passwords to virtually everything (if I could've just handed her my entire iPhone, I would have) and made her a list of all the things she could help me with, because for the first time in a long time I felt free to pause, to disconnect, not worrying that my entire business would stop when I did.

Was the creation of our working relationship super comfy the whole way through? Absolutely not. I had to learn how to sit back and watch her approach projects with her own insight and creative process, rather than being a here's-how-I-would-do-it broken record. We got used to laughing through our little mistakes. Soon, we learned that we could trust each other, speak our minds to each other, and fall back on the fact that we're here to have fun and help people. Like every new relationship, we had to get to know each other the long way, day by day, task by task.

But if you're someone who has a tough time asking for help and support, let me encourage you: it gets easier to be loved, supported, encouraged, and appreciated when you first practice *supporting yourself* by receiving it. Saying the hard yes today means it will come out a little easier tomorrow.

It's simpler now to be able to poke holes in my old ways of thinking, to be able to see the flaws in the beliefs I held. Because of Caitlyn. She loosened my grip of control so I could open my hands to receive. She taught me that we aren't meant to do this life alone, especially the parts where we have a choice in the matter.

A gentle reminder: your trek does not have to be this solitary climb that leaves you at the mountain top to take in the view all by yourself.

Take it from me: there is breathtaking beauty in letting go and letting in. *Letting go* of control can offer that feeling that I'd imagine someone has right before they jump out of a plane to enjoy the adventure of skydiving. It's that decision to make the leap before you can appreciate the ride. It's that one moment of courage that allows the adventure to be had.

*Letting in* means boldly asking for help, maybe even before it comes to you first. Help can show up in the smallest of ways in every space of your life. From getting grocery delivery to paying the neighbor kid ten dollars to mow your lawn. It can come in the form of outsourcing a single task or inviting a full-time teammate to grow your dreams alongside you. Maybe you just need to ask a friend or partner to pick up some slack in the line here and there to free you up.

Asking for help is like a muscle that gains strength the more it gets used. It gets easier the more you do it. And think about it: the stronger a muscle is, the less hard it has to work. The less tired you'll feel. I may not know much about muscles, but thanks to confronting the weakness of my pride, strength is something I have become quite familiar with.

If you're struggling to know where to even begin on your own "asking for help" adventure, start with identifying your greatest need. Pick a need that will give you the biggest sense of relief first, that first taste of freedom, and prioritize finding help with that. Then try to get help with the next biggest thing, and the next, and the next.

HOW ARE YOU, REALLY?

Can you identify an area of your life where you're dropping balls most often? Without judgment, get really honest with where you're struggling to keep up or what's staying at the bottom of your to-do list. Who may be waiting in the wings to help? Where can you let go? Who can you let in to share your load?

Time and time again, every aspect of my life has become enhanced the moment I allowed two things: the letting go and the letting in. I *let in* to experience true freedom, and I *let go* because I saw the hands that were ready to catch it.

I never planned on a booming business, a presence online watched by a million sets of eyes. I never planned on pivoting myself from a one-woman show to leading a team of ten women or building something so much bigger than myself. I never planned I'd become an entrepreneur and then teach others how to do the same—whether in a new course I'm launching or a new podcast episode I'm dropping or a new blog post I'm writing. When I started all this I did so in the pursuit of freedom, with a vision of being in control of my destiny, but I never envisioned I'd also get the chance to create spaces for others to live out their own.

As time passed, my ability to not just ask for but to *seek out* help grew. With each hire, we grew. The company grew, the capabilities grew, the talent grew, the mission grew. And it grew far, far beyond me. We took one plus one and turned it into a million. A million-dollar business, a million watchful eyes, a million more downloads, a million more lives impacted. A million wonderful nuances in the personalities that surround me week in and week out. A million creative ideas, opinions, and endeavors that would have never come out of me alone.

There was magic to be found through restructuring my mindset around asking for and receiving help. I am no longer the only one holding my business in my two hands. I've learned I don't have to be the sole human to carry the weight of it all! As a bonus, life's achievements become much sweeter when I am sharing them with someone other than myself.

It's not just magic or luck; it's science. Psychotherapist Dr. Julie Hanks says, "Asking for help demonstrates trust and helps build bonds of intimacy in friendships. Exposing your human limitations to someone shows that you're willing to be vulnerable to them."[1]

Through vulnerability and heartfelt action, we are building something bigger than me, something bigger than all of us. That's become the entire point of what we do. With our visions aligned and our talents prioritized, we create what you see (and even what you don't see) today. In fact, I see so much more of my team in everything we're making now than solely seeing myself. From the writing to the research, from the webinars to the editing, the team effort happens in order to not only see my vision come to life, but to make the greatest impact. We're all women on a journey together (a literal dream come true, like the *Love Boat* but we're all great friends) while supporting one another on our separate, distinct yet parallel paths.

Each member of my team takes ownership and pride in what she adds and contributes. Each member brings separate gifts to the table. Our different lifestyles, upbringings, experiences, passions, and dreams help us to collaborate in a way that paints the possibility not just for the women out there who look like Jenna five years ago but for women everywhere to see themselves achieving something beyond their wildest imagination.

Don't let anyone trick you into the idea that they are self-made. Behind every successful human is a team of humans who have held space for the vision and contributed their gifts to make something incredible. A team who isn't afraid to ask "How are you, *really*?" and rally around you, regardless of your response.

When we let the words "I need help" escape from the battle within our minds and when they flow out of our mouths, even as a whisper (or an email), we're no longer battling alone. Someone else is there, picking up a sword, saying, "Your fight is my fight, too."

When we ask for help, we expand our circle, our bandwidth, our field of safety, and our potential for so many things while also honoring the gifts that those around us possess. Opportunities for linking arms with other people happen around us *all the time*. Maybe even every single day. You offer to dog-sit for your mother and you run into an old (but newly single!) flame at the puppy park. You ask your boss to sponsor a charity event you volunteer at and she's so touched by the cause, she joins the board. You ask your neighbor for nutrition advice and—boom—you've found yourself a running partner and, perhaps, a new best friend.

Life works like that a lot. When we expand ourselves, our dreams follow suit. They open wide or even change entirely. And it all begins with asking for help.

Behind every CEO might be a man changing a toddler's diaper. Behind every mayor might be a mother-in-law cleaning leaves out of his gutters. Behind every tech savant might be a steady flow of ramen at the ready, and behind every ramen chef might be the best teenage dog walker in town.

Don't believe me? Try asking.

# 13

# livin' the dream:

## HOW TO BE WHERE YOU ARE
## (LIKE, RIGHT NOW)

**Do not stop thinking of life as an adventure.
You have no security unless you can live bravely,
excitingly, imaginatively.**

**—ELEANOR ROOSEVELT**

"I don't think you have FOMO. I think you have FOMC—Fear of Missing Coco!" a friend said to me in the thick of the toddler years.

As a working mom, I can sometimes get just a *tiny* bit weepy over the moments I miss while I'm in the throes of a launch, or hosting a webinar, or hopping on a call with my team. I love my gig, and I love my girl, and I do my best to integrate it all. But, in those famed, croony words of Aerosmith, "I don't wanna miss a thing."

I've been reminded that this is what it feels like to be in the middle of learning the art of presence. Of appreciating where my feet are standing. Of not wishing away a moment, whether I'm checking spreadsheets or washing a pile of bedsheets. Of being all in, fully present, every step of the way.

For me, those moments of presence tend to happen on Saturday mornings, just me and my girl, usually after eating pancakes as a fam. Most of the day is reserved exclusively for bliss-following, cookie-eating, coffee-sipping, and memory-making. Coco orders her own cup of "fancy milk" (whole milk foamed with a dash of cinnamon on top). Honestly, it's cereal-milk-level delicious (I might've stolen a sip from her more than once).

I grab my oat milk latte and take the first careful sip. The baristas wink and nod to us on our Saturday visits, and then we meander wherever our wobbly weekend legs take us. Throwing rocks into Lake Superior and listening to the splash. Reading books, singing songs, drawing pictures of tiny dogs (my specialty!). Trotting down the main street in Grand Marais or wandering through Duluth, looking for puppy sightings, pausing to enjoy a singer on the sidewalk, swinging through the farmers market.

It's not fancy (well, besides her milk), but we fancy it.

It's in these moments I feel like I'm secretly a little bit of a wizard, because I look around me and it seems as though time slows. Instead of the usual blur, I feel like I can see in 5D. It's short-lived, because the fancy milk eventually runs out (or spills) and we have to get home for nap time, but oh how I wish I could freeze time for a second. Soak up those minutes forever and hang on to every little detail. I know that it's *because* of how fleeting they are that I can feel such a longing gratitude for them.

Let me ask you, what makes time stand still for you? Where do you find those pockets of time where you're so hyperaware that the moment you're in is one you don't want to miss? Is it late-night bingo with your crazy aunt? Karaoke after work on a Friday night? Walking hand in hand with your beloved on Sunday morning? Happy hour drinks with the girls? What moments offer you the most presence? What moments do you find yourself fully alive in?

Whatever your moments look like, I'm willing to bet they don't require a ton of stuff. Oat milk lattes, a bingo dauber, a cover charge. The makings of a memory are simple, aren't they? Add presence and you've got a priceless adventure ahead of you. So why do we complicate it? Why do we look for long-lasting happiness by filling our carts and our garages and our closets with things instead of experiences?

While I'd like to believe I've always chosen presence over presents and experiences over things, truth be told, as a child, I loved those purple Polly Pockets *a lot*. Still, there was one specific moment I can remember when I know, without a doubt, I made the right call, I chose the right option.

Growing up, my family lived on four acres in the country, down a dirt road in small-town Minnesota. Mowing the lawn was my dad's thing. It was his happy place between shifts at the papermill. And let me tell you, our yard was *immaculate*—the kind of yard where you could see the John Deere's lines indented, like fresh carpet that's been recently vacuumed.

My dad followed the same method his father used, the one I'm guessing every Midwesterner with large swaths of grass trusts—you mow east to west one week, north and south the next, bellowing *No blade of grass left behind!*

After my dad would mow, we kids would rake behind each mowed line to gather all of the grass clippings and remove them from said perfect lawn. We'd rake until we had little blisters between our thumb and pointer finger, the kind that required Mickey Mouse Band-Aids, and then we'd haul the trailer of grass clippings out of sight down a trail in the woods.

Let me tell you, I *loathed* raking. On my list of Chores I Hate, raking ranked higher than scrubbing the toilet or organizing the junk drawer. It was painful, it was always too hot or too cold, and there was a surplus of surprise bugs. Anytime I asked my friends if they had to rake grass clippings, they looked at me with curious eyes. (My dad would argue that their lawns probably didn't look as good as ours, and I'd just shrug my shoulders in response. No one came to visit us out in the country, anyways! Why did it *matter*?!)

One day, my parents sat us down after crunching careful numbers and they excitedly told us they had a surprise for us! Like a game show on TV, they revealed two options and we got to choose door one or door two. We could either choose to invest in getting a bagger that would attach to the lawnmower and collect the grass clippings, thus eliminating our need to *ever rake those blades of grass again.* Or, we could load up the car and take a family vacation to the Wisconsin Dells. (Recalling this conversation now as an adult has me thinking one thing: *Dang, lawn mower baggers must be expensive!*)

I don't think there was a moment's pause trying to decide between the two. My siblings and I all squealed at the idea of a getaway. We'd stay in a motel! There'd be a pool! There'd be waterparks! And a road trip and car games and car snacks, which are arguably the best kind of snacks when you're a kid! All bets are off. Rules, out the window. Bedtime is obsolete. Our squeals and shrieks of delight told our parents everything they needed to know. The deal was sealed. The healing of our raking blisters could wait. A family adventure it was!

I still remember the five-hour journey, my dad's classic red licorice and Diet Mountain Dew in the front, Gobstoppers for us kids in the back (likely so we'd spend hours sucking them down to the soft candy inside, not able to talk our parents' ears off). Magnetic board games and Tetris on the Game Boy to keep us busy! Oh, what I'd give to experience another road trip in the nineties.

Our lodging wasn't fancy. I still remember the Shamrock Motel with its maroon carpet, floral comforters, and an outdoor pool complete with a mini unicorn waterslide. Yes, shamrocks, flowers, and unicorns. This place was clearly magical (and overthemed). Over the next few days, we went on one unforgettable family adventure after another, from watching my brother absolutely kill it at mini-golf to plunging down every single waterslide at the nearby water park with zero fear. Each night we'd end up back at that small outdoor pool at the motel, where I'd try gymnastics tricks on the stiff mini diving board. "Hey Jen, can you do a cartwheel and then jump in?" "Can you dive in backward?" "What about a flip off the side?" Every day was better than the last.

It was on that very diving board—as I laughed and splashed and lived my best life—that my dad looked at my mom and said, "Wow, she's actually really good at this. She could be a diver."

While I came home from that vacation still being a steadfast raking-hater, I had unintentionally discovered a brand-new love: diving. I took that suggestion and ran (err, dove!) with it. For the next four years, the entirety of my high school career, I walked around with my blond hair tinted that telltale chlorine green. And I learned you can't actually do cartwheels to dismount from the board. *Bummer.*

I think you know the story from there: I went on to dive for the University of Wisconsin–Stevens Point, studied hard, fell in love with Drew, and everything else is history. But sometimes I find myself wondering what would have happened if we had opted to get the bagger for the lawn mower instead of choosing to go on the road trip. So much of my life as I know it can be traced back to that little motel pool nestled in the Wisconsin Dells. What if we had chosen the *thing* over the *experience*?

Now, don't mistake me for a minimalist queen, or someone telling you to feel guilty for owning stuff. My spare closet has tubs unapologetically labeled "Miscellaneous." I've got at least four kinds of spatulas in my kitchen, although I still always reach for my favorite one. And you better believe I'm still holding on to that pair of distressed Abercrombie & Fitch jeans that I pinched pennies for in high school.

I'm not even talking about just buying less stuff from here on out. I'm certainly not a hater of stuff! Please keep buying the things that bring you joy. (Here's where I would sincerely like to shake the hands of whoever invented loungewear, duct tape, and the garlic press.) *Things* have their place, and if you want to live minimally or you have a knack for holding onto all the trinkets, I don't cast a judgmental eye in either direction. I'm talking about the gift of being present in your life, of being fully in the moment, experiencing its richness, aware of its fleeting nature.

Let me explain. What I'm learning about living a more visionary life is that—right now, this very moment—I'm creating a present memory that I'll draw from in later years. Makes sense, right? Not so sci-fi, really, we get it. But what might happen if I flipped the script? What if instead I created future memories that I can draw from *now*? Scenes that are so compelling and beautiful and memorable and realistic, they could carry me forward to a new, unknown place—like my very first vision of that baby girl giggling over syrupy, sticky pancakes?

This is a practice I first learned during a gathering, when my friend Brendon Burchard walked me through this life-changing exercise. We all got quiet as he asked us to get comfy in our seats and close

HOW ARE YOU, REALLY?

our eyes. I peeked to look around the table to see if others were following the rules and then quickly closed my lids. He shared the importance of presence and experience, about how so often we get caught up in the rat race of day-to-day life, running harder and faster as we try to maintain that air of success. He talked about how for so many of us, somewhere along the way, we tend to replace the important moments of our life with work so that we can keep accumulating *things*. Visual representations that our hard work, energy spent, and time invested can mean something, anything.

With our eyes still closed, we were to imagine a few specific scenes from our lives, letting them simply play out like a movie in our minds. We were to think not only about the memories we have already experienced, but also the ones we still want to make, the moments we still wanted to live out.

> ## HOW ARE YOU, REALLY?
>
> What memories do you still want to make? What future moments can you picture yourself cherishing most? What do you want to experience, and with whom? Where do you want to go? What do you want to try? See? Taste? Do?

I remember visualizing the scenes I would want to replay over and over again and, even now, I am blown away by the simplicity of them. My little visions didn't require a lot of things, surprisingly didn't require a passport, and they generally didn't involve work. Sure, I'd need to work to see them come to fruition, but they weren't *about* work. They were experiences that I've either lived or will live that I'm fully present for. *My dad driving a packed pontoon boat with the music a little too loud. Saturday pancake breakfasts at the lake as a family. Quiet mornings throwing rocks into Lake Superior. Drew and I, gray-haired and sun-spotted, pushing grandchildren on a backyard swing.*

These scenes weren't lavish; they were simple. They weren't impossible, costly, or out of my scope of talents or experience. They were a front-row seat to my own life, a glimpse into my dream future. The idea here is that by visualizing the past, we found grounding and gratitude. And in visualizing what we want for our future, we might embrace the simplicity and joy when we find ourselves living those scenes out.

The thing is, we often get tricked by the wish lists consumerism hands us. Our vision boards are filled with not enough plot and too many props—the accolades, the trophies, the new Sorel boots you've had your eye on since the Nordstrom anniversary sale. Those things aren't bad, they just aren't what we'll cherish most at the end of our days.

We wrongly assume that livin' the dream means the KitchenAid mixer, but really, it's the Saturday morning pancakes we'll most want to relive. Those buttery crumbs and lingering laughs still top every wish list I keep. When I look back at the *things* I've bought myself in order to be happy, successful, or comforted, I find a lot of laughable regret. The state-of-the-art standing desk. Every lipstick ever. Fourteen different baby wraps and a box of Hatchimals.

Now, don't get me wrong. Temporary happiness isn't anything to scoff at; sometimes you have a bad week and that very soft comforter you bought yourself is the stuff of legends when you finally crawl into bed. Coco and her Hatchimals are a silly little treat to behold. But in the big, sweeping, generalized sense, the experience of "having many things" is not what it's cracked up to be. Even after years of hearing this wisdom from those who have less or those who have lost it all, we still chase after stuff, don't we? We crave that high of having the thing. Buying the thing. Unboxing the thing. Posting and sharing that we, finally, also have the thing.

But it's not sustainable for us (nor, I might add, for the environment). Dr. Thomas Gilovich, a psychology professor at Cornell University, has based twenty years of research on the very idea that happiness is not sustained from buying things that we want—even if they're things we highly desire or consider to be an extension of our personality. Why? Dr. Gilovich explains, "One of the enemies of happiness is adaptation. We buy things to make us happy, and we succeed. But only for a while. New things are exciting to us at first, but then we adapt to them."[1]

Hear my conversations with experts on the topic of happiness at

WWW.JENNAKUTCHER.COM/MORE

That's precisely why most of the stuff we buy to fill that satisfaction void over the years eventually finds its way to the attic, the garage, the donation bin, or broken in the trash. It was fun while it lasted, but, like us, it turns back into dust (except actually a lot of it doesn't and that's why we have a global trash crisis, but that's another story for a different type of book).

So let me share a personal realization that has been life-altering for me: it's a lot harder for me to find the same kind of regret about my experiences. Even the tough ones. Every single experience has left me with a shift, a lesson, a memory, a passion, or a newfound fire. The heartbreak taught me gratitude. The anger taught me justice. The failures taught me grace.

And the people who walked alongside me? They made it all worth it.

As Dr. Gilovich also writes, "Our experiences are a bigger part of ourselves than our material goods. You can really like your material stuff. You can even think that part of your identity is connected to those things, but nonetheless, they remain separate from you. In contrast, your experiences really are part of you. We are the sum total of our experiences."[2]

Simply stated, our experiences are a compounding investment. Their returns never cease as long as we're alive. And while new tech, a clever toy, or that one Instagram ad that catches me on a particular day will grab my attention, I'm not buyin'. Instead, my experiences and their accompanying lessons have become the plot I use *every single day of my life*. (Especially on Saturdays.)

Every single time I serve pancakes on Saturday mornings, I think of that early vision and I pinch myself that I'm living it. Drew knows by the look on my face and the near-tears in my eyes when I'm thinking of the first time I saw this moment come alive—the Madewell jeans, the Persian rug, the white linen top. When I feel these emotions peaking, I offer myself gratitude for having the audacity to dream of something that was, in some ways, out of my control, and I laugh at how wildly surprising this life can be. While I pass the syrup, I can hear my past self whispering to me, *Jenna. Pay attention. This is what you wanted. Remember? This was your dream. Stay here. Be still. This is IT.*

It's not in choosing one over the other, presence or presents; you can choose and have both. Marie Kondo your linen closet if you want but enjoy the process while you're finding the things that spark your joy. Kiss the parts of your life that no longer serve you a fond farewell and then let them go.

So where do you begin in writing your own future screenplay for your life? I get it, you're already busy and taking a few minutes each day to envision your future might sound like an absolute waste of energy. Maybe you've rolled your eyes at every vision throughout this book; every bit of woo-woo that's been accompanied by the work. Maybe you find yourself pushing back on the very idea. *Aren't you a grown-up now? Who has the time? Where do you get the mental space? And how can you even begin to dream when your emails keep pinging or your toddler won't stop pretending the kitchen pots are bongo drums?* I get it. It feels silly, all this daydreaming.

But here's the secret that isn't really a secret—when you take a few minutes to dream, to ask yourself what really matters to you, you get all that time/energy/space back (and then some). Because you're trading in today's worry for *tomorrow's wonder.* You're replacing the doubt with the dream. When you let yourself relax into what you want next and who you're becoming, you're also acknowledging who you already are. You're no longer worrying about hurrying through your week anymore, chasing the weekends. For that moment, you're *in* the moment. You get the ultimate return on investment: the present of *presence* so you can *experience* the experience.

I no longer relate to that old Fear of Missing Coco. Because when I'm with her, I'm *with* her. Time stills. The minutes get fatter. The moments expand. Whether it's a slow Saturday morning or a frenzied Tuesday afternoon, I can feel that familiar pulse, that quiet drumbeat. *You've been here before. You've envisioned this.*

*You're—quite literally—livin' the dream.*

# what you're going to do about it

what a journey we've already been on together. Pages upon pages, lots of questions thrown at you, and yet here you are. thanks for sticking around. We are about to launch into the part where the hammer-meets-nail, and you get to take a swing toward actually building the life that supports you and the world around you.

Regardless of where you find yourself when this page is opened, I hope the journey through this book has filled you up with things you didn't even know you needed. You get to embrace this next section with gratitude covering you from head to toe.

Now it's time to dig deeper into the nitty-gritty practice of implementation. This is where you take what you know, all those tough questions you've been asking yourself, and put some good ol' action behind the answers.

Words are powerful and lessons through storytelling make for a great stage play, but this isn't a production. It's your life. Here is your invitation to roll up your sleeves, and make things happen. Commit to turning those answers that are springing forth into reality.

Pick up your hammer,

Jenna

# 14

# what brooke shields doesn't know:

## WHY YOUR STORY MATTERS (A LOT)

**When we women offer our experience as our truth, as human truth, all the maps change. There are new mountains.**

**—URSULA K. LE GUIN**

"Mommy, tell me a story about when Coco was a baby!" she whispers to me at bedtime. Coco's got a thing for storytelling these days (and also for describing herself in third person). So, I tell her everything—the sound of her coo, the curl of her toes, the sparkle in her smile. She wants to know what I was like as a baby, what her daddy was like as a baby, what our rescue dogs were like as pups (origin stories we'll never know, but don't worry; I've got a good imagination).

It's her way of understanding life, and the new life that grows inside of me. By the time this book reaches your hands, there will be a babbling baby in our midst—another soul to learn, another forehead to kiss.

Another story to tell.

We all have the desire to be remembered, to leave a legacy of some kind, and to make some sort of mark on this world. Most of us want to leave this spinning planet better than it was when we got here, right? But so many of us spend our days busy and distracted, dripping with kids, work, or responsibilities, on hold with our Internet service provider while wiping the coffee grounds and toast crumbs off the kitchen countertop. Just an average Tuesday morning, you know?

But what if I told you that your legacy is unfolding right now, today, even while you're waiting for Jim, the technician, to restart your router?

We tend to overplay the notion of legacy in our culture. We often think of it as a status thing, like our name on a building, a million-dollar donation to a good cause—heck, even a hashtag would do the trick as long as it's far-reaching, right? *The bigger, the better!* Legacy feels weighty, monumental, bigger than life.

We see it reflected on TV and in movies where discussions of legacy happen in a floor-to-ceiling library in some illustrious mansion between a grandfather and grandson, and there might even be a prized ring or wooden box involved. Sunlight is pouring through the windows. Definitely some kind of stringed instrument crescendoing, scoring the scene. Whether the predecessor wants it or not, there it is, a big, promising legacy handed to them in mahogany or gold. I know that's the Hollywood version, but you don't really hear "legacy" come up in everyday conversations. It's not really discussed at the dinner table, and if it is, it might be met with eye rolls, like "Dad's talking about his retirement and legacy again!"

But legacy is all around us, every single day. Legacy is the mark we made, the mark we are working on making right this very moment.

It's our story, no matter how big or small we think it is. It's not about conquering the world, curing a disease, or building a mass of wealth. Legacy, plain and simple, is what you leave behind.

Legacy is a grandfather, telling a tale of his first canoe ride while a grandson catches bass in his old fishing boots. A daughter, digging through the attic and stumbling upon her mother's old journals, letters, and photos from high school. You, walking through the city you love most, encountering stories on every street—names carved into the corner maple tree, or preserved in the sidewalk cement, or scratched into the diner's booth.

Legacy starts in the simplest of ways: with a story. A good old-fashioned tale usually starts with "Once upon a time . . ." and that line isn't just reserved for princesses or fairy tales. When we have the space to confidently share our stories that reveal our passions, illustrate our transformations, and pass down our hardest lessons, we open ourselves up to being fully known.

Trust me; I've got proof. A story wrapped up in a single sentence. A changed life in just a dozen words: "I knew if she could do it eight times, so could I."

These words were whispered to me on a night in New York City. While most days I work from home in my yoga pants, some days I get to fly across the globe to enter rooms with pretty table settings and fancy dress codes. That's where I found myself on this particular evening, at an event where women from all walks of life were invited to celebrate the work they were doing. From women in media to philanthropists, nonprofit leaders to influencers, we gathered to kick off a new year, a new decade, in the company of other women who were dead set on impacting their world. With my trusty Spanx on under my sweater dress, I sat at a table surrounded by some of the most brilliant, accomplished women I had ever met. Wisdom gathered around the table. Years upon years of it. I was astounded.

As I overheard snippets of conversations being shared, trade secrets being swapped, encouragements being doled out, and connections being made, I wished there was a way to preserve them all. To save this moment in time, not just for us to relive but for future generations to draw from. As I looked around the room, I realized that so much of the valuable knowledge these women had within them would leave the earth when they did. Their years of pivots and pain, trial and error, triumphs and treasures—it would all get buried right along with them like the gilded glory of an ancient king. All I could think about was how much this world could gain from each and every one of them while we all still had the chance.

There was one conversation that left a mark on the evening—and my life. I had been chatting with Jen Foyle, a global brand president for a major clothing company. She's kind and captivating, but has an obvious, thick shell around her that likely got her to the place she is today—a trailblazer and a boss. As she asked me where my daughter was, I smiled—"She's in Hawaii with her daddy. I flew in just for the event and can't wait to get back to the beach!"—and clinked my glass to hers. She then looked me in the eye and said, "Did you know that it took me *eight* rounds of IVF to have my daughter, Maggie?" I totally froze and shook my head. I had no idea.

I could, of course, relate in some way. The painful, confusing struggle of not having your dream happen, and the pain of trying again with the same result was all too familiar for me. I felt all the words bunch up in my throat, wondering if it was too bold to reach over and grab her hand. I finally exhaled and asked her how many times she'd thought about giving up in the process. Expecting her to answer something along the lines of "A million and one." But she looked me in the eye, whispering strongly: "*Never.*"

I was dumbfounded. In vitro fertilization (IVF) is an intense process. It's emotional, incomprehensibly expensive, exhausting in every possible way, and it can make anyone believe they'll be eternally stuck in a hope and grief cycle. It threatens to wring you dry, chew you up and spit you out, and a baby isn't even guaranteed. I was frankly stunned to hear a woman could throw herself in the ring that many times without crumbling. I couldn't help myself. I asked bluntly, "How the hell did you keep going?"

Then she told me something I didn't expect. She said, "After the seventh try, the doctor told me it was time to give up, that it was over and that a baby just wasn't going to happen for me. I told him I wanted *one* more go around, one last try, because once upon a time on the TV, I heard Brooke Shields's fertility story. She bravely shared with the world that it took her eight rounds of IVF to finally have her baby. I knew if she could do it eight times, so could I."

I paused, trying to take all of that in. Thoughts filled my head as I sipped my drink again, trying to buy myself an extra moment before vocalizing any response: "Can you imagine if Brooke had never shared her story? If she had kept *that* piece of life hidden away. Would Maggie be here today?"

"Wow, I guess I never thought of that. No, I would have given up. One hundred percent" was her answer.

(BRB, gotta go email Brooke Shields to let her know that a fifteen-year-old girl living in New York City is here today solely because she had the courage to share a painful piece of her life. And in doing so, she gave a stranger hope, a story to learn from, a reason to not give up.)

Minutes later, Jen kicked off our event and shared our conversation with the room full of women, some of them her employees and others her friends for years. Up until this night, she had never told a soul what it took for her to have her baby. Her right-hand gal found me later in the night and said, "I know her like the back of my hand, and I had absolutely no idea that she went through all of that."

Vulnerability is contagious. As the evening progressed, I witnessed women all around the room ask questions and open up to one another. Slowly, we changed the topic from work or titles or achievements to enter that uncharted *How are you, really?* territory with one another. Conversations around the table shifted deeper into love and pain and grief and struggle as we all began to really *go* there. To not let the night pass without learning one another's stories, not just the highlight reels—the real ones. There was this unspoken commitment to make the most of this rare momentum we'd built through our story-sharing, truth-telling, and unabashed vulnerability. A desire to etch a piece of one another's legacies on our hearts. I watched hope, curiosity, and belief take up residence in that room with the soft hum of true and honest conversation.

This is exactly why our stories matter. It's why the tales of every-day women—our trials and our triumphs, our loves and our losses—can fill up rooms and stadiums and entire communities with enough oxygen to go around, and then some.

When it comes to telling our stories, we often pass off the responsibility to the one with the loudest mic, or the best voice, or the biggest audience, or the greatest accolades. We feel that in order to make an impact we need a signed degree with a gold foil stamp, a bunch of letters after our name, or an online presence in the thousands. But that's simply not the case. Life is teaching us lessons every day. We are shaping our legacies, one brave choice at a time. Most of the life-changing things I've learned didn't necessarily come from people with multiple degrees. I learned that *that* part didn't need to be a qualifier. Many lessons came because people decided to share their stories and experiences. I mean, it won't surprise you I don't have a degree from Body Confidence University, and my undergrad wasn't in podcasting.

Beyond posts of cellulite or TMI stories going viral, I have read countless stories that people bravely place into the hands of my DMs, telling me they stepped *out of* not only their comfort zone because of how I show up, but also *into* their own beautiful life. I've read tales of women who have taken one small spark of hope from one of my blog posts or from a podcast episode and fanned it into their own awe-inspiring flames. I've encountered stories of women who didn't lose hope after loss because they caught a glimpse of my smiling, giggly miracle.

So, let me approach you with a little tough love, because if you left this world today without sharing your story, then that would be a tragedy. Tragedies happen all on their own, without our permission, without warning, so when the pen is in our hand, why not write a good story?

I want to be super clear: *You* could be Brooke Shields to someone. You could be responsible for the existence of someone's long-awaited Maggie, or for someone's newfound confidence, or for making another human feel a little less alone because they see a bit of their own story reflected in yours.

What if the things that have happened in your life, those moments where you find yourself diving deep into a world you didn't plan to be a part of, those passions that come out of left field and wake you up in the morning, the obsessions you can't shake loose—what if they were the exact things that give you this chance to use your story to change the course of someone else's day . . . or even their life? What would it look like if you took all of the things you've been through and dared to share what you've learned along the way to save someone else time or heartbreak? To help someone rebuild? To help someone find joy? To help someone feel seen?

### HOW ARE YOU, REALLY?

What stories do you need to tell? What moments have transformed you? What dreams have you fought for? Celebrated? Learned from? Write one down today. Keep it close to you until you encounter someone who needs to hear it most. (Even if that someone is yourself.) When you find that someone, share that story with all your heart.

Pause here to unclench the pressure of feeling like every story has to be a "good" one. They don't always have to end with "happily ever after." Not every part of your story is for *everyone*. Some pieces are just for you, maybe for now, maybe forever. Not everything that happened to you wove a beautiful color of thread into your life. There are undoubtedly many things you should have never had to face. And even more still may come your way. Your story isn't yet finished, which means you can ditch the pressure to wrap it all up and tie it into a pretty bow. Not every story needs to be shared in order to have meaning.

As we learn from the moments we've been through, the movements that carved out who we have been and who we are now, the cuts and scars that line our bodies, the words that we have replayed, rewritten, repurposed . . . we make new stories for ourselves.

As we share our stories, we liberate ourselves into seeing the potential of that pain and rebuilding we've walked through and how it may be used for a purpose. Even a seemingly small purpose. A story of healing delivers a little piece of your healing to someone else. I firmly believe that good lessons have a certain "law of physics" to them: *they multiply.* As we internalize a bit of what we've learned, we leave a mark on not only ourselves, reminding us that we're worth listening to, but on our communities, and by extension, our world.

It all starts with a deep breath and the courage to speak into trusted spaces. It's diving below the surface of the normal responses to the question "How are you?" and getting a little messy, going instead for the "How are you, *really?*" This is one of the many reasons I chose this title for my book. Because it might be awkward to ask or answer that question, but when asked, it invites raw honesty.

So where do you find the courage to share your story? Start with the spaces you're already in. Maybe it's when you're recounting to your child the story of the first time you felt left out. Or telling a friend about the time you went on a terrible date but liberated yourself to be who you truly are and not who the stranger across the table wanted you to be. Or unboxing your career struggles over a pile of nachos with a coworker. Your words don't have to be big, or perfect, or tidy to mean something to someone else.

Your story not only liberates you, but it invites those who are listening to participate. The moment Jen shared her story that night in New York City, the whole room was invited to move past the "How are you" straight into the "really" part. When you say, "I feel safe to share these words with you." Or "I love you, so here is the story I want to tell you." Or "I have something to say that I think you might need to hear," everyone around you can see they're free and safe to do the same.

The silly stories that make you smile, sweat, cringe, or cry share a bit of how you've become who you are. When you share your failures, every mess has the potential to turn into a message. When you share your scars, you expose the parts of you that have worked so hard to heal. When you share your triumphs, you invite others to celebrate the victory with you. And while your life may never be covered in a docuseries one day or live on the pages of a book, your legacy, your story when shared has the power to make someone else feel a little less alone. In a world filled with a billion hollow connections, true vulnerability like that is a gift.

While I'm sure on the night of our New York City gathering, the global brand president didn't plan to disclose her fertility journey to a room filled with strangers and friends, I am led to believe that someone in that room (besides me) thinks of that story often. Just as Brooke Shields changed her life, Jen's story might have done the same for someone else.

So now it's your turn. It's time to remind yourself where your passion came from. It's time to hear yourself vocalize the stories of your roots and point back to your beginnings. It's time to crack open corners, tell the secrets you've been keeping too long. This is your official invitation to be Brooke Shields to someone, to embolden a new spirit of bravery to do the scary, beautiful things with their life.

Clear your throat. Repeat after me.

*"Once upon a time . . ."*

# 15

## just one step:

### WHERE TO START, AND HOW

**Reinvent yourself over and over and over and over and over until you find home. There is no time line for the soul.**

**—MALEBO SEPHODI**

"But how do you keep showing up imperfectly?" a girlfriend recently asked me. I laughed. My first response was "Is there another option?" Because in my experience, life isn't going to give you one.

Waiting for perfection will have us waiting forever and wasting a whole lot of time. Waiting for perfection might mean staying in a relationship, a job, house, or a city you know you outgrew long ago. Waiting for perfection might mean missing out on a beautiful, bold future to stay comfortable in a narrow view of now.

There's an old Voltaire quote that I force myself to cling to when my perfectionist side wants to take the reins: "The best is the enemy of the good." Straightforward. Hard to ignore. Cuts me to my core. These eight words speak volumes to me in the moments I want to freeze up before I can fail, because in all of the stalling to make sure there's *no* risk, I don't even get a chance to try.

My friend Emma knows a thing or two about this quote.

Emma's what you'd call an idea girl, bubbling over with business plans and smart inventions and million-dollar concepts she's constantly mapping out in her head. From visions of facilitating local events to empowering and connecting women across the world, Emma's ideas are beautiful and bold and powerful. But they are just that: *ideas*. Merely thoughts that live in her head without the world knowing or being able to experience the dreams she holds.

I first met Emma at a business retreat a few years ago, and we bonded in the hotel lobby over a shared love for hot lemon water. A few days into the retreat, she asked if she could pick my brain about a few ideas she felt stuck in. So on the last day of the event, we met for an early sunrise walk before catching flights back home to our families.

As we sipped our morning lemon water tonics from paper cups, she described every obstacle that stood in the way of her (dozens of!) ideas. We talked, and I listened, and in the first mile alone, it was clear to me something bigger was at play here. She was afraid. She wanted a fail-safe. She wanted a 100 percent guarantee that every action she took moving forward would work. She wanted to know that if she really went for it, she'd stick the landing. Most of the obstacles she described that could potentially hold her back were what-ifs living in her brain, bottlenecking her thoughts like rush hour traffic, paralyzing her from taking action.

This wasn't just an Emma problem, this was a human problem. I've seen it time and time again. She was essentially overcomplicating her plans as a means to keep waiting a little longer to act on them. A goal of perfection leading her to procrastination that delayed any form of her progress. The visions stayed so big that they might as well have been a mission to Mars. Listening to her, I felt my hands start to get sweaty, and it wasn't from the sunrise hike. Just thinking about how many ideas take residence in incredible human minds like Emma's made me feel a fraction of *her* anxiety. Her fear of failure was holding her back. And fear? Well, the sources may differ for each of us, but the feeling in our bodies is usually the same.

"I'm getting anxious listening to all of the ideas you aren't taking action on," I told her. "You're letting potential problems and your desire for perfection be your excuse to procrastinate on your dreams. What if you picked one thing that was easiest for you, and just started? It doesn't have to be your life's greatest calling or an idea that will go on to change the world, but right now you need to prove to yourself that you're capable of taking imperfect action, of simply getting started, and making progress."

She nodded, wide-eyed. We both knew where it was she wanted to end up, but we also both knew she'd never get there unless she moved forward with *just one step.*

So many of us often complicate this first step. We zoom out until it looks like an insurmountable task, at least for now, at least until we "get our life together," until we have the money we need, until we can clear our schedules, *until, until, until.* We work on the idea itself, rather than doing the work that turns the idea into the thing. We let ourselves believe that the idea is so big we need to become an entirely different person before we can even approach it!

But when we do this, we forget to look down there at our own two feet. Our shoes, the ones we laced up this morning, ready to take just one step. A small one, perhaps! But a step that gets us just a tiny bit closer. And maybe on the fifth step, we trip. Maybe on the twelfth step, we fall pretty hard. Maybe on the thirty-eighth step, we stumble. But we keep getting up, because falling doesn't adhere us to the ground. We can turn our ideas from a giant mission into a day-by-day journey simply by doing the thing.

That "thing" could be anything. Whether launching a book club in your neighborhood or launching your own book into the world, whether adopting a child or adopting a new life philosophy, whether changing up your diet or changing up your hair, every new path begins with one single step. One action to inch you closer, to scooch you further, to move you onward in the direction of your dream. But here's the catch: No one can take action for you. *You* have to be the one to take it, even if it's with trembling knees.

Unfortunately, life doesn't always present us with a smoothly paved route or perfect rhythm every time we're running down a dream. We don't always know what the proposal is supposed to say, how to fix our marriage, or what to do about the scary diagnosis. We get flustered. We get lost. We start making excuses. And we miss out on the grand adventure, having never made any progress to pursue a better path.

The position you're in this very moment is one you can leverage to get you to the next spot. The tools you have within your reach are the ones you're meant to use to create your rough draft, your round one, your prototype's prototype. Over the years, I've learned that most of the time, we don't get to have the grand experiences or even the shiny things if we aren't willing to utilize what we're working with right now. Your million-dollar life may come, but until then? Go ahead and start with your hundred-dollar life.

Trust me, I'm no stranger to scrappy first steps. When I launched my very first podcast episode, I was sitting in the front seat of my

2008 hybrid. In the car parked in my garage, with a microphone and two spare bedroom pillows balanced over my steering wheel, I hit record. That podcast now has hundreds of episodes, tens of thousands of monthly listeners, and millions upon millions of downloads.

To this day, I can remember what that first hour felt like. I can smell the leather of my seats as I sat, freezing into a human Popsicle during that Wisconsin winter, determined to not open the door until I had finally started. I had no high-tech microphone, no previous experience, and no clue what "production value" was. I simply hit record and that was the day *The Goal Digger* podcast was born.

The day that I decided it was time to gather up all the guts I could to simply hit the record button on my first episode was the day my idea finally came to life—even in the midst of my hesitation. Even though I had no idea what I was doing. Even though it was nowhere near perfect.

Sure, starting a podcast may have been a calculated guess, but it was one that felt *right*. One I didn't hitch my identity to in terms of numbers and money. One idea that had me curious enough to try something new with zero guarantee it'd work out. On that day, I decided success for me was just hitting record and saying a few words.

Truth was, I was so insecure about my own voice—literally *and* figuratively! Would I come across as someone who had something to say that other people would actually want to hear? Would I say "Um" eight million times? Would I lose my train of thought or forget how to form a coherent sentence? It didn't matter. Because sharing my thoughts, my ideas, and the things I've learned with the world? That was enough for me. That was the imperfect action I encouraged myself to take.

Does your imperfect action include
launching a podcast? Find your step-by-step
beginner's guide to podcasting at
W W W . J E N N A K U T C H E R . C O M / M O R E

My podcast could've failed, flopped, or fizzled out. I could have tried for ten episodes and found out it wasn't for me. But even then it wouldn't have been a failure. I wouldn't have counted it as a loss. Failure, like success, exists only in the ways we define it. Who gets to decide what counts as a success or a failure? We do.

It's safe to say my podcast is nowhere near perfect; it is riddled with mistakes—even to this day. Time and time again life has gently reminded me that this notion of "perfect" is just that, a notion. An illusion. It's not even real! As simple as that is for me to type, it's not at all easy for any of us to learn.

It's easy to say, "Humans make mistakes!" But what happens when you put your name in that sentiment and make it personal? "Jenna makes mistakes." Yep—apply it directly to *you*. It stings a little bit more, doesn't it? But it's true. You make mistakes. I make mistakes. I'll bet even Oprah makes mistakes (maybe, although I can't really bear to think of that).

Mistakes aren't just something to fear or something to hold us back. They arrive with knowledge that propels us forward. If you choose to not embrace your ever-evolving, ever-learning, ever-mistake-making self, you're withholding those potential gains from yourself. But you're also withholding that knowledge from everyone else. You're letting those around you carry on without your contribution. You're existing in your own shadow, safe and sheltered from all mistakes, but never stepping out to feel the sun or experience the fun of taking risks.

When we allow ourselves to experience the fun of taking risks, everything becomes an experiment. We become the mad scientists of our own lives! We lose the desire to label everything as a success or a failure. Instead, everything we do yields a result that gives us information. And information empowers us to make decisions on the next action we'll take.

I'll be honest, I've always been a done-is-better-than-perfect kind of gal. Imperfect action has always been my way of movement, even when I don't know what results the action will yield, even when it sounds easier to stay still and avoid the risk. But avoiding risk and staying safe aren't the same thing, are they?

What if by staying safe, you're risking never evolving? Never growing? Never trying? Never creating your own happily ever after? Don't get me wrong, there are certain situations in which I would love to know the ending before I read chapter one. Where I'd love to know that everything is going to be okay; that *I'm* going to be okay! But ideas don't always become realities that way.

It's perfectly reasonable to want a master plan for every starting line of life. And when you're embarking on something new, you're likely going to crave an immaculately detailed blueprint (or, at the very least, a syllabus). But when you're learning or attempting something new, you're accepting the mystery. Along with the unknown, you get the full right to say, "Hey, I've never been here before! I have no idea what I'm doing!" You get to poise yourself as a beginner, open and willing and teachable. Fully ready to launch off the starting block to find out if the water below is tepid or icy or absolutely, perfectly—*finally*—refreshing.

So, what do you do when there's no countdown or starting pistol going off telling you it's time to begin? You refine the vision. You ask for help. You bring people into your conversations. Read the feedback. Hit record and see what happens next. You might feel it's not going to matter. You might want to close up shop after day one because of the belly butterflies. You might need to nervous pee because of the sheer feeling of doom that you're going to let other people down. Do your thing anyway. Find your footing, choose your pace, and honor that part of you (however small or hoarse-voiced it is!) that is asking you to try something just a little bit scary.

These days, we tend to want to fast-forward the "getting better" part. We don't want others to see us trying; we only want to show the success. It's like our digital lives have become a peer-reviewed journal, and we'd rather stick to what we know than risk failing—or worse, failing *publicly*! We worry about people seeing us try something new, we worry about the judgment, we worry about not getting it right or not having an Instagramable outcome from day one. But there's a reason the ol' grid is made up of many, many squares. If there's room for square 4,351? There's room for a square *one*.

With every major pivot in my life, I'm brought back right back to square one. I love being reminded of what it felt like at some of my own starting lines, because I know I have many more awaiting me. The fear, the feeling that I'm not worthy of the race, the wonder of what results my experiment will yield . . . and in spite of it all, getting into the starting position and running like crazy anyway.

When I recorded that first episode in my car parked in my dark garage, I wasn't thinking about episode five hundred. I had no idea what topic I'd be covering years from then! I had to narrow my focus, lower the stakes, and keep my sights on the first episode. I had to take the first step, the one I could control in that very moment: hitting record, talking about the thing I'd planned, exiting the garage, eating soup for dinner, and maybe laughing at the whole ordeal with Drew over said soup. I just had to let my courage be louder than my doubt for one hour. One single hour, then I could hit stop, get out of the car, and go back to wondering what the heck I was doing or if it'd work out!

That's how progress begins: with one brave hour. Moving forward is knowing that you can commit to just one step at a time, and then deciding to take another, and another. Like when you're in a thigh-quaking, back-tweaking workout, and you know you're not even halfway done, but you're 99 percent ready to give up and call it a day. Then the trainer yells at you, "You can do *anything* for fifteen seconds" and you take a deep breath and actually believe them. Imperfect action feels like this, and if you're like me, it comes with the same amount of sweat!

There are countless stories that teach this one simple truth: So many of life's greatest journeys involve winging it. Giving it the ol' college try. Just doing the dang thing. Walking toward a bend in the road without knowing what's ahead, but with 100 percent assurance that it's better than being stuck where you're at.

These tiny actions and small steps are happening everywhere, all around us, this very minute. World-changing, best-selling novels are being scribbled on the corners of napkins or in the margins of another book. Billion-dollar companies are sprouting up from folding tables in garages. Future comedians are making people laugh around their own dinner table. Fashion designers are learning their craft with hand-me-downs and scissors.

Get scrappy. Get resourceful. Get creative. Get *going*.

What will *your* first step look like? Will you type "how to get a grant" in your search bar? Will you ask your midwife what books she'd recommend on learning homeopathic healing? Will you join your local Toastmasters to brush up on your public speaking skills? Will you borrow your neighbor's power drill and build a bookshelf?

I've met many humans over the years who have told me about all their ideas that are "in the works" as they await the perfect time for them to be launched into reality. Truth be told, most of those ideas never enter the world; they simply *stay* ideas.

Actually, strike that. I wish that were the case, but the reality can be far more painful. More often than not, those unexplored ideas become a source of shame, stress, and pressure as they become unlived dreams. Resentment doesn't need much of an invite to start to seep its way into our lives. It's far more common than not for women to feel like the "good days are behind them" or that they're only busy with living unfulfilled lives. If you're there right now, don't shut out these thoughts even though they're painful. Plunge your arm deep into the dirt and wrap your fingers around the roots and start pulling them up. Look at what seeds they sprouted from.

This feels like a good time to ask: How are you, *really*? Are you angry your life didn't turn out the way you wanted, the way it was supposed to? Are you frustrated or scared the dreams that have been sitting in your heart all this time are still just dreams, and perhaps getting heavier by the year? And here's one of the questions we must approach with however many extra dashes of bravery necessary: Who do you think is responsible? Who or what have you found yourself blaming for a loss of fulfillment? What is keeping you from action?

Maybe you shoved the early seeds of a dream deep down into your pocket because planting them didn't make sense at the moment. Maybe saving your dream for later was the pragmatic thing to do, the "right" choice at the time. Maybe waiting was wise all those years ago. But I want to tell you to plant those seeds now. Don't wait until the perfect season. Because if you wait any longer, the dream won't grow. Resentment will. Bitterness will. Like root rot on that aloe plant you've had in your bathroom for too long, your past will try to tangle you up and keep you from your present, sabotaging your chance at trying to grow the life you're yearning to live now. Look down. You're not in the soil; you're above it. You're the gardener of your own life, and you get to choose what to plant. You get to enjoy what grows.

Your life is still happening and is therefore not labeled as unfulfilled. There are many, many blank pages left for you to fill in. That's the epicenter of why we're having this conversation in the first place. I'm not scared that you're not *doing enough.* I'm not telling you to make sure you fill up every breath and opportunity with more doing—that's the antithesis to my very being. In fact, I'm waving a big warning flag in the air to signal you to notice what you are doing (or not doing) and make sure it's what you actually mean to do.

After years of seeing others live their lives on autopilot engineered by someone else, and almost doing that very same thing myself, I want to see more of us uninstall that programming. I want us to feel the freedom to explore new things, to make mistakes, and to let those mistakes roll off our backs as they teach us how to move forward. Perhaps that first intentional step will be one you find yourself looking back on and saying, "I didn't know it then, but that one decision changed my entire trajectory, it led me here."

I know mine did. Not too long ago, I scrolled way back and hit play on my very first podcast episode. I cringed a little (okay, a lot), remembering how I muttered into my earbud microphone in a voice that no longer sounds like my own. (Ugh, I spoke with my "phone voice"!) While my voice and delivery have evolved and improved over the years, I am so proud of my humble garage beginnings—and I still cling to them now. I'm so thankful I took action. I'm so proud I went for it. I'm so grateful it all led me *right here*.

Moments of inspiration would've never turned into reality if I tried to plot the perfect path. If I had spent months and months researching the perfect microphone, maybe I would never have hit record in the front seat of my car. If I had decided that those three hundred dollars were too much to spend on the camera I used to start my photography business and kept searching for a cheaper one, I could still be in my windowless office. And if I had never opened up a document and started typing these words, this book wouldn't be in your hands today.

### HOW ARE YOU, REALLY?

Which of your ideas are stuck in your head, going nowhere? What's really holding you back? Where is fear of failure rearing its head? And what's the first imperfect step you can take to make your big, unwieldy idea into a you-sized reality?

Don't lock your goals in your heart, in a place where they live only as a "goal." Where they only serve as a weight holding you down, rather than a launchpad ready to lift you up. Bring your ideas forth. Hold them up to the light. Ask them what action is required of you. And *listen*.

Remember my friend Emma? The moment we faced her own *How are you, really?* question together was the moment she realized that she had two choices: she could keep putting off her ideas for someday, or she could start somewhere small today.

She chose the second option and, once she'd returned home from our retreat, attended a local networking event for women in business. As she nervously walked through the door, she was ushered to a name tag station and instructed to write not only her first name but her dream career underneath. She laughed as she tried to write "Organizer of Women's Retreats Worldwide" in the tiniest letters she could manage.

Soon, the event leader hushed the crowd and motioned for everyone to take their seats and welcome the evening's speaker. Emma made her way to one of the last empty chairs, squeezing into a row in the back. Offering a quick hello to the women next to her, she glanced over at their name tags. To Emma's right, scrawled in Sharpie, she saw: "Travel Agent." And to her left? "International Hotelier."

A reminder for you: You needn't know the future in order to give a good idea a whirl in the present. Just start with something good, something honest. Let the path reveal itself from there.

(And don't forget to bring a Sharpie.)

# 16

# when a woman knows her value:

## HOW TO MAKE IT HAPPEN

**Life is not easy for any of us. But what of that? We must have perseverance and above all confidence in ourselves. We must believe that we are gifted for something, and that this thing, at whatever cost, must be attained.**

**—MARIE CURIE**

At the risk of sounding like I'm quoting the December page of an inspirational calendar, I think that *everyone* has a gift to share with the world. I get that you might not believe that. I can imagine you might be thinking, *Yeah, yeah, but you don't know me.* It's natural to question if you truly have a gift, something special that could help change lives or leave an impact on the world. But you're here, right now, reading these words. And I know that means you're going to make a few things happen while walking around on this planet—and I know that means you've been given a few gifts to make those things happen with. You might not be able to see those gifts for what they are (yet), but take heart: the rest of us *can*.

Big or small, your gifts are glaringly obvious to the rest of us. Maybe you can lighten any mood with a perfectly timed joke. Maybe you've got a knack for making complex data seem understandable, simple even. Maybe you know exactly what to say to make someone feel loved, appreciated, and seen.

Or maybe you're like my mother, who is the living-and-breathing epitome of resourcefulness.

Over the years, my family and I have developed this inside joke about one of my mom's stealthiest skills. While she is unfailingly kind, she can also be fiercely persuasive. I mean, I've seen her melt even the most ironclad, ice-cold people. She's so disarming and approachable, but seriously potent—in that Minnesota nice way—when she needs to be. I've witnessed my mom's scrappiness time and time again through-out the years. (In just a few short paragraphs, you will, too.)

Whether scrappiness or humor, encouragement or wit, our gifts can show up in a variety of ways. But the truth is, we sometimes get in the way of them showing up at all. Instead of displaying them loud and proud, we tuck them away in storage, unused, collecting dust. We are typically the first ones to discount them, dismiss them, or discredit the impact they could make. Our gifts come so easily to us that we're quick to write them off. We assume *everyone* possesses the same skills. Our natural talents—these unconscious competencies we all have— live so close to our zones of genius that we shrug them off as common sense. And we move throughout our daily lives never noticing, recog-nizing, or celebrating their value. Ignoring the fact that they could be life-changing for someone else.

How many times have you downplayed your gifts? How often have you shrugged your shoulders and passed the buck to someone who you perceive to have more skills, more worth, or more resources? How many times have you failed to recognize your own value? I'll go ahead and answer that last one: often. Way too often.

I'm going to be really honest here. Before all the steps of "building a life you love" either beckon you forward or tempt you to turn and run, you must transform *the way you see your own value.* This is a step you're prepared to do with what you have right here and now. This is another place where the *woo* meets the *work.* It's where you allow who you are and what you have to make a mark on the world you live in.

Back in my earliest gymnastics days, my parents signed me up for my first class as little more than a desperate attempt for their three-year-old to release all the energy she contained. But what started as a once-a-week hobby of cartwheeling like a puppy on those blue folding mats soon spiraled into my full-on passion. After a few years, the owners of the gym had a conversation with my parents, telling them that if I wanted to pursue gymnastics more seriously, I would need to switch to a different facility. I had outgrown their level of expertise and training.

I proudly waltzed around my bedroom after class, still wearing my leotard under my winter coat, quite pleased with myself when my parents came in to discuss the idea with me. I thought they'd be over the moon, but their delivery was riddled with a quiet hesitation.

Switching me to a new gym would mean a higher tuition cost attached to the new center's expanded offerings. My parents knew this heightened cost would stretch them too thin financially, which they thoughtfully explained to me. But even with this knowledge, they never flat out told me no. In fact, I could see the gears turning in their minds.

Even as a kid, I picked up on these subtleties. I noticed. Maybe this was partly due to being the kind of child who had a little ping in her intuition when she knew she was being sheltered from something. Perhaps it was the fact that my parents always led with honesty and didn't shy away from sharing the realities of being a responsible grown-up. Regardless, I could tell this wasn't an easy decision for them.

My parents both knew how much of an obsession I had with gymnastics, as I'd developed some big dreams, like going all the way to the Olympics. And while those Olympic-sized dreams were beautiful, they also came with a cost for my parents, both in their time and their wallets. After a few days and nights (of not so patiently) awaiting their decision, my parents, with a careful steady tone, let me know they were going to let me make the switch to the new gym after all.

Of course, I was elated by the news and what it meant for me and my future as a gymnast! I walked into the new sprawling space and I was a kid in a candy store—endless balance beams, a foam pit to jump in, trampolines, and the bounciest floor built especially for back handsprings. No more folding mats, no more small-town community center, and a big *hello* to the place where I would become the type of gymnast I saw on television. (Hiiiiiiii, Shannon Miller!)

While I started living out my big back handspring dreams, my mom was steadily crunching numbers and figuring out a plan to make this all work financially. She'd already said yes, even though she didn't have all the answers. She'd leaped full force into the uncertainty, knowing her value, her worth, and her resourcefulness would follow her. And it did.

During one of my practices, sitting upstairs watching the action below between the railing posts, my mom lifted her eyes from the blue carpeted springy floor and noticed there was a kitchen. A really *outdated* kitchen. If I'd have been sitting next to her on those bleachers, I'd have witnessed the famous "Sue Spark" in her eyes, her mind's wheels turning quicker than a flash.

After practice, she came into the locker room (probably in an attempt to force me to bring home all my piled up stinky leotards that definitely needed a wash). She slowly wandered the space, taking in the bright red and yellow lockers with chipping paint, a bathroom in need of repair. I sensed she wasn't peering around the gym searching for lack. Instead, she was searching for *opportunity*. And she had found it.

A few weeks later she made an appointment and sat down with the owner of the gym, Mark, to offer up a proposal. The night before the meeting, she sat at the computer, her face illuminated in the glow of the screen, as she typed in Microsoft Word a detailed plan for how to help beautify the gym and, hopefully, save the family budget.

Now, before you start overqualifying my parents and underqualifying yourself (something a lot of us tend to be experts in when we're faced with the reality of making our dreams happen), my mom wasn't an interior designer. She was a nursing instructor. And my dad? He wasn't a contractor; he put in long hours at the local papermill.

But on the day of the meeting, my mom boldly sat down in Mark's office, explaining her observations and handing over her printed proposal. She calmly asked him if he had any interest in rejuvenating the neglected, dusty corners of his gym. As Mark sighed with relief, my mom quickly discovered this was something he had always intended to prioritize, but never had the time or money to focus on. They agreed on the terms, talked through specifics, and then he shook her hand, saying, just like they do in the movies, "You've got yourself a deal."

That night my mom was back at the computer finalizing a contract that allowed me to go to the gym tuition-free if my family agreed to make the much needed updates to the space. One week every year the gym would close down and my entire family, grandparents included, would scrub, sand, paint, tear down, and build up different pieces of the gym in order to earn my ability to keep chasing my dreams.

I'll be honest, sometimes I wished it were easier, that I wasn't so aware of what my dream was costing my family. I cringed whenever my coach announced we needed a new competition leotard, or when my grips for the bars ripped and I needed a new pair. There was always a hesitation partnered with guilt that probably didn't exist for the other girls. But I saw my family's sacrifice and I honored that. It wasn't lost on me that not everyone could easily cut a check each month. One teammate's mom became the receptionist at the gym to help pay her way through, and another teammate's mom coached the little kids to soften the cost. (The bottom line: moms can be such rock stars.)

Looking back, I am so thankful that I had a front-row seat to watch my mom rise to this challenge of believing there could be a win for all of us when it looked like there would be none. Not only did I get to pursue my dreams, but my teammates got to enjoy a better facility and my coach got to release some of the stress of managing the space. All of this was possible because my mom looked at the situation objectively. She didn't shy away from the challenge or take the easy path and pull me out of gymnastics due to lack of funds. She got creative and scrappy, and it worked—not only for me, but for the whole community.

That's what knowing your value *is*. That's what refusing to give up *does*. That's what declaring your worth and taking up your space and showing up for life with open hands can do. Because open hands open doors. Barriers, like neglected corners of the gym, exist everywhere. We're generally aware of them, but we're also quick to disqualify ourselves from being a part of the solution. But once you allow yourself to look at a potential problem as a potent possibility, and once you release the doubts and the what-ifs and the I-can'ts, you're changing the narrative entirely. You're not looking at your current circumstance as *what it is*; you're looking at your current circumstance as *what could be*. And that's when you transform a would-be loss for one into a will-be win for all.

What does that look like for you today? What situation are you in right this very moment that you might be able to look at objectively? Is it an insanely frenzied dinner hour where your baby's screaming while you try to throw together a meal? Is it a grocery bill that's too high? Does your son want private (read: *expensive*) music lessons in pursuit of his dream? Perhaps there's a win-win hidden in what you might be considering a lose-lose. Look at the gifts you've been given. Look at the *people* you've been given. Now, look for the overlap in need. Who could use something from you? Where can you offer your unique skills? What help can you accept in return? What resources can be exchanged to create a better scenario for everyone?

Can you invite the latchkey kid over to play patty-cake with your baby while you cook a hot meal for her family and yours? Can you barter work hours at the CSA in exchange for fresh produce? Can you wash your friend's dishes while she teaches your son how to play the piano? Whatever the barrier, whatever the road block—you could be holding the green light to what happens next in your life in your own hands.

When we ask ourselves *What value do I have to offer in this situation?*, our skills and passions, however large or small, emerge from the woodwork. Whether your gift reaches around the world seven times for twenty generations, saves a single life, or even helps a group of people have a happier day, it's an idea I want to see and help become reality. I'm counting on it. (We all are.)

## HOW ARE YOU, REALLY?

What are your greatest strengths? What value do you already possess that can help make your vision real? Are you making excuses as to why your talents wouldn't be welcome or useful? Why? Where can you get creative and resourceful to move forward?

Knowing our need, recognizing our value, and sharing it with the world is how a woman in need of a great idea for her Princeton thesis ends up creating Teach For America—and twenty years later—has trained more than 24,000 teachers in low-income schools, reaching three million students.[1] It's how an environmentalist of the Anishinaabe nation works tirelessly to file lawsuits that will recover lands withheld from Native American communities.[2] And it's how a factory worker filled positions while men were away at war, growing a force of working women by 50 percent in four years and proving that a woman could, in fact, excel at a "man's job."[3]

Recognizing your own value and stepping into someone's need—whether on your own behalf or the world's—can be scary. But once you know your worth, it's absolutely worth it.

You're probably reading these lines and are somewhere in the process of disqualifying yourself from being able to make a dent or a difference. It's likely that you are imagining someone else as the solution, casting yourself as a stand-in character, an extra and not the lead. If you're still thinking, *No way; not me! I don't have anything to offer!* I'm going to, respectfully, call your bluff.

> Don't believe me? Find the one-of-a-kind value you can offer this world in forty-five seconds or less. Take the Secret Sauce quiz at
>
> WWW.JENNAKUTCHER.COM/MORE

Think of someone you love. I bet if I asked you to tell me something you value about them, you could rattle off a handful of gifts, skills, traits, or areas of specialized knowledge without batting an eyelash.

Maybe it's your best friend, who has a knack for throwing parties, or your mother-in-law, who's an out-of-this-world baker. Perhaps it's your neighbor, who's great with flower arranging, or your sister, who always knows how to make you laugh. It could be that person you went to school with who knew how to dress every body shape or the clerical assistant in the office who was a pro at budgeting.

The people you love bring so many amazing gifts into your world, right? *Well, so do you.* Every person you know—yes, yourself included!—has specific traits and sparkling insights to share. So, if you can lift up those around you, applauding and celebrating what they can do, give yourself the same gift, for goodness' sake!

To this day, my mom has never stopped finding ways to add value to and for the people in her life. She keeps her ears open looking for opportunities to contribute and offer distinct worth in unique ways. Her latest feat? Figuring out a way to support me and Drew through my baby's birth. With pandemic restrictions on hospital visitations and a limited number of people who can be present at the birth, my mother weighed her options: accept the new rules and cut her losses, or figure out a way around them (fairly). So she got creative, snagged an opportunity, did the work, and completed her official doula certification. With over thirty years in the nursing profession, that piece of paper is just a reminder of all the work and knowledge she's held for decades, but her willingness to take the necessary steps to be present for me makes me teary-eyed. (Well, that coupled with pregnancy hormones!) Looks like Doula Sue will be holding my hand the whole way through another baby's birth—just like she has held my hand my whole life long. What a lucky baby, to be caught in those loving, strong, resourceful arms.

So what would it look like if we *all* channeled our inner Mama Sue? I'm not talking about being obsessed with fixing every problem (not everyone wants you to be their hero). And I'm not talking about seeing issues that aren't there, creating dissatisfaction in your life where there might not need to be. Being a Mama Sue isn't about shoving yourself into places you don't necessarily fit or feeling like you're the *only one* for *everyone*. I'm talking about gazing out into the world with a self-awareness and attentiveness to what's going on beyond our little corner of it. My mom has been an incredible example to me of what it looks like to pay attention for *your* cue. Knowing you hold the screwdriver means that when someone holds up the screw, you know it's your turn.

Are you good at seeing the outlier? Maybe you'd be that warm light of friendship to the person at the party struggling to join in on the good times. Are you a wiz at taking a complicated idea and breaking it down into something easily understood? Maybe you'd be *the* ultimate instructor for teaching a computer class for senior citizens. Are you that friend with spatial awareness and a knack for organizing? Maybe you could plan an organizing day with a friend where you help them tackle that spare bedroom or pantry situation they've been dreading.

Can you see how small or big this can become? Your *cue* comes in all shapes, platforms, and volumes. But when we understand what our own specific gifts are, it gets easier to see those *you*-sized gaps that only you were created to fill. You start to see opportunities everywhere.

My mind often goes back to that first contract my mom created with my gymnastics academy, and how she listed her offer right there, on paper, in black and white. Looking back, that's some kind of wasabi-level boldness. See? Work mixed with woo.

My parents have taught me a million valuable lessons through the years, but this one always hits me deep when I think about the sacrifice, courage, and attitudes that created possibility in a situation that otherwise would've been labeled as impossible. Their loving example created a double blessing for me. Not only was I supported to live out my gymnastics dreams, but I was taught the importance of finding the places where I can make a difference and the confidence to voice the difference I'm willing to make. They showed me how to take a potential no and find a way to create a yes. They showed me how to unleash the permission for me to pursue whatever would come after it. And, they showed me how to paint steel lockers and make them shine.

When the full weight of this story comes rushing back to me, I can't help but get teary-eyed. My parents, who I still know to be so very wise with their resources, decided to prioritize the possibilities of my passion over the cost of it. They chose the unconventional, uncomfortable path on my behalf. And my favorite part is that they still clung to their own character and took a nontraditional path in doing so, not hesitating for a second about other people judging them.

In short? *My mother knew her value.*

Looking back, I'm grateful my mom didn't hide the fact that we had to be resourceful in times when we lacked resources. Every contract she drafted proved to herself and my family we truly had something to offer, we just had to extend the invitation.

I don't know what stands in the way of your invitation. Perhaps you got the news your dream job fell through, the grant was rejected, or the scholarship funds were diminished. Maybe the radiator went out in your car. Maybe your beloved pet got sick. Maybe your application for a mortgage got rejected. But wherever a problem pokes its head, so does the opportunity to be a part of the solution. When you believe in your own value, the solutions are easier to find.

Imagine, today, seeing yourself as someone with value that exists whether or not others can see it or comment on it or judge it. Someone with power and a vital role to play. Someone who deserves support, recognition for their work, and an equal chance to take up space in the sphere they belong in.

When you understand that point alone, you start to see yourself differently. You start to ask yourself questions like: Where can I share myself? How can I spread my worth to someone else? What person, place, or community needs me right now?

You can become the go-to person for something you *want* to be recognized and utilized for. You wake up to the investments and exchanges that are happening in your everyday life. You start to see the places where you're excited to jump in and contribute. You begin to exercise your gifts that bring value to yourself and others, and the more you see people showing up for what you bring to the party, the deeper your confidence grows.

This is where you unleash yourself, too. Right now, you may feel tethered to a destiny you'd trade for literally any other. You may feel stuck to a career or relationship or city that feels like wearing shoes two sizes too small. You may feel like the world will never learn to value the skills you have. You might believe that bridging the gap between the life you can have, giving and sharing of yourself, and where you are right now would feel like crossing the Grand Canyon on a tightrope. *While juggling.*

I know how easy it can feel for a dream to seem too far to reach. And I know how hard it can feel to pull off a Tsukahara on the vault.

But when a woman knows her value? Turns out she can land both.

# 17

# it's complicated:

## HOW TO INVEST IN YOURSELF, AND WHY IT MATTERS

**The more you honor your spirit and soul, the more that energy grows around you.**

**—LION BABE**

"I just can't decide if I should hire it out," my friend Rachel told me in an audio message. She sounded desperate, confused, and absolutely exhausted. "I know I can do it myself, but I have so much going on right now. Am I just being lazy?"

She was in the beginning stages of launching a second coffee shop in her hometown. Her first had been a runaway success, and she and her husband knew they'd want to expand to the northern side of the city eventually. They'd already purchased the building, but it was sitting empty. In the throes of running the first coffee shop day in and day out, that dream kept getting pushed to the back burner. Between juggling her three kids and a full staff, she and her husband couldn't find the energy to start the necessary renovations.

I pushed send on an audio text back to her: "Rachel, how much is your time worth? Like, what would you say is your hourly rate for doing everything you do in a day? Is it more or less than what it might cost to hire out the remodel?"

I watched those three dots forming her response. "Wow," she wrote. "I guess I never asked myself that question." I hadn't, either, for a very long time.

My relationship with money hasn't always been a positive one. If I had to choose a category using Facebook's terms, "It's complicated" would have definitely fit the bill when I got my first job. Money has broken up marriages, started wars, and torn people apart, so how could we *not* feel sensitive about it? Money *is* complicated. Not because of who you are, but because of the way this world works.

Our questions surrounding money have a way of piling up. What does it actually mean to "spend wisely"? Where's the line between saving and squandering? And if a lottery winner can, and statistically will, go bankrupt, is there any hope for the rest of us? So many of us weren't really taught about money management, *much less* what investing in ourselves could look like.

Now, without going deep into a "culture of money" talk (we can save that for another book), I'll tell you this: money will master you if you let it. Either by holding you hostage to every nickel and dime or tempting you to follow every whim you have no matter the cost or outcome. But once we strip away all of our big, scary feelings about it, money is just *one* of the ways we exchange what we have for what we need. Just like we exchange our time, energy, wisdom, and experience. Whether you pay for a remodel like my friend Rachel did, or you take an online course, or you hire a babysitter, or just get yourself a laptop that actually works, these exchanges are essentially saying yes to investing in *you and your life*.

There's a good chance that you have placed much of your energy into having money, saving money, stewarding money, or the pain and fear of losing money . . . and in those quests, you may have completely devalued your time. There's a reason we call it *spending* our time or *saving* time. And there's a reason we say things *drain* our energy. Your life's currency, your breathing and being alive, is your time. It is of immense, immeasurable value, and the daily, tangible weight of what that means is what you have to determine before you move forward with spending another hour of it carelessly. Yes, it's *that* important!

But I'd be remiss to assume that time carries the same weight for all of us. As if we all have the same access to time. As if we are all able to quantify our time equally. There are people with private jets and people with three-hour commutes. There are people tending to not only their schedules, but the schedules of their children and elderly parents. There are people who are working a full-time job to pay their way through school so they can get out with as little debt as possible. There are people with passion to do great things *and* ADHD.

The reality is that we're all doing the best we can with the time we have—from single parents to caretakers, those who juggle multiple jobs to make ends meet, and those whose starting line is drawn onto a very different landscape. While the idea of prioritizing time is important, it's also important we recognize that while we all share the same amount of hours in the day, our circumstances separate how we are able to fill those hours.

Because the truth is this: as complex as our relationships with money are, we don't give enough thought to the cost of our time. Time isn't just money, time is life! It's not *actually* all about the Benjamins. It's *also* about Big Ben. Our minutes, our routines, our alarms, our schedules. The way you spend today is a reflection of how you'll spend your life. I've watched so many people lie to themselves about when they'll start "truly living." And I've watched so many people hustle their way to success only to arrive and realize it was never really about the money after all. It was about having the ability to *choose* what mattered most to them: time or money.

As we move through our own stages of life, we will inevitably change what we value. At the beginning of my career, money was what I was after. I had to be willing to trade my time to earn back money both to pay off those pesky student loans and fund my dreams. That's why, long before I could afford to budget for learning opportunities like conferences or courses, I consumed every ounce of the "free" stuff I could find: the YouTube videos, the podcasts, the blogs, the free webinars. Before I could ever afford to hire a business coach, I took on mentors (granted they were well-established folk, like Amy Porterfield, who at the time didn't know I existed). I leaned in, I took notes, and I watched. Any chance I had to learn from someone doing anything that interested me was a chance I would take, and since these resources were free, all it was costing me to learn was my time.

But it took *a lot of time*. Sifting through so many voices, determining which content was valuable for me, and applying sound advice to the context of my unique business added hours and hours onto my to-do list each week. Once my season of burnout hit, the scales tipped. I was finally ready to place *time* as the priority in my decisions. In my quest to experience freedom and rest, I was willing to trade that hard-earned money to get back my time.

As my business and bank accounts grew, so did my opportunities to invest in my own education as an entrepreneur. I've always known the power of being in proximity to other people who think like you, dream like you, and work like you, but living in a village of 1,200 people in the middle of Wisconsin didn't provide many opportunities to get in rooms with people who were on anything resembling a similar journey to mine.

I had heard the term "mastermind" thrown around by other business owners and really it sounded like an expensive, exclusive society of people who come together and brainstorm, learn, troubleshoot, and share in the hopes of elevating everyone. The whole "a rising tide raises all boats" type of experience. You're essentially paying a fee to not just learn from the leader of the group, but by joining you're also intentionally placing yourself in a room of other people who might be at a similar place in their life or career as you.

That's why, six years into my entrepreneurial journey, I made the pulse-quickening choice to invest in joining a mastermind. If proximity was power, then I was ready for it. I was ready to open up and talk about how everything was going, to share my problems and obstacles and to help others overcome theirs, too. I didn't even know who else would be in the room, but my gut told me investing in community, education, and support was the next right move for me.

Masterminds are like a concentrated brainstorm-business-class-therapy retreat with wine and, inevitably, a very braggy person or two. (It happens.) Maybe that's why they are often booked at places with very beautiful, soul-soothing sunsets. When we are wrestling with our problems, it is helpful to be reminded of the perspective that we're little specks on this dirt clod hurtling around a fireball, you know? California (and its sunsets) was calling and I was prepared to answer.

But here's the thing you might not know: masterminds aren't cheap. The websites for these events always boast for like fourteen pages before telling you it's going to cost you about the next few decades of your Costco membership. They honestly boast for a reason, though. I'd heard more than enough times how powerful and important these experiences were and I was tired of juggling my issues on my own. I made the decision; this was going to be the first large investment I put down in the name of learning and putting myself at the table with other entrepreneurs, and it would hopefully reveal a gateway to dreaming even bigger for myself.

They say it's not about what you know, but who you know. Time and time again, I've found that to be true. I can literally trace connection to connection from casual gatherings I've attended, even just a dinner with a few new faces. Connections that have changed the trajectory of my life. Like the time I met someone in passing in a hotel lobby, quickly exchanged numbers, and weeks later was invited to take part in a project that landed me on a stage in front of thousands of new faces. Or how one yes was responsible for my little family jumping on a free flight to Fiji to not just work but to experience a slice of the world we never dreamed we'd see.

The lesson here isn't necessarily that you should join a mastermind to see if it pays off. And believe it or not, the lesson isn't even about the power of education. (Though I do believe in both.) The lesson is that every dream will cost you something. It'll take time, money, energy, or all of the above to take an idea into reality. Every vision holds risk. And when you decide the time is right for you to make a move toward your truest answers, remember that *you* aren't the risk.

*You* are the investment. And *you* get to determine the level of time, money, energy, and skills you're willing to invest.

I've said it before: first steps are hard. When it comes to investing in yourself, that first step can feel all kinds of awkward. Uncomfortable. Maybe you think that doing something for yourself is . . . futile? Or maybe you think it's just too disruptive for everyone else in your life. But whether you've sidelined your dreams to stay at home and raise your babies or the way you were brought up caused you to label yourself and your ideas as worthless, it's time for you to sit in the investor's seat of your life and honor the ideas that have weighed heavily on your heart.

While you might not feel *Shark Tank* ready to bet on your own vision yet, the goal is to build up the belief that you can be a savvy investor, one who is ready to make a bet on yourself. It can be hard for us to see ourselves or our ideas as worthy of investing. While it's easy to look at anyone else and see why they're worth betting on, it's time to accept the same goes for you. Look at yourself: your ideas, your resourcefulness, your personality, your experiences, your particular outlook. Bet on yourself with whatever it is you've got.

There is no one-size-fits-all investment for you to use for the rest of your life. You'll have different priorities at different times in your life. There's no denying that you'll experience phases where you're willing (or even forced) to trade time for money just like I did. And then maybe at some point you'll find yourself willing to trade that hard-earned money to buy back your time through different means. We know the importance of simply starting and we can only work with what we have right now. So, make a plan based on your present reality. Trust yourself to know the answer and follow that answer into action.

HOW ARE YOU, REALLY?

What is your life's currency? Where do you have excess? Depletion? What do you want more of, and be honest—time, energy, or money?

Once you define your currency, protect it with everything you can. Otherwise, you'll eventually waste your precious investment on whatever pulls at your attention, insecurity, or comfort zone first. It'll take budgeting. It'll take boundaries. And it'll take a whole lot of honesty. Are you wasting your hard-earned money on Target candles and clearance sweaters? Can you cut date-night costs by dining in? Can you shop secondhand for a few months while you build up your savings?

While you're budgeting your bank account, don't forget to budget your clocks. Are the items on your to-do list necessary or are they time-wasters? Are they urgent or are they distractions? Do you see things regularly pop up on your calendar that you feel are no longer for you? Instead of adding to your to-do list, create a not-to-do list where you can get really clear about the ways you might be squandering one of your greatest assets.

Budget what you've got now to get what you want and need later. Human creativity knows no bounds. And eventually, you'll be able to leverage what you've built with your sweat, money, energy, and time into that next thing. Gymnasts turn their sweat on the mat into championship trophies. Baristas turn a lot of weeks of spilled, burned milk into the most gorgeously poured rosetta you've ever seen. Gardeners break their backs over dirt and seeds and water for months until they're eating a dinner from the literal fruits of their labor. And I will work for a year on a course to make sure it's the best damn thing possible, so that when I release it into the wild Internet, people can learn in my digital classroom while I step away to be with my family and take extra-long bike rides.

When actress America Ferrera began to invest in her dream life, she first spent *hours* of her time. "I used to have to ride, like, three buses to get to an audition. This was pre-Uber, not that I would've been able to afford Uber if it had been around. I had to ride the bus, I had to walk, I had to ride my bike, I had to beg my siblings for a ride."

But later, once she could, she invested her money to gain back those hours. "With my first paycheck, I went and bought a car. It was a 2000 Mitsubishi Mirage. . . . I think it cost me $12,000. [It was] a huge rite of passage."[1]

Where are you, right now? What investment will bring you closer to your dream life? Is it having your dinner delivered once a week so that you can be present for bath time with your kid that night? Paying someone to weed your flower beds even though you're more than capable but you're craving time to snuggle up and watch a movie with your person? Or, like my friend Rachel decided, writing a check to a local contractor so she could finally fling open the doors to her coffee shop dream just a few months later?

Choosing your currency isn't a single destination. It's not a test that you need to pass once. It's something to be revisited often. As you and your circumstances evolve, how you get to spend your life evolves, too. And your return on investment? Well, that evolves, too. In ways you'll never see coming.

Remember that mastermind I'd initially invested in to grow my business, contribute to a community, and bond over common entrepreneurial challenges? I'd thought the experience would become a major asset for my career, and it was. But the greatest reward wasn't a business breakthrough: it was a personal one.

Let me explain. When I experienced my second miscarriage, I came home from hearing the news and ran into my kitchen, digging through drawers until I found a piece of paper with a phone number that said: *I will help you with your fertility.*

Those words had been written down and given to me by a naturopath fertility doctor I met in that very first mastermind over a full year earlier. At the time, I didn't think I needed her help, but for some reason, I held on to that scrap of paper. So I dialed the number, got in contact with her, and she was the one who led me through all the bloodwork, the dietary changes, and lifestyle transitions required to conceive Coco. When I think about *that* sort of return on investment, I can't help but tear up.

Investing in ourselves will always reap benefits, even when they're not the ones we expect. I joined that mastermind thinking of my business, but, of course, it was a compounding investment—multiplying and expanding until it enriched every corner of my life, and beyond.

Investing in yourself today allows you to step confidently into tomorrow, chasing the things that will make your eyes sparkle even when you're old and gray. The things that will make even more room for living a life that isn't just awaiting a fresh batch of paid time off. A schedule that isn't depriving you of sleep, but one that lets you spend your energy well so that rest isn't something that has to be earned.

Imagine yourself saying, *I believe in you, I will back you, your vision is one that must come to life.* If you have the stamina and space, speak those words out loud to yourself. There's power in letting that air pass over your vocal cords so you can hear how good it feels to believe in yourself. You get to speak *and* be heard all at the same moment. Like how different it is before and after someone finally says the words "I love you."

Like how different it is when you change your status from "It's complicated" to "In a relationship."

# 18

## what's your enough point?:

### HOW TO SAY HECK NO

**It's not the load that breaks you down; it's the way you carry it.**

**—LENA HORNE**

One morning, my neighbor Simone and I were walking up a gravel hill, pushing strollers side by side when I said, "But maybe more isn't always better." As we talked about life and motherhood, her booming rental of the tiny house on their property, and her vision of building more properties to rent in order to expand their business, I asked her what she needed to hear: "How will this change things for you, *really*?"

As she turned her freckled face to the sun, I watched as she started chewing on a response. We kept walking as she quietly processed the question, actually giving herself a few moments to really think. The silence and open air made room for both of us to hear what was going on in our own heads.

As anyone would, I imagined what gears were turning for her. I wondered if she was seeing what I was seeing in her life, or maybe she was seeing something entirely different. From my perspective, I saw a woman who continually placed the finish line of success farther and farther away, always out of reach only to keep her striving and doing. Rare were the moments I saw her utterly relish in and enjoy her hard work and achievements.

I had watched her little family live in a construction zone, a long road of projects with hardly an end in sight. Spending every spare minute sanding, tiling, and grouting in order to turn their dreams into a reality. Weekends were project days, and weekdays were catching-up-with-everything-else days. I could see how much she and her husband, Andrew, were yearning for rest, for peace, for a house that felt like home and not just another project waiting to be done. I knew because when you love your friends, you pick up on things like that . . . and I also understood because I've kept my own finish line out of reach, too.

Ever been there? Are you there right now? The finish line set so far out of sight but realizing you're the one that keeps pushing it? Wondering how your pursuit of a dream has turned into a little bit of a never-ending hellish nightmare? The truth is, you're in very good company.

Once, while speaking at a conference, I finished my morning session and scoped out an empty seat in the auditorium so I could catch the rest of the speakers that day. I found a chair, plopped down, and whipped out my trusty notebook. The day was jam-packed with speakers but I was thoroughly enjoying myself.

Somewhere around late afternoon, I guzzled down a lemonade during a break and looked through my notes. Scanning the pages, I noticed a similar thread winding through each of the speakers' stories. Mine included. Every single one of us thus far, in our own way, had a tale of success that turned into burnout and then (eventually) led to a major breakthrough.

Maybe we were all achievers on the Enneagram, maybe it was because we all had that "entrepreneurial" way of living life, or because business owners have that knack for hustling ourselves all the way into the ground. Or perhaps it was because of our shared industry. Maybe there was some rare star alignment happening when we were writing our presentations. Or maybe, and this one felt the truest, it's a story arc we all know how to tell and relate to because transformation through trial is basically a guarantee if you happen to be a human.

I laughed as this common theme kept popping out at me from my pages. I thought to myself, *Is it some kind of* requirement *to burn out before we get the breakthrough? Is this what we're teaching?* And while I'd love to think we can learn from everyone else's mistakes to avoid the pain, sometimes we can't. We can read all the books, listen to all the podcasts, and go to all the conferences, and still make mistakes on our own journey. Lessons are really just words, and it's hard for them to sink in until we feel them for ourselves. Some people can hear about how the stove is hot, others have to touch it. Meaning, even if we're warned, we still might need to experience it to understand it.

Success is not all pushing forward, full steam ahead. Or, like for my friend Simone, success isn't a finish line you have to keep pushing forward, away from where you are, so that you're never allowed to cross over and enjoy. Sometimes it *is* falling apart, losing steam, and feeling like we need to step away from the work we're doing just to breathe, before we can course correct or experience the breakthrough that's on the other side.

So how do you get to the other side? How do you move forward when your life feels too big, too wieldy, too out of control? How do you pick up the pieces when things feel too scattered to sustain? And what happens if you can't?

I'll start with a cliché that somehow still does the trick for me: just because you *can* do something doesn't always mean you *should*. I know that sounds like a catchphrase your mother might've spouted at you in high school when you stayed out too late, but it's got that profound snap of clarity to it that I need to hear *often*.

Have you ever considered that idea, especially in your adulthood? The fact that you *can* do a million different things. It's one of the coolest parts about growing up. Our interests grow, too. We get smarter! (Hopefully.) We get better at stuff! (Again, hopefully.) We not only grow in our skills and abilities, but we also get to choose how we're going to use them. Or *not* use them.

I know how easy it is to let our desire to start a new project, to expand a dream, or even our very good intentions to just make some part of life better . . . snowball. New passions are swirly and exciting, like the early stages of falling in love when you want to be together 24-7 and leave your toothbrush at their place. We want more and more and more, until we don't. We want to feel needed, or productive, or indispensable, until we don't. We want it all and we want *to do* it all, because we can! Until we don't.

Or maybe, until we can't. Until we find ourselves in that place where we're double-booked because we're juggling too many calendars. Where the things we really want to try—a new recipe, that new barre class, a weekend trip to the lake—all get pushed to the margins because, well, *people are relying on us*. And the to-do list just keeps growing.

It's easy to see how we trick ourselves into it all. Maybe everything on your list—the HOA treasurer, the bake sale, the FB moderator for that one trunk show—stays there because you've been told you're the best person for the job. Maybe you show up because you think no one else will. Maybe you feel like you don't have a say in the matter (and maybe that's true).

But maybe you've taken on all of your responsibilities because—even though you love each of them for different reasons—you believe the lie that more is better. That busy is best. That joy and fun and rest can all keep scooching down on your priority list so you can make room for the *important* stuff.

That's it, right there: the fact that we label work as the important stuff and joy as something to just toss onto the calendar if there's room. *That's* the shortcut to burnout. If you're reading this and thinking, *That's me. I'm there right now. Burnout city!* I want you to know that it's okay, and that you're not alone. A *Forbes* study reported that over 52 percent of respondents experienced burnout of some kind in 2020.[1] That's over half of us in one year's time!

And while we shared a collective experience in 2020, there are many paths that lead each of us to being burned out, bone-tired, and overloaded, and sometimes we need to crash into it before we recognize we missed (or ignored) the warning signs along the way. If my conference notes had one other thing to say, it's this: our breakdown or burnout might be a sign that a breakthrough is coming.

I remember one particular weekend from years ago like it was yesterday. It was the day where I could no longer ignore the warning signs in my own life. I'd shot a wedding on Saturday, spent the night at my in-laws, edited all day Sunday, and finished the weekend by squeezing in a Sunday evening engagement shoot at an apple orchard. Drew was kind enough to join me as my unofficial chauffeur and camera bag holder.

Drew and I used to go to the same apple orchard ourselves just for fun, when we'd need a little Sunday post-church escape, complete with apple cider. We'd slow down and mosey around, splitting a caramel apple before heading home. But on this particular evening, as my finger clicked the shutter and I brought the energy, directing with enthusiasm, making magic behind the lens, I asked myself: *When was the last time I played in an orchard, instead of worked?*

When we got back into our Honda to make the drive home, I turned to Drew, laptop in my lap, and asked him, "Do you think they could tell?"

He looked at me, a little bewildered, and responded, "Do you think they could tell *what?*" I sat there as my eyes filled with tears, "Do you think they could tell how absolutely exhausted I am?" He chuckled, reassuring me that there was no way they had any idea; in fact, even he had no clue I was feeling that way. I was 100 percent on for that couple; the photos were proof.

But I closed the computer as tears dripped out of the corners of my eyes. With a weariness sinking deep into my bones, I grabbed Drew's hand as I felt the walls I'd built crumble around me. There it was, finally. In that moment, I became keenly aware of just how far I'd let myself go, how long I'd pushed my engine to run on empty, how many yeses I had said without pausing. My head against the window, my eyes leaking, my exhaustion hitting me all at once. If there was a scientific term to describe me in that moment, it would have been "a total hot mess of a burnout."

With his hand in mine, I paused long enough to realize that with each and every yes I was saying to work, I was inadvertently saying an equal and opposite no to the things that I cared about the most: my husband, my time, my family, and my memories. My *self*. There was no time in the schedule to bask in the joys of what I was achieving. No time to rest. No time for play. Life had become a blur as I kept up with my pace, charged up my batteries, and clicked the shutter on other people's lives every single weekend.

The thriving career I had built was centered on documenting moments ensuring other people would never forget their own memories and that made me proud, but what about making more of my own? That was a "more" I could get behind. That was the more I needed most.

When was I supposed to live and enjoy life's moments? When would I get to make and preserve my own memories? When would I finally sign the contract for my own life with express permission to wander an apple orchard, leaving my camera behind, to just, you know, breathe and eat a damn apple?

In case it's unclear, my burnout didn't happen overnight. (Does it ever?) It was slow and sweltering. Adding a deadline here and an event there until my commitments had become a full-on bonfire, raging out of control with little room to breathe. I didn't realize until it was too late, but I can see now exactly how it happened. Somewhere between shooting my first wedding and the night of my undoing, I had tricked myself into believing that boundaries were for weak people, whatever that meant. I thought I was the kind of person who could face the "hardship" of stress and exhaustion without having to do anything about it. I thought I could just power through a little bit longer, and then I'd take a break once things slowed down.

But things never slowed down, because *I* didn't slow down. Every time that small voice inside me asked me to slow down, I would tell myself it was just the temptation to give up, lose my momentum, or cash in a "break" too early, like it's something I had to suffer through to earn. Like it was the voice of pessimism. And me? Well, I was an optimist! An overcomer! An achiever! Stopping, turning back, slowing down, saying no? I wanted those options out of my playbook. I wanted to prove to myself (and everyone watching) that I didn't need breaks. I wasn't tired. I didn't need a rest; it wasn't time to sit on the bench.

On that Sunday night, I felt a shift inside of me. In my breaking down, I had finally broken open. A realization that all my on-paper goals weren't all they were cracked up to be, that more wasn't always better, and that even if it was, I didn't have any space left to give it. The cost of putting my achievements and goals in the driver's seat caught up to me.

I looked down at my metaphorical life map and saw just how off course I was. I was officially lost. While the visions I was chasing and the achievements that I thought were defining success for me left my bank account holding a few more digits, I hadn't yet learned the lesson that life wasn't just about money—it's about time, it's about energy, and it's about enjoying all three. I had leaned so hard on equations that I dismissed my emotions. I'd forgotten success is only success if it *feels* like success. And I was so burned out I wanted to burn it all down.

Thankfully, this is when I crawled into bed, the melatonin kicked in, and sleep won before I could chuck my camera out the window or ctrl+alt+delete everything on my laptop.

You might be here right now: exhausted, depleted, tempted to burn the whole thing down, too. But it's important to note what happened after I slept off the melatonin. I didn't quit, but I also didn't just go back to my regularly scheduled programming. I had to discern if *everything* needed to change or just *something* needed to change. While you might be tempted to start an entirely new life, maybe you should start with a good night's sleep, a nourishing meal, a hot bath, or even just twenty minutes of quiet to listen to your response when you ask yourself *How are you, really?*

The next day, I woke up to a sore back, a mushy brain, and a stronger sense of grace for myself than I'd had the night before. Scooting up to the kitchen table, I grabbed a notepad and started doing math. I ran the numbers, I looked at the bank accounts, I imagined different scenarios, and I created a spreadsheet (yes, with a color-coded *chart*) so that the minute Drew got home from his nine-to-five, I had a plan to reveal.

"Hey babe, we need to talk," I said as he walked in the door. We sat down at our table together (an Etsy find that really reveals the unashamed obsession I had with "farmhouse" before Joanna Gaines made it cool) and I walked him through my plan. I had drafted up a response to my burnout; it was a direct answer to the question "Is more always better?" And the spreadsheet spelled it out clearly, with a loud, resounding *Nope!*

"Screw money. Trust me, we were way happier when I made half of this income! There's no way I can survive another wedding season like this one, so I'm prepared to live on less if that means I get more life. I hope you're with me on that," I said to him. It's likely that I was probably waving my hands around during that mini-speech and might've even ended with a hand slammed down on the table. (Good thing she was sturdy.)

Drew never once interrupted me. He didn't deny my statement. Didn't fight on the bank account's behalf. I watched something resembling relief slowly come over him as I was speaking because he was also seeing the breakthrough. The shell on a life I was pretending to enjoy was finally cracking, and he was smart enough to peek a few chapters ahead in our life's book to know that this whole "undoing" happening to me could be one of the best things ever.

It was clear that I'd need to take a break from all those "Hell, yes!" text replies and email responses if I was going to pull this whole *less is more* thing off. After our dinner table talk, I munched on a bowl of almonds and wrote out a list of boundaries on what I would agree to for the next year (knowing that this meant some hard noes on others) and communicated them clearly to him and to myself. I wouldn't work on Sundays. I wouldn't shoot back-to-back weekend weddings. I wouldn't give discounts. And I would keep at least one weekend each month entirely cleared for family time.

Even writing those boundaries down now, it sounds as if they would have ruined me. That they'd sink any chances of success in my career. I mean, a whole weekend every month? That's a quarter of my potential earnings! No one gets married on a Tuesday! But those boundaries didn't close off my ability to be successful. They *saved* me. Those boundaries helped me claim time as my currency. Those boundaries gave me my life back.

If you ask me what's been the most transformative tool in my growth, I'd tell you without hesitation: boundaries. Boundaries gave me the time to make memories out from behind the camera— memories for my own self, and my own enjoyment, and my own life. Boundaries helped me come home to who I was beyond work. Boundaries allowed me to pivot the way I ran my business and scale to heights I didn't even know were possible. I'm honestly surprised that I don't yet have a tattoo that says *boundaries*, because they're the hero of my life, my well-being, my sanity . . . the real MVP of my story!

HOW ARE YOU, REALLY?

In which area of your life do you feel a burnout
approaching? What boundaries can you
experiment with? Where do you need to say no?
What's your enough point?

Take the time to consider what lines you need to redraw in your
life. Maybe it's sharing what you will and will not commit to in a relationship. Or having a meeting with your boss to discuss your workload,
overtime, or expectations. It can be as simple as an autoresponder in
your inbox. It can be as easy as deleting an app that sucks your time
away without you noticing.

You may not be able to shift everything all at once but give yourself the chance to get the lay of the land and start *somewhere*. And as you
redraw each line, remember this: the task of transformation, of shifting our boundaries, is no small feat. It requires patience for yourself—
sometimes the hardest person to have patience for.

The truth is, boundaries aren't solely for keeping people, or whatever powers that be, *out* . . . they're a tool that can keep you *in* your life.
Boundaries protect yourself from staying in constant motion because
that's when we stay so busy and distracted we stop listening to our
souls, checking in with our bodies, or hearing our intuition.

During my own experience with burnout, I worried that if I listened to the inner voice telling me to slow down, it would cause me to
get too comfortable, complacent even. I believed the lie that if I was to

allow myself to truly feel content it had to mean I was being complacent, that I had lost my drive. At first, when I allowed myself to slow down, it felt like the achiever in me was broken. Slowing down didn't feel natural. Slowing down felt counterintuitive. Slowing down felt like accepting defeat.

It's those very thoughts (or, rather, *lies*) that keep us believing our worth is found in our output, that we have to say yes to everything. When I really pull these beliefs apart, I recognize that somewhere along the way, I was told that happiness was entirely up to what I could *achieve*, and therein I would find some wellspring of importance, success, and purpose. But that notion led me to a boundaryless life, a life where I felt like my pursuit for *more* was endless, a life where the finish line was always out of reach. And if I couldn't ever *have* enough, then I certainly wouldn't ever *be* enough.

So, what's the difference between then and now? I still work hard, I still push myself out of my comfort zone, and I do things like set yearly goals for my life. But the difference is that my goals work together as a galaxy, lighting up other areas of my life. Like stars in my own constellation, each one is there to point toward what I am about and what I value, some a little brighter than others, but all important. I am far from complacent. I still get to do all of that achieving I love so much. But I also get to be content with what my life feels like at the end of the day.

Yes, sometimes I still become goal hungry and creatively passionate about new ideas! Sometimes I bite off more than I can chew. Sometimes I'll dive face-first into a project that I give a lot of my time to, but I have learned to tune into and listen for when my inner voice is telling me to slow down, to take a break (or a nap), to linger here a little longer (and sometimes it's actually Drew's voice asking me to step away from work and go on a walk with the fam).

When I remember that burnout, I remember how I felt exactly none of the satisfaction that was initially promised to me by the world. I remember feeling bone-tired. I remember feeling exhausted, like a shell of myself. I remember wondering, *Is this it? Is this really what I've worked so hard for?*

Only a short venture into my own handcrafted career, into my "freedom," I found I had created even more arbitrary goals to pursue in hopes that I would never disappoint anyone, and that I would hit every single one of those shiny metrics our culture sets. Because that's what success looks like, right? That's what success sounds like, right? *Busy! Productive! Booked solid! Crazy rich! Sorry, no time, gotta run, catch ya later?*

But is that *really* what I wanted? Once I created the space to check in with myself, it all became clear: in my quest to *look* successful, I'd forgotten to ask what it might mean to *feel* successful.

That's why redefining success helped me establish the boundaries I needed. Shifting the question from *Is this considered successful?* to *Do I consider this successful?* changed the whole game. We're visionaries, right? We're people who pin pictures to digital bulletin boards, so we know how we want our lives to look.

No wonder it's easy to get lost in how our success appears to the outside world. It's like every version of success that mainstream society hails as worthy is all about making sure that success is something that is seen. Heard. Velvety and expensive. Shining and able to be hung on a wall, worn around a wrist, or driven really fast. No wonder we feel empty when we reach our milestones (the ones we pinned to that vision board).

It's easy to photoshop the dream until it's unrecognizable. That's why there are many millionaires who are miserable. That's why they'll spend an arm and a leg to go on a retreat to the Amazon for two weeks to try and reconnect with their soul. It's why there's a mass exodus in the workforce (a crisis, as it's been called), because people are calling BS on being overworked, underpaid, and drained of everything that makes life worth living, in the name of success. It's why we're all recalibrating our concept of happiness and where it can actually be found. Because we know, throughout the stages of all our hard work, we want our milestones to *feel* as wonderful as they're supposed to.

Our goals on paper are valid and beautiful, but as we set them we need to also lean on the emotion of life. The question isn't what should success *look* like to the world, but how should it *feel* in my world? Remember? Feelings are meant to be felt.

So how do you know what success will feel like for you? Here's a starting point: Instead of chasing giant goals on paper, shift your focus to finding an "enough" point. Remember: *more* isn't attainable! Ever! There is no end to more! It's not feasible to think that every single day we're supposed to wake up and *be more* and *do more*. It's not sustainable and it only propels us forward on our path of burnout. Instead, when we operate out of a place of *enough,* we find where to stop, we establish where we can confidently draw the line, we protect our best yeses, and we know when to call it a job well done.

For help finding your "enough" point,
head over to
WWW.JENNAKUTCHER.COM/MORE

Two years ago, I was on the deck of my friend's home in Puerto Rico overlooking the ocean. I remember standing on the rooftop, champagne in hand, when one of the guests shyly approached me with a camera and said, "Hey, didn't you used to be a photographer, too?"

I laughed and told her I did, and, as one does when meeting a new friend with a shared experience, we talked nerdy gear talk for a bit. Then in a hushed voice she asked me, "So, how did you get out of it?" I smiled and paused, trying to figure out if she meant "how" or "why." I knew my response probably wasn't going to be what she wanted to hear either way. I told her that my decision to maneuver away from the photography game meant I needed to define my "enough" point and draw that line in the sand.

If she really wanted a change, she had to commit to firm boundaries, to saying no more, to charging rates aligned with her goal, to not saying yes to every opportunity, and to getting really honest about what she truly needed to bring in financially in order to free up her time. I challenged her to focus on not making more money but freeing up more of her time, and the only way to do that was to focus on boundaries around booking and just book up to her enough point so that she could claim back her time.

I think she was disappointed I hadn't hacked the system or invented a new method to get out of shooting on rooftops while everyone else was drinking champagne and enjoying the view without it being obscured by a lens. But I told her what I told her, and I'd tell you the same.

Scaling back may seem like very odd and backward advice for me to give you, especially in a book where I'm telling you to wholeheartedly and unapologetically chase after the life of your dreams! But this is where we get specific. And honest. *You don't have to change the game.* I certainly didn't! You don't have to revolutionize or start a movement. You just have to choose what rules you're playing by and what rules you aren't.

Once I finally understood where my yes belonged and where boundaries were needed, I became obsessed with operating out my enough-ness, which, in turn, freed up my greatness. Those boundaries didn't hold me back like I was afraid they would. They didn't contract anything. They expanded *everything*. As my schedule widened, my life opened up to something far beyond "work."

I had the freedom to rest. The freedom to have fun, to experiment, to *enjoy my life again*. The freedom to be. I claimed back margin and blank space, and I claimed back enough time to be filled with whatever the hell I wanted to fill it with. And I finally kicked back and watched a few Netflix marathons (and found out why you all love them so much!).

So, what does it look like to find your hell yeses and your hard noes? I wish I could tell you that your burnout and breakdown are finally over, and your breakthrough has arrived. I wish I could tell you that those equations I used to do the math and the color-coded charts at my kitchen table would solve it all for you, that you could just plug in your issues, crunch the numbers, and *bam*! There's your answer.

But I don't know your answer. I only know the question: *What is your enough point?* Where will you allow yourself to feel contentment without worrying that you've become complacent? How will you establish what you *truly need* so that you can start to go after what it is you *really want*? How will you define success? How do you embrace your enough? How are you, *really*?

My heart aches over the many moments I've tried to blow past my own enough point, time and time again. Sometimes my cheeks flush when I remember days of scrambling to keep it altogether when I was on the verge of throwing it all away. The crying-in-the-bathroom moments. The nights I stayed up late comparing myself to people on the Internet instead of sleeping. The months on end of putting the pedal to the metal without ever stopping. It aches returning to those memories of being perennially exhausted, overworked, and undervalued (by myself!).

As I write this very sentence, it's not my heart that aches anymore. It's my back. Not from hauling camera gear through an apple orchard or lugging my laptop from destination to destination. My back hurts because today I went on a hike with my little family for a few hours through the woods (and carrying a toddler is surprisingly heavy). Two very different aches, both born as proof that boundaries can make a life—or break one.

Some of my boundaries are nearly a decade old now, gathering a little of that hard-earned dust, which I love to see. But some are brand spanking new. I still have to make adjustments often, because I'm still growing. (Because I'm still alive.) And guess what? It still hurts. I don't like telling people no every single time I do it. I don't like choosing one good thing over another. I don't like disappointing someone I love because they might not understand, but it sure as hell is worth it to protect my best yeses.

Remember my neighbor from the year's early-morning stroller walk? Well, a few months later, she did something pretty miraculous by human standards: *she changed her mind*. She and her husband decided to pull back from their full-speed-ahead momentum. They paused their project, they said no to more, and they postponed their idea for expansion, because they truly knew they'd hit their own enough point. Their income was stable, enough to make plans to move somewhere else warmer and wilder: the first step in the life they've long desired but believed was still far off in the distance. As I type these words, they've quit their jobs, rented out their house, and packed their suitcases to live in Brazil for six months so they can recalibrate and have time to figure out what's next.

As it turns out, the dream was close *enough* all this time.

# 19

## soul savasana:

### HOW TO BE

**The most valuable thing we can do for the psyche, occasionally, is to let it rest, wander, live in the changing light of room, not try to be or do anything whatever.**

**—MAY SARTON**

When was the last time you went an entire day without logging into your email, checking Instagram, or posting a new status on Facebook? If it was just yesterday, congratulations! If I had confetti, I would delicately toss it over you and golf clap. But if you're thinking, *Whoa, I can't even tell you*, then lean in a little closer, because we probably both need a hug.

I thought I would end this book with something like a proverbial nightcap. If page one is the crack of dawn, well, then we've now arrived at dusk. Time to whip off your bra (if you wear one), boil up some water for your least stale sachet of Sleepytime tea, and make sure your waistband isn't constricting your body from being the shape it truly wants to be.

Honestly, I need this peaceful little tuck-in as much as you do. Working has always been my compulsion. My instinct. My . . . default. I've wondered on many occasions if it's biologically built within me, like a little chunk of code in my DNA. On days where I don't *have* to work, I'm a genius at creating lists upon lists of New Urgent Things that 1000% Need to Get Done Right This Minute. My knack for inventing reasons to skip a nap, a lunch break, or an entire Sunday is uncanny. (Drew isn't a big fan of this little trick of mine.)

It's why I used to hate savasana at the end of a yoga class. It killed me to lie flat on the floor, sweaty from a yoga sesh, awake for an eternity that was really just five minutes. My mind would spin, and I tried to count the minutes away in my head or think of a catchy tune I could sing to myself. (Ahem, if you're ever in need, might I suggest "Doo Wop (That Thing)" by Ms. Lauryn Hill? Exactly 5:20.) My muscles would twitch. My to-do list would call out to me, humming *You need to go grocery shopping and the bathroom is a mess! And remember those eleven questions you have for Brooklyn! Don't forget the dryer sheeeetsssss!*

Second by second, I'd anxiously wait for the moment when we would finally sit up, bow our heads in respect, and get on with our day. If it wasn't considered disrespectful, I would have totally been the person who'd snatch up my mat and run out the door while everyone is just getting into position, checking "work out" off my daily list, and moving on to the next thing with vigor.

It actually took me a few years to really fall in love with yoga and understand it. Up until that point, I'd never understood the phrase "practicing yoga." I ignored that first word, an important one, that tells you you're never meant to master it; you're only meant to show up, to try, to practice. But things finally shifted when I stopped approaching yoga as something to succeed at, to be good at, or to conquer. Once I was able to focus solely on myself, my body, and my breath, instead of everyone else and their abilities, I started to come alive with the movements, even savasana. *Especially* savasana.

Learning this was a lesson for me, the productivity queen, to commit to spending an hour breathing into spaces that need it. Getting to bend in a quiet room meant I could listen to my body and my mind without interruption. Slow, intentional movements, bringing my attention back to every flex, every breath, every heartbeat.

Still, when it came time to reap the benefits of all of the work I'd just done? For the longest time, I couldn't. I just couldn't be still with myself. Being still wasn't the thing that made me uncomfortable. It was what came with the being still. I couldn't believe I had actually earned the right to lie there, resting. I worked and worked, trying to achieve my way through every new pose. Stretching was my way of *earning* the right to rest, and then when the time came to rest, I still fought it.

It's a pattern I have in my life, in yoga, and in my career. I intentionally withhold joy from myself because I have to be sure that I've truly earned it, that I worked hard enough to earn the right to rest. But the voice of that withholding didn't always sound mean or aggressive. It sounded like a coach, which is a voice I'm quite familiar with, and as an athlete, quite adept at responding to. I'd feel the voice telling me that the world doesn't need another quitter. That I was better than that. It sounded like someone in the heat of battle, saying, "Give this your ALL! It's NOW or NEVER! Chaaaarge!" And somewhere along the way, I let that voice shape a belief in me that the weight of the world was resting on my shoulders. And it was up to me to keep carrying it.

This idea that everything in my life had to be earned latched itself into my subconscious and stayed there for many years, in the shadows, cloaked in the smiles of a seemingly totally fine "overachiever." Until one day, I decided to use my own achievement tunnel vision to hack the system. What if rest *was* the goal? What if I put rest squarely on my to-do list, like *all caps style*? What if I penciled it right in there with all the deadlines and reminders and appointments? Better yet—what if I wrote it in ink, like I did for the rest of my goals?

Since I like to go big or go home, once I decided to "do" rest, I went big. The first time I wrote down the goal that I wanted to take a month off work, it felt inconceivable. I'm not even sure where that exact goal or number of days came from, but as I was going through a "dreaming about the future" meditation-y exercise, it came tumbling right out of me and onto the page of my journal. In response to seeing that on my list, I decided to figure out if or how that would even be possible.

At the time, Drew and I were childless and in the middle of the uncertainty of trying to get pregnant, so I let my brain run wild with this newly formed dream to see where else it would go. I next wrote, "I want to live somewhere else one month out of the year so my children can see the world and experience different cultures." I envisioned having a baby or two, sitting at some outdoor café in France while my kid gobbled down a croissant and started calling me "Maman." Just writing that idea down sparked something in me, enough to share that idea with Drew.

I remember saying to him, "Wouldn't it be so cool someday if we were able to take our kids places and not just visit but sort of live in a new place for a month? Imagine doing life in different places and growing up learning about different cultures, languages, and land-marks!" While he undoubtedly thought the idea was neat, the conversation was left in the ether for "someday," the place where many *cool* notions go to die.

A few days later, I was still thinking about that idea, but I had to clarify a really important question: Why did I tell myself I'd do that once we had kids? Were children a prerequisite for me to embrace a vision? What if Drew and I just did it for *us?* That night I pulled open my laptop and started looking at Airbnbs on Maui and following the directions of the exercise that got me there, I priced it all out: flights, a car, a studio apartment . . . you name it, I budgeted it.

When we realized it wasn't truly out of reach, we committed. We gave ourselves ten months to make this dream feasible and, spreadsheet in hand, we were ready to do the work of saving up, scheming new visions for Drew's work, and preparing my business for my first extended leave. I worked to prepare all the content for my podcasts and blogs in advance, scheduling all the things to run while I rested. We carved out a few weeknights every month for planning and with mouths hanging open in shock, soon enough we had done it. We were going to Maui, a place we loved and couldn't wait to explore together, for an entire month. It would be my first Soul Savasana.

Months later, after a few long flights, we settled into the rented condo, cleared out the single dead cockroach we found, and set about making it our home for the next thirty days. This was it! My season of rest! I was so ready.

You can guess what happened next. It was a mere forty-five minutes into my "sabbatical" before I felt an itch to pop open my laptop to "just check in" and make sure everything was okay. I caught myself just in time, before I got sucked into work, pulling Drew out of the condo with a Corona and lime as we ran across the street so we could watch the sunset.

The truth is, we all stink at resting. I once read a study featured in the *Washington Post* that found over 55 percent of Americans don't use all their paid vacation time each year.[1] Literally time we're being paid to rest! Time we've been given. Time we've worked for. Time built into our lives to recalibrate. And over half of us won't step out of our routines and comfort zones of work or productivity to relax and enjoy something that we have, in fact, *earned*.

I'd love to pause here for a gentle reminder: you need not *earn* your right to rest in order to deserve it and need it. Rest needs to be a part of your life beyond the rare gift you grant yourself only when you've had a "good week." The human body requires it and rest must happen regardless of how much you did (or didn't do) for the day. Your worth isn't measured by what you've produced. You aren't a machine; you are a human being. Rest is the fuel for living.

Did you know that sleep is when our brains make long-term memories? This is when our minds have a moment to churn all the day's experiences into thick, delicious life butter. Sleep is when our minds get the chance to make the vision of our lives even more vivid. And rest? Well, it adds another wash of paint on the canvas. Our experiences are solidified. Our hopes and dreams have a chance to be repaired after what might've been a day of taking a few punches.

So, rest isn't just a required ingredient you need in order to do *more work*. Rest isn't just a break. It is where you enjoy the person you've been busy becoming. Rest is where you catch up with yourself. Rest is where you become more *you*.

There's an age-old tale where a Buddhist monk visits New York. His Western host helps him navigate the city, and he tells the monk they could save ten minutes by making a complex subway transfer at Grand Central Station. So, they do it. And when they emerge in Central Park, the monk sits down on a bench.

"What are you doing?" the host asks.

And the monk replied, "I thought we should enjoy the ten minutes we saved."

And here we are, running around like chickens loose in Grand Central Station, adopting every latest trick to earn time and save time, and what do we do with it once we've got it? *We use it to run around some more.*

Why? Because rest makes us anxious. Stillness scares us. The mind starts to spin and think about everything we're not doing. Worrying that we're dropping the ball. Or that the longer we're away from the work we do, the more replaceable we get. The less valuable we are.

Chances are, you've been here before. Telling yourself you'll rest only to fill up that preserved time with *more*. Like when you finally put the baby down for a nap and waste that precious time for yourself mindlessly scrolling on autopilot. Or when you scarf down your lunch at your desk, barely tasting it, so you can take those extra minutes to work ahead on your next task. Or when you finally get that weekend off or take that well-deserved PTO and you fill it with . . . something productive. Like cleaning the garage. Or "catching up" on projects. Or getting a "jump start" on the week ahead.

Are you there today? When it comes to rest, how are you doing? Like, *really*? What do you do when so much of your identity is intrinsically tied to what you accomplish? How do you stop rushing through life, trying out every productivity hack so you can take the mere minutes you saved to become *even more productive*?

For most of us, time to rest *is* actually available. We just refuse to capitalize on it because we don't know how to manage what might happen in our brains when we actually do slow down! Whether it feels like wasting time or losing our position in life, whether we're simply scared to ask ourselves *How are you, really?* and have to face the answer, we don't know how to fill our time with things we don't consider productive.

The thing no one tells you is that it takes practice to learn how to truly rest. Even when I carved out my own Soul Savasana, island time didn't take over the moment we landed. It took me awhile to settle in and get used to days without a schedule. To let my text message inbox fill up while I battled Drew in a game of Scrabble or asked for another round of chicken skewers. To let the sunshine tell me to enjoy the day without needing to know how many minutes I'd been soaking up its heat. To let a conversation flow for hours, not worrying about the next thing I've got booked. With the passing days, the urge to post, check, or create started to soften and I found myself devouring books just for fun by the pool. Every time my brain told me I should be doing something, I replaced that thought with *I* am *doing something*. I am resting.

By the time the first week ended, I found my groove as Resting Jenna, an identity I hadn't known or explored for years. Maybe ever. Being still felt like I was meeting myself again, getting to know the parts of me I'd tucked behind my work blinders; it was a chance to reacquaint myself with who I was beyond what I was creating.

After a blissful month on the island making memories, we found our seats on the flight back home. I stared out the window as we left the island, seeing the view fade in the distance and shifting my focus to see my own reflection staring back at me. I *looked* rested, whole, content. I saw a few new freckles and smile lines on my skin. I willed myself to remember this version of me: Resting Jenna, a person who can be still, a woman not afraid to feel things, a sum far bigger than the parts of the work I create.

That was the first time I allowed rest into my life in a big, meaningful way. I gave myself the time to practice it (as silly as that sounds) and it's now not only something I'm more comfortable with, but something I have learned to crave. Just like your computer requests a reboot moments before it crashes, I can keenly feel my body, soul, and spirit calling me to turn inward and slow down. It calls me to not try and run away from the feeling of exhaustion, but to be still. I've learned that choosing stillness is an action that is intentional. It's not laziness, it's not complacency. It's putting out the welcome mat and beckoning rest into your life.

Learning to rest is a practice, and it needn't require a state-of-the-art playing field. If you're not in a season where you can swing an out-of-state hiatus, here's my permission to eat a DIY Dole Whip on your front stoop—no fuss or flight necessary. As always, start with the tools you've got.

Rest doesn't usually look like it does on Instagram. It doesn't always look like palm trees and beachy waves, room service and robes. Trust me, our minds can spin wheels just as fast in paradise as it can at home. It won't always look like those quiet, slow mornings with your chamomile tea and morning pages and an hour-long journaling practice. In fact, it may *never* look like that, and that's okay.

For some of us, rest doesn't even look peaceful. It might actually look a little more like war. Rest is the battle cry. It's the anthem as we trade in our clenched jaw and furrowed brow for a big, deep breath and softened shoulders. Over and over and over, it's fought for in the smaller, more mundane moments—the split second where you hear the baby fussing on the monitor, and you take a beat and set an intention before you start the day. The neck stretch you take before filling up your water glass. The body scan you perform before reacting to a harsh word from your spouse. The few pages you read for pleasure before your head hits the pillow.

I have a friend who's a high-achiever, and my challenge to her recently was to think of rest as a couch-to-5K challenge, but in reverse. Can she work her way, minute by minute, to a mile of quiet? Can she start today with a moment of silence before she brushes her teeth? A few moments of peace tomorrow before she lets out the dog? Ten minutes of meditation before she brews the coffee? (JK, you can still have your coffee first.)

HOW ARE YOU, REALLY?

How often is your mind silent? How often do you grant yourself the chance to pause the chaos and listen to what's been speaking to you in the quiet? Can you put a Soul Savasana on the calendar, right now? What might happen if you did? What might be revealed to you? (Hint: Everything.)

My Soul Savasana changed me into someone who now integrates purposeful presence into everything I teach (and live). But I can only speak to the power of ditching the hustle because I have to do it over and over again. It's a beast I have to face frequently. My support system—including my family—often steps in to gently remind me that we're not in a hurry. When I say the words "No rush!" or speak about how very few things in life are truly urgent, it's really an echo of the wisdom shared with me regularly.

I get that it's odd that I'm closing out a book all about chasing your dreams by telling you to chase rest and get more z's, but the truth is, it's the only way you can sustainably move through this life. Remember the song lyric "A dream is a wish your heart makes, *when you're fast asleep*," because I think some wisdom lives in that ol' tune. Rest is an essential part of making your dreams come true.

Life is, of course, full of nuance; it's filled with this/and, rather than either/or. We get to walk in an abundance of options and opportunities for how we want to pursue the richness of being fully alive while preserving our souls in the process.

We can rest *and* work. We can dream *and* do the dang thing. We can set goals *and* boundaries. We can want more *and* define "enough" for ourselves. We can hold on to our values *and* change our minds. We can start, come back, and hit reset. We can power through and power down and power off. We can break down *and* still break through.

The beautiful thing about this life is that we can get it all, it's just up to us to define what "it" is.

Over the years of yoga, I've learned how to practice Soul Savasana without wanting to sprint out the door or count my minutes away. The same goes for resting. It takes a little bit to find comfort in it, to figure out who you are beyond what you do.

Rest is like entering a sacred secret place only you can go. Even with a screaming newborn on your chest or a toddler pulling at your pant leg. Even with your mile-long deadlines and your interrupted sleep and every ounce of self-doubt dragging you underwater. Even when working through the storage boxes in your subconscious mind is a whole job and a half (thank God for therapy). Even with what feels like an impossible dream—whether taking a pause for ten minutes on a New York City park bench or taking flight for a month on Maui.

What I know is this: your own Soul Savasana is so close and it's calling you, even in that seemingly silent void. It's just there, within reach, the place where your truest answers will make themselves known. Your greatest ideas. Your hard-earned wisdom. Your soul-banging intuition.

It starts right now. Right here. Are you ready?

Be still for five minutes. Lie flat. Close your eyes. Breathe in. You have just one question to ask yourself, and just one question to answer.

How are you, *really*?

# epilogue

## THIS JUST MIGHT BE IT: WHAT TO DO NOW

**Another world is not only possible, she is on her way. On a quiet day, I can hear her breathing.**

**—ARUNDHATI ROY**

Thea greets me outside in the breezy Lake Superior air. I worry that she just caught me taking a selfie sitting in the front seat of my car wearing my cute new floral mask. As we walk inside, I see a mouse scurry past the French doors. I gasp, but don't say a thing, hoping the rodent moves along to the ice cream shop next door.

Once inside, I fill out the paperwork quickly: *No, I don't have any allergies. Yes, you can touch my feet. No, I'm not claustrophobic.* As I check each box, I keep one eye trained on the corner of the room, praying the mouse doesn't reappear and surprise me. (Or tempt me to do more than gasp. Somehow, I feel like we have an *understanding.*)

Thea mentions in a calm voice behind her own mask that she is not only a massage therapist, but an "intuitive healer." She says it like it's blasé, not a big deal, incredibly normal. I want to ask her a million questions, but my aching shoulders remind me that I want to get my muscles rubbed even more. She leads me back to the dressing room, and she steps out while I quickly strip down to just the mask on my face. I lay on the table under the warm blanket and opt to close my eyes rather than stare at the ceiling.

Thea walks back in and something about her presence instantly calms me. I melt into the table with each squeeze of her magical handiwork. I find my mind wandering, wondering if that "intuitive" side of her is reading my mind the entire time. My brain goes back and forth between pure bliss and pondering. Halfway through, I slowly flip onto my belly, quite certain I am flashing her in the process (if anyone knows how to gracefully execute a massage flip, I'm all ears) and I take my first deep breath without my mask. Pure, pepperminty oxygen fills me, and I remember how sweet unfiltered air feels.

As we finish, rather than the low, quiet hum of a voice that tends to be heard around a spa post-massage, Thea talks directly to me. I detect a hint of reluctance.

"I know, I know, I have to finish, but we aren't done yet. You're still tense in your shoulders. We have to end, but please don't get up too fast, we just did a lot of work."

She exits the room quiet as a mouse (pun intended) and I lie there, very still, a little afraid to move, heeding her advice and wanting just one minute more of those oozy melty-body feelings.

". . . we just did a lot of work." I will myself off the warm table and dress, hastily throwing my jewelry into my wallet and rushing through the usually slow process because now all I want to do is talk to Thea. I know it's likely she has someone else lined up to get massaged-and-mediumed any minute.

I meet her back outside, scanning the room to see if the mouse has returned from the ice cream shop. "I kind of wish you and I could just . . . sit and talk for a few hours?" I tell her. "There's so many things I feel drawn to ask you. Your energy is unlike anything I've experienced before. I mean, that massage felt kind of life-changing, and I'm not just talking about the muscle rub."

She graciously thanks me and then her eyes meet mine and I see a little boldness pop up in them. She asks, "Would you be open for me to tell you what came up energetically during your massage?"

I match her, boldness for boldness.

"Tell me everything, Thea."

She speaks, and every word lands on me like a soft, knowing hand on my shoulder.

She tells me I'm fighting my creativity. That there's something I know I should begin but I am shying away from it. I'm resisting an important project, and I'm delaying the start. I'm trying to veer off the path because I'm afraid of it, and I'm metaphorically turning my hips to try to navigate around it, and her hunch is— I already know what I need to do. And I know it could change a lot of lives.

"Stop fighting it and surrender to it," she says gently. "Begin."

So, I did.

I sped home and met Drew in the kitchen. He probably imagined he would greet me with greasy hair and the impression of the headrest around my eyes, but instead of entering the room in a blissed-out state, I started blurting out words out of context. I was going a mile a minute. Spinning. Full-on run-ons.

"Wait a minute," Drew stopped me. "Slow down. How did a massage therapist tell you that you need to write a book?"

The truth is, I've had this folder in my Gmail titled: "If I Write a Book" for the last five years. Becoming an author would naturally come up in conversations here and there, and while the idea was certainly flattering, it never truly inspired me into action. It sat, dusty as an option, never feeling like a worthy project for me to take on. Never exciting enough for me to take steps and turn a book into reality. It was always one of those "maybe someday" ideas whose someday I wasn't totally convinced would ever arrive.

While the final destination of holding a book that I wrote in my own two hands gave me goose bumps, the path to getting there never felt aligned with the way I exist, create, or spend my time. Why would I want to trade time away from living my life in order to write about it? How could I possibly help others find their own answers if the one I was living was based around numbers of words, deadlines, and contracts? Could I handle writing a book with everything else I had going on and still keep my anti-hustle vision firmly in check? Like, *really*?

Eventually I learned that there would never be a magical spot that appeared on my calendar saying, "Now is your time to write." A fairy bookmother would never appear with a wave of her wand and say, "You now have the magical power of book writing! This will be easy!" Time wouldn't slow down and a window of opportunity wouldn't carve itself out so that I could do what I thought would be this big, hard thing.

But with that nudge from Thea, I knew what I had to do. I had to write this book. I was all in . . . except I still didn't want to follow any of the traditional rules of writing a book and getting it published. I didn't hire a book agent. I didn't write a book proposal. I decidedly didn't give myself a deadline (very strange for my personality!). I didn't peek inside that email folder for incoming book deal offers or pitches from editors. I shied away from sharing my plan with even my closest friends.

In my years of leadership, I've learned the things we teach are the things that we (the teacher) need the most. When I speak words to you, they are likely the words I've needed to hear myself. Writing a book meant I would have to get honest about all the lessons I've learned, but also all the ways I am still learning. Just like we all have to do, every single day. Blinking in the sun, celebrating our hard-earned answers while staring full-faced at the questions ahead. That's the beauty of living.

Whether we like it or not, as long as we're awake, we are a permanently enrolled student in the school of life. We're always being taught, even on the boring days. Even on the quiet ones. *Especially* on the quiet ones. Everything around us is speaking. Every moment is a lesson.

But to learn those lessons requires application. Movement. Progress. When you work on your dreams, you're inherently going to be working on yourself. You're going to need to be honest the whole way through, and honesty, even with ourselves, can be tough. That's *heavy* work. You've got a real journey ahead of you. The human you look at in the mirror every single day is a complex being! One that requires patience. Don't fret that you're about to flip over the last few pages of this book and think, *So, now I have to have it all figured out?!*

Fight the impostor syndrome that's about to tell you that everything you just read couldn't have been about you. That you have to keep faking it and making it for everyone else. That what sounds great on these pages is only applicable for other people. That you're not ready, not worthy, not skilled, creative, energetic . . . that you're not enough.

If this book gave you anything, I hope it gave you the permission to ask yourself the questions, and give yourself the answers, that make a crystal-clear case as to why you are more than enough. And you always have been.

It was actually with these very thoughts in mind that I set out to write a book that was *authentically me*. I didn't want to put a deadline on what could potentially be a creative lifeline. I didn't want to monetize a blank Google doc! I didn't want my story to be formed in a way that wasn't authentic to me. I wanted to be the one that owned my words. I wanted to write the words that would *tell*, not words that would *sell*.

So, I did what I've encouraged you to do this entire book through. I closed my eyes. I got very quiet. I got very still. And I got very, very honest. Instead of pursuing profits or aiming for a spot on the best-seller lists, I asked myself, *Is this a peaceful pursuit? Will this make an impact? Is this the best use of my time? Is this aligned with my values? Is this a part of my legacy? How am I, really?*

I knew the answer was yes. And that I was ready. And Thea did, too.

I opened up a Google doc, titled it, "I'm going to write a book" and began. No flourish, no big announcement. I did all of this without even my mom ever knowing (*Hi, Mom . . . surprise!*). In my usual less-than-formal style, I sat up in my favorite leather chair after dinner and just started with the first stories I wanted to tell. As I began to write these stories, I felt a weight coming off my chest. Each story propelled me toward telling another and then another. My confidence started to grow as I watched my once blank Google doc expand into pages upon pages. I was reminded of those feelings of excitement around simply starting.

I say this to remind you, lovingly and encouragingly, that our work is never complete. We will never fully arrive. We will never stop needing the nudges, prompts, and reminders to stay awake to our lives.

Hours passed, then days, then weeks, then months, then a year. Slowly and surely, the book in your hands was written in the way I wanted to write it. These pages are filled with the real me, and while I did have to step up my grammar game, it's become something I am so insanely proud to put out into the world.

A few nights before I would type the last word of this manuscript, I remembered the mouse from that early spa appointment with Thea. As someone who is always searching for signs from the universe, I needed to know: Was there a meaning with that mouse I saw scurry past the door? I bristled at the thought—*Don't be crazy, Jenna*—but still, curiosity got the better of me. Soon enough I found myself hitting the search bar in my browser, the results staring me right in the eyes.

"The mouse symbolizes running away from problems or hiding from the challenges of life."

Perhaps you grabbed this book hoping to find the answers you've been seeking. Maybe you were praying that somewhere buried in these pages was the permission you've been waiting for to actually pursue your dreams. To quit the dead-end job. To move your body. To stand up for your neighbor. To fight for climate change. To be the surrogate. To leave the relationship. To start the relationship. To change your life.

It's not always going to be easy, and it feels scary at first, but it sure as hell is going to be worth it. You're not waiting for rescue any longer. There's no ticket needed for admission for the life you want. You have permission to explore what you love. Take that deep breath and let the fresh air of your freedom, your clarity, and your dreams fuel your next move. No more waiting for a life you'll live *someday*. You're living it right now.

Life is more than a hunt for money, power, and influence. The lives worth celebrating, and the ones who lived them, aren't just for the history books. If anything, we've been learning that history books still get the stories wrong. The stories of celebration are happening in every single life. The ones that 7.674 billion people are living right alongside us.

Life in and of itself is utter magic. We have it, we multiply it, we share it. And that makes it worth celebrating. That makes *your life* worth every step forward. Every leap, crawl, and reach. Every dream that you have is a bit of your life's beauty saying, *Wanna see what I can really do?*

And while your dreams take you to places you've never been, life will delight you with its little curiosities every single day. Celebrate them and listen to them. Peek into the tiny moments and learn from them.

Life is picking up crumbs with a licked finger off a plate where a slice of cake used to be. Life is cry-laughing on the phone with your best friend until the place between your ear and your jaw burns. Life is finally hacking the perfect chocolate chip cookie recipe and screaming to your spouse to come taste batch number twenty-eight because you, the cookie genius, cracked the code! Life is sitting on the porch and letting the breeze cool the sweat on the back of your neck on a hot summer night.

Life is answering the call to show up when someone you love is in pain, and letting others hold you through your own. Life is letting the tears out when they're knocking at the door. Life is sitting beside your baby's crib and watching them breathe. Life is buttoning up the shirt for your last shift at the last job you'll ever let steal another ounce of your joy.

Life is deleting that phone number. Making the first move. Letting the acne show. Cleaning out your purse. Listening to the same playlist since high school. Calling an old friend to relive the nights you felt the wildest. High-fiving yourself in the mirror because you've got your own back.

Everything that got you here—the good and the ugh and the yikes—propelled you all this way. It all mattered. It all counted. In the words of Thea, "We just did a lot of work." And my goodness, look how far you've come, even when you didn't think you could.

Keep going. Your work, just like my work on this book, will need to be done in silence with no one watching. You'll need to do it your own way, in your own time. You'll need to do it in a way that feels right, not just *looks* right.

I cannot promise to give your body a rub down while simultaneously revealing the truths hidden deep within you, or to send a mouse out to scare you into understanding that you've been avoiding *the thing* that you were put on this earth to do.

But if you've been searching for a sign, *this just might be it.*

With love and hope,

*Jenna*

# appendix 1

Truth be told, every *How Are You, Really?* prompt in this book is for you. But, it's also for your people. The same questions that can bring forth answers within us can also offer clarity and depth for everyone else around us.

So, in the spirit of community, I've gathered each prompt for you to share with those in your inner circle—all in one handy spot. Maybe you'll go through them every Thursday afternoon at your favorite Thai place. Maybe you'll rally your ladies for a monthly Zoom chat. Maybe you'll spout off a few questions during your next book club meeting or after barre class. Or maybe you'll post your own answer in your next Instagram caption. (Def tag me @jennakutcher if that's happening! I can't wait to read it!)

However and whatever you decide, use them. These prompts are powerful, and potent, and every single one leads to a new possibility— in your life, and in every life around you.

# appendix 2

I will not tell you you need to have a morning routine to be successful, or happy, or to lead a life that feels fulfilling. In fact, for the last few years, I've lived in guilt that I didn't have this precise five-step process on how to wake up and be, you know, *amazing*.

If you're like me and you've wondered why you just can't wake up two hours earlier to journal and sip your lemon water slowly and meditate and get in a yoga flow before you sit down to do your work, then take a deep breath. (And if you're not like me and you absolutely *live* for that quiet A.M. sunrise—go get 'em, early bird!) Maybe there's another side of the population who simply rolls out of bed, grabs their phone for a ten-minute scroll to see what possibly happened while they were sleeping, and rushes out the door with a sloshing mug full of coffee that's already gone cold.

And maybe, even more so, there's a population that craves both the structure of a lifelong habit with the flexibility of a daily choice. Maybe there's a simpler plan for the rest of us—a group of people who might find release in the idea that sticking to (or skipping out on) a routine doesn't need to be a make-or-break moment in your week.

Maybe there's beauty to be found in the idea that we're given many beginnings in a twenty-four-hour period, and there's always a chance to jump start the day—wherever you are.

No matter the feeling, no matter the minute, no matter the reason—these jump starts are all great first steps. How do you know which one to take, and when? You need only to ask yourself one question (and I know you know it by now): *How are you, really?*

Remember: you have a neon sign within you, guiding you, nudging you, and pointing you toward what's worth paying attention to. Our feelings are like bright, flickering arrows that, if we're willing, can guide us toward what we need to do next.

And so, this is not a routine. It's a *rhythm*. It's finding the feeling, sitting with the feeling, and seeing that feeling through. It's offering gratitude for the information, and it's moving forward based on that information. Taking action from a place of intuition.

This is not a quick list of things to accomplish so you can be better in twenty-four hours or less. This is a short list of things to try so you can *feel* better—any time at all.

These jump starts have made my days delightfully better. They've made my conversations richer, my presence stronger, and my intuition laser-sharp. Some have grown my confidence. Others have taught me rest. My hope is that each will offer you the same.

Get yours at

WWW.JENNAKUTCHER.COM/MORE

May we ask with curiosity.
May we answer with kindness.
May we live in love.

**WHEN HOW YOU *REALLY* FEEL IS WIRED:** Charge your phone in a different room in the house. Better yet? Make a charging drawer or cupboard so your devices are out of sight, out of mind.

**WHEN HOW YOU *REALLY* FEEL IS SLUGGISH:** Get outside, even for just ten minutes. Notice the weather, notice the sounds, notice the smells (hopefully they are pleasant!), and be a part of the outside world.

**WHEN HOW YOU *REALLY* FEEL IS EXHAUSTED:** Invest in a good pillow and good curtains. Seriously, if being a mom taught me anything, people sleep better in dark rooms and with a little white noise.

**WHEN HOW YOU *REALLY* FEEL IS INSECURE:** Correct your mean girl whenever she starts to get noisy. As hard as it is, direct her thoughts to the thoughts you'd tell someone you love to believe about themselves.

**WHEN HOW YOU *REALLY* FEEL IS LONELY:** Reach out to three people and send a message! If you need a starter prompt, begin with: "No need to respond, just thinking of you." Send encouragement, a funny GIF, an old memory, anything.

**WHEN HOW YOU *REALLY* FEEL IS UNINSPIRED:** Read more! I'm glad this book is in your hands and that you made it this far! Try to make reading ten pages of any book every day a practice in your life. I promise it will transform you.

**WHEN HOW YOU *REALLY* FEEL IS POWERLESS:** Don't run from personal development; run toward it. I swear it's not all toxic positivity. Self-help can be an invitation to learn more about how to be the best version of you.

**WHEN HOW YOU *REALLY* FEEL IS OVERCONNECTED:** Log off social media more often, and without apology. I promise no one is refreshing your feed. It feels so good to experience moments without worrying about documenting or sharing them. Delete the apps if you have to.

**WHEN HOW YOU *REALLY* FEEL IS UNFOCUSED:** Ground yourself before you walk into a room. Literally, feel your feet on the floor or notice as you walk through a door to pay attention to where you are in the moment.

**WHEN HOW YOU *REALLY* FEEL IS CONFUSED:** Define *one* thing that will move you closer to your goal. If you can't do that, write down the end result you want and reverse engineer what it will take for you to get there by making a list of smaller actions you can start with.

**WHEN HOW YOU *REALLY* FEEL IS INTIMIDATED:** Take the time to rewrite the story. Yes, really! Sit down and write it out! Chances are you're telling yourself a story on a loop; one that doesn't support your belief in yourself. With a pen in your hand, write out what it would look like for you to achieve and succeed.

**WHEN HOW YOU *REALLY* FEEL IS OVERWHELMED:** Do what I call a brain dump. Write down all of the thoughts in your brain, no matter how random, whether it's the item you need from Target or the deadline that's looming. Then release them from your brain! They are safe. They're not going anywhere. You don't have to carry them anymore.

**WHEN HOW YOU *REALLY* FEEL IS DISCONNECTED FROM A SIGNIFICANT OTHER:** Start a habit of spending five minutes— *uninterrupted and undistracted*—where you catch up on each other's day. Greet them at the door and put your listening ears on before rushing to the next thing.

**WHEN HOW YOU *REALLY* FEEL IS CYNICAL:** Adopt a practice of mindfully thinking of things you are thankful for each and every day before you close your eyes. It doesn't matter if it's a small thing or feels insignificant. Training your brain to be grateful can (and will) shift your entire perspective.

**WHEN HOW YOU *REALLY* FEEL IS STUCK:** Start documenting. It's easy to forget how far you've come or what you've achieved. Whether you set more goals on paper or write one line a day about what you did, document your life. I know you think you'll remember all of this, but I promise it becomes a blur and you'll wish you had written down the many moments of positive action that brought you here today.

**WHEN HOW YOU *REALLY* FEEL IS BLAH:** Drink more water . . . seriously! Go fill up your cup with water (and no, your cold coffee doesn't count!). Right now! Off you go.

**WHEN HOW YOU *REALLY* FEEL IS LETHARGIC:** Stand up and move your body. Stretch your muscles. Shake it out. Breathe into those neglected spaces. Create your own reason to take a mini Soul Savasana no matter where you are.

**WHEN HOW YOU *REALLY* FEEL IS REJECTED:** Get out of your bubble and help others in need. Whether you volunteer locally or research a cause globally, poising yourself in a position to help others can shift your perspective and prompt you to a place of gratitude.

**WHEN HOW YOU *REALLY* FEEL IS ISOLATED:** Join a community. Whether it's a Facebook group or your local mom's group, being an active participant can inspire action in other areas of your life. Place yourself in rooms where you can make a difference and feel a sense of belonging!

**WHEN HOW YOU *REALLY* FEEL IS READY:** Hit play on *The Goal Digger* podcast and listen to my voice! I promise to keep pointing you back to the messages and themes of this book, I promise not to use my phone voice, and I promise to keep sharing the lessons life is teaching me.

# acknowledgments

I'm not going to lie: I put off writing this part until the very last minute. The probability that I will forget to acknowledge someone here is very high and frankly overwhelming. How can you possibly thank the village of humans who champion your work and make it possible for you to do what you love every day? It's entirely impossible, but here I am trying.

In the past, I've heard that writing a book is a lot like birthing a baby into the universe. Since I've now done both of these things, I have to say, I agree. Writing a book is a process that requires time, energy, growth, and being stretched in ways you didn't know you were capable of before releasing new breath, new life into the world.

And since I wrote this book while simultaneously growing a wiggly human being, handing in my final manuscript just days before my second daughter was born, I feel like I am closing this part of the process as an entirely new woman and a very proud mama (on so many levels!). Just like I had humans by my side reminding me to breathe through the labor pains and to push just a little harder, I had an amazing team of humans who held my hands and who sweat right alongside me throughout this journey.

I have to start this off with thanking the guy who has stuck by my side for over a decade, loving every iteration and evolution of me along the way. Drew, you are my best friend, my partner, the best teammate I could ask for, and I would literally live like a single college-aged dude if you weren't in my life following behind my little creative tornadoes and piles every day.

The way you graciously listen to my wild and crazy ideas, the way you didn't question me when I said, "It is time for me to write a book," and the way you supported me and our family through the process speaks volumes to the man you are. I'm so glad I kissed you during *Home Alone*!

Thank you for not judging the fact that I sustained my life, this book process, and the baby in my belly on chicken nuggets and Coco's mac and cheese, and thank you for shining a light on this vision, reminding me it would all be worth it on the days where I got slightly overwhelmed. I know you think I'm a sap when you catch me getting teary-eyed every time I make pancakes (which happens to be often) but I also know that when you notice my watery eyes and smile, it's because we know we're living out that scene we held for our lives, it's because we're awake to the life that we're living. I can't sum up what you mean to me, but I'll sure try to every night before our heads hit the pillow. I'll do my best to remind you, affirm you, encourage the chasing of your dreams, and I promise to love you well, for the rest of my days, because one lifetime will never be enough.

To my Coco, I know I carry a lot of titles, but it is my greatest joy on planet Earth to be called your mama. You grew, evolved, and absolutely transformed through my writing process, and I love the little girl you are and who you are becoming. Thank you for cheering me on when I was working, thank you for making me play "Baby Shark" in the corner of my screen while I was writing so we could sit together, and thank you for loving books as much as I do. I clung tight to a vision of you someday reading these words, and I'll savor each moment until that day comes. You have taught me that the wait is always worth it. You are my greatest inspiration, the light of my life, the giggling girl from my vision, and my rainbow that came after the storm.

To this baby in my belly, who turned out to be Quinn Louise, you gave me the push I needed to make this dream come true. On the path to writing this book, you were my purpose. So much of this process unfolded because of you. You were always a dream of mine and getting to write a book while anticipating meeting you was exactly what I needed to chase two dreams simultaneously. I like to think that my heartbeat grew stronger just as yours did, throughout this process. Thank you for giving me the ultimate deadline to get this done and thanks for literally being my sidekick throughout this entire process. I know that by the time I write my next book, I'll have so many stories of all the ways you've changed me, inspired me, and taught me.

To my family, my goodness, whenever I try to sum you all up, it's impossible. I recognize how absolutely rare it is to have a family in your life whose daily text threads make you smile but also who celebrates and champions you every step of the way. You all have been a pivotal piece of my story and a huge source of my motivation. Mom and Dad, I'm waiting for that parenting book I've been begging you to write because you somehow raised three independent, confident, driven children who genuinely love one another (and who have a knack for picking out the best partners and birthing the greatest kiddos). I am so thankful my pancake vision led me home to all of you, because I can't imagine a life without our spontaneous nights, pizza parties, and weekends at the lake. I love you all so much.

One of my greatest desires in this book writing adventure was to live out my values through the process. I wanted to walk the walk, I wanted to live my life in a way that stayed true to all of the words I have written in these pages. I wanted the process to be fun and lifegiving, and thankfully, I gathered a group of women who not only rallied around the mission of this book but who also made sure that the way we navigated every step of the process put our lives first and the work second. Writing this book truly felt as good as it looks!

To my amazing book doulas, Brooklyn and Erin, I truly couldn't imagine going through this process without you. I never want to write a book without you two by my side. Thanks for making this process far less painful and way more fun!

Brooklyn, I'm so thankful LinkedIn brought you into my life and I'm also thankful I didn't hire you as my podcast producer! I saw something in you that I couldn't put my finger on, but I trusted it and I am so thankful I did. You were the only human I shared my Google doc with and you didn't scoff at my idea that I wanted to write in secret, without telling another soul. You were my copilot, the yin to my yang, and a human who constantly balanced me with your fresh perspective. I love you so, BW.

Erin, you entered the scene as my fairy bookmother (after years of me telling you, "No, I'm not ready!") and you jumped on board at such a critical time in the journey, guiding us through the hard parts of the process with encouragement, enlightenment, and eternal joy. Your voice notes propelled me to keep on going, your organization made my heart sing, and your additions enriched this book in ways I can't explain but can feel.

While your email sat in my "If I Write a Book" Gmail folder for years before I read your words, Margaret Riley King, I am so thankful that the universe plopped us into one another's lives at just the right time. You are more than an agent (and a bad ass one at that!). You are a friend, a visionary, a force to be reckoned with, and an advocate for telling stories that matter. To my editor, Carrie Thornton, I liked you from the moment I met you! Thank you for championing this book, this message, and the timing of it all. Your gifts elevated this book to a whole new level! I am so thankful to have walked through this journey with you two, and beyond the book, we got to experience life and what it looks like to live out the words inside of the book throughout the process.

To the entire team at Dey Street, thank you for bringing me into your fold of brilliant minds, talented writers, passionate creatives, and heart-forward humans. It is such an honor to play a role in the legacy you're weaving throughout the publishing industry and beyond. I am so grateful to be among the many voices you and HarperCollins have championed throughout this century.

To my wildly talented and passionate team of women who have stood by me and my business day in and day out to ensure that our mission to serve the world is lived out, I couldn't do this without you. It takes a village to create what we do and every day I thank my lucky stars that I get to create alongside you. Thank you for holding down the fort when I would disappear into "Book Land" for a few days to work on this book. Thank you for keeping my head on straight while I juggled the work and writing, all while combating pregnancy brain. (It's real, I swear!) Every facet of my brand and business is backed by an incredible woman on a mission, and this book is a celebration of all that we've built (and the way that we've built it) together over the years. No one will quite understand the family we've built within this brand, but I always smile when we sign off Zoom calls and everyone yells "I love you" and we know that we mean it.

I'd be remiss not to acknowledge my Creator here. I don't really believe in happenstance; I move through life believing everything happens for a reason and I can only do that because of my faith. I channel that same God-given confidence that I had as a five-year-old often, because in order to keep creating and showing up in the way I do, I have to believe that I was made for a unique purpose, made to answer a divine calling, made to use my work as a form of praise. While my practice and definition of faith has shifted and evolved throughout the years (and I anticipate it will continue doing so), I am so grateful for the role it and the role God have played throughout my life but especially throughout the parts of the journey I've shared in these pages! Thank you, Lord, for this chance to tell my story that's been handwritten by you. I pray these words are used for your glory. Whenever someone asks me why I am the way I am, whether it's about my work or my messiness or the way my lip crinkles when I smile, I still respond, "Because that's how God made me."

And to the close-knit community of women that surrounds me, inspires me, and cheers me on: thank you. Every woman mentioned in this book landed on these pages because of the ways they have shown up in my life. From my college roomies who once dressed up like me and went out in sweatpants to celebrate my birthday to my neighbors who fulfill my lifelong vision of exchanging milk and eggs in the driveway when we've suddenly run out, from my entrepreneurial friends who inspire me to enjoy the chase to the friends who sat on my porch eating brownies when I was in the darker days. I am so thankful to be able to walk through life with women who are fierce, who don't hate my incessant voice notes, and who aren't afraid to share how they *re-ally* are.

I've learned so much throughout this process and just as I have a team backing me and all the ways I show up in the world, this book has an entire team of editors, publicists, marketing experts, designers, sales representatives, and everyone else behind the scenes of this process who have truly helped this book move from being just an idea in my brain to something you can hold in your hands and welcome into your lives. It's truly a miracle.

Finally and forever, to you, my reader. In my sunniest visions of pancakes and Persian rugs, I couldn't have possibly imagined a community of readers and listeners so brave and true and good. Because of you, I get to learn. Because of you, I get to lead. Because of you, I get to *live*.

How am I, *really*? Wildly, unabashedly grateful.

# notes

**CHAPTER 1: THE SOFTER QUESTION: HOW TO FEEL YOUR FEELINGS**

1. Lara Fielding, "Listening to Your Authentic Self: The Purpose of Emotions," HuffPost (blog), October 20, 2015, https://www.huffpost.com/entry/finding-your-authentic-pu_b_8342280.

**CHAPTER 2: GOLDEN HANDCUFFS: HOW TO DITCH THE SUPPOSED TOS**

1. Nicolas Cole, "9 Sad Reasons People Stay in Jobs They Don't Like (Even Though They Always Talk About Leaving)," *Inc.*, October 21, 2016, https://www.inc.com/nicolas-cole/9-sad-reasons-people-stay-in-jobs-they-dont-like-even-though-they-always-talk-ab.html.

**CHAPTER 3: HALFWAY TO A DREAM: GOING AFTER YOUR GOAL**

1. Amy Blaschka, "Want to Make Big Progress? Science Says to Start Small," *Forbes*, November 12, 2019, https://www.forbes.com/sites/amyblaschka/2019/11/12/want-to-make-big-progress-science-says-to-start-small/?sh=10961f72594e.

**CHAPTER 4: THE COZY CORNER: HOW TO HEAR YOURSELF (AGAIN)**

1. Paul Hemp, "Death by Information Overload," *Harvard Business Review*, September 2009, https://hbr.org/2009/09/death-by-information-overload.
2. Carolyn Gregoire, "10 Things Highly Intuitive People Do Differently," HuffPost.com, March 19, 2014, https://www.huffpost.com/entry/the-habits-of-highly-intu_n_4958778.

## CHAPTER 5: MOTHERS STUDYING MANDARIN: HOW TO HAVE SOME FUN AGAIN

1. Fernando Alfonso III, "The Long Lost Hobbies People Around the World Are Revisiting During the Coronavirus Pandemic," CNN, April 5, 2020, https://www.cnn.com/2020/04/05/world/old-hobbies-quarantine -coronavirus-wellness-trnd/index.html.
2. Kristen Wong, "How to Add More Play to Your Grown-Up Life, Even Now," *New York Times,* August 17, 2020, https://www.nytimes .com/2020/08/14/smarter-living/adults-play-work-life-balance.html.
3. Mihaly Csikszentmihalyi, *Flow: The Psychology of Optimal Experience* (New York: Harper Perennial Modern Classics, 2008).

## CHAPTER 6: RUMBLE AND QUAKE: HOW TO CHANGE YOUR MIND

1. Robin Hilmantel, "Ina Garten: I Don't Believe in Making Goals," Time .com, February 4, 2016, https://time.com/4198968/ina-garten-making -goals/.
2. Jenna Kutcher, interview with Dr. Maya Shankar, "Navigating Change with Help from Cognitive Neuroscience," *The Goal Digger* podcast, podcast audio, episode 479, July 19, 2021, https://jennakutcherblog .com/maya/.

## CHAPTER 7: A BATTLEFIELD OF CUTS: HOW TO LISTEN TO YOUR BODY

1. Kathleen Lennon, "Feminist Perspectives on the Body," *Stanford Encyclopedia of Philosophy,* Fall 2019 Edition, August 2, 2019, https:// plato.stanford.edu/archives/fall2019/entries/feminist-body/.

## CHAPTER 8: MARRIED TO MR. SIX-PACK: HOW TO SPEAK TO YOURSELF

1. Elaine Mead, "What Is Positive Self-Talk?," Positive Psychology (blog), February 18, 2021, https://positivepsychology.com/positive-self-talk/.
2. Kristin Neff, "Self-Compassion: An Alternative Conceptualization of a Healthy Attitude Toward Oneself," *Self and Identity* 2, no. 2 (2003): 85–101, https://doi.org/10.1080/15298860309032.